Nonfiction Matters

Reading, Writing, and Research in Grades 3–8

Stephanie Harvey

Foreword by **Shelley Harwayne**

Stenhouse Publishers
Portland, Maine

Pembroke Publishers Limited
Markham, Ontario

Stenhouse Publishers
www.stenhouse.com

Credits
Page 64: "President's life is an open book" by Margo Hammond. January 20, 1993, *Rocky Mountain News*. Reprinted by permission of *St. Petersburg Times*. Copyright © 1993.
Page 67–68: "Smoke 'em at 'Creek,' but not at 'Big Mac'" by Chuck Green. September 13, 1996. Reprinted by permission of *The Denver Post*.
Page 76: *The Unhuggables* by Victor Waldrop, Debbie Anker, and Elizabeth Blizard. Copyright © 1988 by the National Wildlife Federation. Reprinted by permission of the National Wildlife Federation.
Page 82: "Author's Note" from *Encounter*. Copyright © 1992 by Jane Yolen. Reprinted by permission of Harcourt Brace & Company.
Page 83: "A Killer Down Under: Australia's Box Jellyfish." Copyright © 1994 by William Hamner. Reprinted by permission of National Geographic Society.
Page 85: *The Secrets of Vesuvius* by Sara Bisel. Copyright © 1990 by Sara C. Bisel and Family and The Madison Press Ltd. Reprinted by permission of Scholastic Inc.
Page 141: *Survivors in the Shadows*. Copyright © 1993 by Gary Turbak. Reprinted by permission of Northland Publishing.
Page 157: "Sea Turtles: In a Race for Survival." Copyright © 1994 by Jack and Anne Rudloe. Reprinted by permission of National Geographic Society.

Library of Congress Cataloging-in-Publication Data
Harvey, Stephanie.
    Nonfiction matters : reading, writing, and research in grades 3–8 / Stephanie Harvey : foreword by Shelley Harwayne.
        p.   cm.
    Includes bibliographical references and index.
    ISBN 1-57110-072-5 (alk. paper)
    1. Literature—Study and teaching (Elementary)—United States. 2. English language—Composition and exercises—Study and teaching (Elementary)—United States. 3. Reading (Elementary)—United States. 4. Interdisciplinary approach in education—United States.
I. Title.
LB1575.5.U5H37   1998
372.64—dc21   97–36584
                                         CIP

Published in Canada by
Pembroke Publishers Limited
538 Hood Road
Markham, Ontario L3R 3K9

Cover design by Richard Hannus, Hannus Design Associates
Manufactured in the United States of America on acid-free paper
06 05 04   20 19 18 17 16

To Edward and late-night revising

Contents

Foreword

Steph Harvey is an unforgettable educator. She is a gregarious, inquisitive, compassionate woman with boundless energy and a story for every occasion. I'm unable to imagine her asleep or simply relaxing. She seems to have read every novel and newspaper, traveled to every country, attended every cultural event, and worked in every public and private school in Denver, Colorado.

It is fitting that Steph Harvey has written *Nonfiction Matters,* a powerful tribute to the world of nonfiction research, because she lives the life of a nonfiction writer. She finds this universe and everything in it incredibly fascinating. She becomes totally immersed in people and places, making lifelong commitments to her favorite topics. Ask her about Tibet or Shakespeare or the Broadway theater and be prepared to take notes. Steph knows a lot and is eager to share.

Through many years of professional visits to Denver, I have been privileged to spend time at the Harvey home. On my first visit, I was impressed by two very large works of art. They were body images traced and painted by her son, Alex, and daughter, Jessica, when they were kindergartners. Steph mounted, matted, and framed these bright and bold tempera masterpieces and hung them prominently for all to see. Steph knows how to pay tribute to children's art, particularly children with big questions, passions, and concerns. More important, she knows how to inspire all children to join the ranks of students and inquiring minds. With heartfelt sincerity, Steph Harvey also pays tribute to teachers, elevating and honoring their work and encouraging them to take their own areas of inquiry seriously.

As the principal of an elementary school, the Manhattan New School, I am particularly delighted that Steph has slowed down long enough to record her ideas on the teaching and learning of nonfiction research. I was privileged to read her chapters in progress and informally shared the highlights of her content with my colleagues. On many Monday mornings, I began conversations with, "Listen to what Steph says about . . . ." My colleagues were impressed with Steph's ability to present rich, practical, classroom-based ideas while staying true to the best theoretical research on reading, writing, and the inquiry process.

With zest, flair, and a contagious energy, she reminds us of the importance of nurturing wonder, the role of mentors, and the reading-writing connection. She helps teachers expand their strategies for helping students tap resources, offering guidelines for conducting interviews, writing letters, and doing field observations. She tackles the big issues of management and assessment head on, pushing us to rethink our usual ways of working. We are grateful for her thorough presentation of the role of technology in the research process. Steph's detailed description of e-mail, Web sites, and public bulletin boards revitalizes our notions of inquiry possibilities. We also marvel at her expertise in the area of reading comprehension. She offers many helpful suggestions for turning students into active readers, giving special attention to those students who struggle with their reading.

Steph doesn't merely assign nonfiction writing, she teaches nonfiction writing, offering invaluable crafting lessons. We could design several months of mini-lessons based on her comments about precise language, quotations, dialogue, sequence, transitions, and clarity. Above all, Steph inspires us all to become "curators of our own collections," thereby inviting all students into the world of nonfiction research.

As a school community at the Manhattan New School, we are delighted that *Nonfiction Matters* is now available in its polished, published form. We expect that our entire staff will read it for an upcoming professional book-talk. We will share the pages upon which we used our highlighter pens, placed a sticky note, or wrote in the margins. We will no doubt talk about Steph's effectiveness and expertise as a teacher of nonfiction reading, writing, and research. Above all, we will talk about how *Nonfiction Matters* has made a difference in our teaching lives.

Shelley Harwayne

Acknowledgments

When I'm writing I'm always aware that this friend is going to like this or another friend is going to like that paragraph or chapter, always thinking of specific people. In the end, all books are written for your friends.

Gabriel Garcia Marquez

I've never written a book before, never seriously considered it. But I know now that I've written this one for my friends. The mind wanders during long hours in front of the screen spent choosing words and constructing meaning. As I battled syntax, struggled with clarity, yet relished the solitude of writing, I heard the voices of friends, colleagues, and mentors weighing in with their opinions on a word, a phrase, or an idea. I kept wondering what they would think of this line or that one. I tried harder because of them. And I thank them.

To begin, my profound gratitude to the teachers who so graciously opened the doors of their vibrant classrooms so that together we could study teaching and learning. The conversation that emanated from our joint work has changed me forever. My heartfelt thanks to Mary Urtz, whose thoughtful questions about the quality of the nonfiction being written in her classroom began this book before I ever imagined it (I'm in awe of Mary's tranquillity and her instinctive gift for teaching); to Leslie Blauman, who listens to her students in ways I never dreamed possible and whose teaching continues to evolve to meet their needs and challenge them in the process; to Ponderosa teachers Carol Mooney, Kathy Marquet, Norton Moore, Lorraine Becker, and Marsha Fulton, who laced our work with humor and thoughtful reflection; to their principal, Connie Wallace, whose knowledge of instruction, love of kids, and skill with schedules and organization made it possible for our work to go further and deeper than we believed possible; to

ix

Cris Tovani, who showed me the benefits of explicit strategy instruction for middle and secondary school students as well as younger kids; to Debbie Miller, who sets a new standard when it comes to learning from kids; to Carol Quinby, whose teaching of nonfiction literacy strategies serves as a model of excellence for bilingual classrooms everywhere; to Gloria Mundel, whose commitment to inner-city middle school teaching is a constant source of inspiration; to Sue Kempton, the kindergarten teacher who pops in and out of this book because so much of what happens for kids in her classroom should continue through high school; to Glenda Clearwater, who never forgets the connection between reading and writing; to Jody Cohn, who reminds us to look through different lenses; to Karen Ruzzo, who took time to share a remarkable project with me; and to librarians Kathy Higgins, Fran Jenner, Carol Newman, Susan Oakes, and Evelyn Scott, for sharing their knowledge of information literacy with someone who needed lots of information.

Mounds of thanks to the kids in these lively classrooms—thanks for the work, thoughts, and enthusiasm they bring to learning. Without them, this book would not exist. And thanks to their moms and dads for the endless permissions and copies of student work.

A special thanks to the Public Education and Business Coalition, a committed group of people who dedicate themselves to the cause of improving education for a broad spectrum of kids across the Colorado front range and to their executive director, Barbara Volpe, who expressed sincere interest in this project from its inception. It was through the PEBC that I had the opportunity to work with an extraordinary group of teachers and staff developers. Many of the ideas in this book were born out of discussions and collaborations at PEBC staff developer meetings, study groups, workshops, and institutes. My heartfelt thanks to my colleague Anne Goudvis, whose cell phone bill escalated with every chapter; to Liz Stedem, my great friend, who read early drafts, responded, and gave me one of the book's best stories; to Ellin Keene, who completed her own book a year ahead of me and helped me negotiate the hoops and hurdles; to Chryse Hutchins, who reminded me of the power of sharing our stories with kids; to Nancy Burton, who challenged me to think about technology in a much broader way; to Kathy Haller, whose appreciation for individual student differences is a constant reminder to me; to Colleen Buddy, whose thoughtful, reflective practice continues to amaze; and to the members of my PEBC writers group, Laura Benson, Wendy Cameron, Sue Kempton, Pat Lusche, Sheila MacAuliffe, Debbie Miller, Joan Schroeder, Cris Tovani, Kristin Venable, and Julie Weaver, who all could and should write a book of their own.

It was Shelley Harwayne who convinced me I could write this book. I was stuck before I even began. Shelley helped me see the connection between passion and inquiry and nudged me to start there. She read drafts and sent voice mail messages that spurred me on even in dark moments. She is a true friend, and I wrote much of this with her in mind. Thanks to Judy Davis and Joanne Hindley, my friends at Manhattan New School, who opened their rich classrooms and thinking, not only to me, but to my entire family on our New York visits; to Diane Snowball, whose dinner conversations never cease to enlighten; to Tom Newkirk, who trusted I could do this and encouraged me to continue; to David Pearson and Jan Dole whose work in reading comprehension theory contributed to the thesis; and to Don Graves, whose experience and wisdom underpins much of this book.

Thanks, too, to Sue Lubeck and the staff at The Bookies, Denver's preeminent children's bookstore, for their cheerful disposition and willingness to search for remote bibliographic references and information whenever I rang them up.

And many thanks to Stenhouse Publishers and my editor, Philippa Stratton, whose great ideas and charming e-mails always brought a smile to my face.

It takes a rare occasion to thank teenagers aged seventeen and fourteen, but I am particularly indebted to my kids, Alex and Jessica. They are prominently featured in the book, which shouldn't be a problem unless they happen to read it! I love them unconditionally, and thank them from the bottom of my heart.

And in the end, this book was written for my best friend, my husband, Edward, who read every word and struck as many of them as he yearns to strike of the words I speak. Truthfully, I couldn't have done it without him. Thank you, Edward.

1

· ·

From Passion to Presentation

In 1992 I attended a workshop led by Howard Gardner, the eminent Harvard psychologist. Dr. Gardner welcomed a crowd of more than two hundred educators, then scribbled a line of small dark letters on the overhead projector. These letters emerged on the screen as the question, "What is the purpose of education?" He asked us to take a moment and comment in our notebooks.

I was confounded. I twitched nervously, shifting from side to side in my chair, the auditorium silent except for pens skittering across paper. What was everyone writing? I drew a blank. A few minutes to sum up the complexities of my twenty years in education? The task overwhelmed me. Ten minutes later when Dr. Gardner solicited comments, my notebook lay bare on the desk before me.

Volunteers from around the room shared admirable, altruistic accounts of the purpose of education: to develop thoughtful citizens, to instill compassion, to give unlucky individuals the chance at a better life. After a dozen or so responses, Dr. Gardner acknowledged the merit in this spectrum of purposes and then offered his own take: "For me, the purpose of education is to enhance understanding."

I have never forgotten this simple response to what appeared to be such a complex question. Not one audience member mentioned the word *understanding* when addressing the purpose of education. Gardner told us about his daughter, an A+ student in advanced high school physics, who as a freshman in college discovered that although she could do the math and complete the assignments, she didn't understand physics. Years of high marks and stratospheric SAT scores did not guarantee understanding. If we don't understand what we learn, what is the purpose of learning?

1

Teaching for understanding has become a top priority for me. Students and teachers gain understanding through inquiry. Inquiry projects born of learners' passion and curiosity encourage students to understand what they learn, rather than merely retell it. This understanding leads to insight, which occurs in kindergartners as well as Ph.D. candidates. Insight leads to new questions not possible before.

Author Amy Tan writes, "I can never remember things I didn't understand in the first place" (1989, 6). Inquiry requires that we dig beneath the surface to explore a topic, dwell in it, wonder about it, and find out information. This deeper understanding is forged with long-term memory. This book describes active learning whereby students explore their passions and curiosity, pursue topics of interest, ask questions, conduct primary and secondary research, read for meaningful content, organize and synthesize information, craft authentic reports, and present and report findings—and gain new understanding in the process.

Who Am I?

• • • • • • • • • For the past ten years, I've worked as a reading and writing staff developer both in private practice and for the Public Education and Business Coalition, a Denver-based nonprofit group dedicated to providing private support to public schools. I have met hundreds of teachers, some with whom I've worked closely, conducting demonstration lessons in their classrooms over the course of a year, others less intimately in study groups, workshops, or institutes. My connection with so many exceptional teachers energizes me and infuses me with new teaching ideas.

I wish all teachers had the opportunity to leave their rooms and recharge themselves by observing another teacher's instruction. I spent fifteen years in my own elementary classroom. I understand the isolation. No other service profession is characterized by the degree of seclusion that plagues education. Imagine lawyers without paralegals, or surgeons operating alone. Teachers do amazing things inside their classroom walls, but nobody except the clients inhabits these classrooms.

The teachers and students portrayed in this book come from inner-city, suburban, and rural classrooms across Colorado and other parts of the country and encompass a broad socioeconomic spectrum. The classrooms portrayed are grades three through eight, but teachers in both primary grades and high schools have adapted the content for use in their classrooms as well.

Why Nonfiction?

• • • • • • • • • Several years ago, I walked into the fifth-grade room of Mary Urtz, a highly committed teacher with whom I'd been working for the better part of a year. Kids in the class were reading and writing primarily fiction, the occasional memoir thrown in. Their teacher and I had provided instruction in those genres, with favorable results. I found Mary hunched over a pile of papers, reading intently.

"How's it goin'?" I asked.

She raised her head and removed her glasses, looking uncharacteristically glum. "You don't want to know," she answered. She explained that her fifth graders had taken their first shot at report writing. The curriculum required a report on a country, and the early drafts lay dying in a stack in front of her. "Here take a look. They are so *dull!* No life whatsoever."

As I read, my own experience with traditional school reports came rushing back in waves. Remember state reports? Each student in the room draws a state out of a hat. Audible groans reverberate from unfortunate souls who draw states that offer no connection or allure. Cheers burst from the lucky kids who draw hot spots like Hawaii, California, and Florida. The teacher assigns a list of subtopics that bears a striking resemblance to the structure of a *World Book* article, and then each student rushes to the library to check out a lettered volume of an encyclopedia, those with states beginning with the overrepresented *N* stumbling over one another to get to the stacks first. Kids read the encyclopedia entry and perhaps a book from a series on states, and then spend hours rearranging words to avoid plagiarizing, a terrifying offense that might land them a dawn execution. A week or two later, the final reports—sounding the same year after year, differentiated only by the name in the top left-hand corner—are turned in to await FDA approval as a surefire cure for insomnia.

The truth is, I not only wrote these reports in school, reducing Louisiana and Nebraska to the lowest common denominator, but assigned some later as a teacher. They read like encyclopedias, which is not surprising since we used encyclopedias as models. Assignments like these relegate students to the status of mere "word movers," rearranging information and reporting it back (McKenzie 1996, 32).

"What do you want to do?" I asked Mary.

"I want to teach them to read and write nonfiction. Their fiction has voice, and although it may ramble a bit, it's fun. The nonfiction they write would put an owl to sleep, it's so dull. I want to teach them to write compelling nonfiction, like you read in a *National Geographic* or a picture book by Jean Fritz. I *know* they can do it," she stated emphatically.

I knew we had not paid enough attention to nonfiction in this classroom or in many others in which I had worked. Nonfiction is the most widely read genre. In *On Writing Well,* William Zinsser says, "The great preponderance of what writers now write and sell, what book and magazine publishers publish, and what readers demand is nonfiction" (1990, 54). As we thought about how to better instruct for nonfiction, we began to see the need to understand it more clearly ourselves.

In the belief that you can't teach what you don't understand, Mary and I, in conjunction with a group of other interested teachers, undertook an in-depth study of nonfiction reading and writing. We began by reading everything we could get our hands on. William Zinsser, E. B. White, Eudora Welty, Donald Graves, Don Murray, Annie Dillard, Ralph Fletcher, James Kilpatrick, became our and our students' writing teachers.

As we studied, we saw that the best nonfiction writing emerges from topics the writer knows, cares, and wonders about and wants to pursue. Nonfiction inquiry demands that learners select a real topic that interests them, develop some questions about it, read for information, search for answers through research, report information, and ultimately gain new insight.

Want to see how this plays out in the classroom? Let's fast-forward to a sixth-grade class during presentation week, the culmination of ten weeks of nonfiction inquiry in which each student has investigated a culture that is meaningful to him or her. The final products are as diverse as the students who created them.

Bringing Greece to Life

Anika hauled the audiovisual cart to the front of her sixth-grade classroom and plugged in the VCR. Parents, relatives, school personnel, and other kids streamed in and squeezed into folding metal chairs. Anika flipped on the VCR. A pink neon sign flashing *Retsos Restaurant* through a dark, rain-soaked night filled the screen. There was Anika, standing under an umbrella at the entrance to the restaurant. "Hello," she announced. "Welcome to Retsos, my favorite Greek restaurant! You can learn a lot about a culture from its food and mealtime behavior. Come in and I'll show you."

"First meet my mom and dad, aunt and uncle, and two cousins," she said as the camera panned the dining table. "To start, we have a Greek salad sprinkled with feta cheese. That's goat cheese. In Greece, they have hardly any cows, so they get their dairy products from goats. I like it best of all the cheeses. The main dish is moussaka, the Greek national meal. It's made mostly out of eggplant and ground lamb. In America, they sometimes use beef, but to be really Greek, you should use lamb like they do here at Retsos, because beef is scarce in Greece and lamb tastes great. If you noticed, when the waiter served the moussaka, he served my uncle first, because he is the oldest person at the table. The oldest is always served first in Greece, no matter whether it's a man or a woman. And you are never supposed to keep your wrists in your lap, but instead up on the table. My little cousin better watch it! Elbows are okay at home, but not out at a restaurant."

Anika continued her description. When the five-minute video ended, she talked (from note cards) for another five minutes about some additional elements of Greek lifestyle and culture. Her research included interviews with members of her extended family and the owner of Retsos. A written report accompanied her presentation.

Anika was no mere "word mover." Her presentation both entertained and informed the audience; no one else could have done it exactly the way she did. Both Anika and the audience would remember the information, because it was couched in the context of a family meal.

Although Anika had struggled through some rough spots along the way (many of the books she consulted were dry and detailed, taking notes was tiresome, and she never found an organizational strategy that suited her style), Anika's enthusiasm on presentation day came through loud and clear.

She credited the success of her project to her background knowledge and love of Greek culture. Her passion for Greece drove her to ask questions and find out information she didn't know. Once invited to explore her interest in Greece in daily notebook writing, she began to ask important questions, narrow her topic to Greek culture in America, read for content, interview relatives, take notes, choose a genre, craft a piece, structure a presentation, and convey her findings. Her teacher provided explicit instruction in every phase of research and guided her through the process.

When students are encouraged to follow an interest to its conclusion, they learn a lot. Students and teachers I've worked with have found that nonfiction inquiry:

- Is an opportunity to engage in authentic research.
- Encourages planning, sustaining, and revising work over an extended period.
- Helps one become an active learner who applies what she or he has learned.
- Generates a high level of enthusiasm and engagement.
- Replicates the process of making decisions and acting on those decisions.
- Allows one to pursue a special interest.
- Is an opportunity to search for answers to questions.
- Is an opportunity to develop expertise.
- Is an opportunity to learn and use reading strategies specific to nonfiction.
- Is an opportunity to engage in research and to experiment with primary sources such as interviews, surveys, and Web pages.
- Is an opportunity to organize information.
- Is an opportunity to write clearly and concisely in an interesting way.
- Helps expand vocabulary.
- Is an opportunity to practice persuasive writing.
- Provides authentic homework.
- Is an opportunity to practice public speaking.
- Is an opportunity to prepare a final presentation using a variety of tools and resources.
- Is an opportunity to participate in process and product evaluation.
- Exposes one to a wide range of interesting topics and allows one to hear many different thoughts and perspectives.

The Teacher's Role

P. David Pearson suggests that a teacher's role is "to act as a sort of tour guide to help students see richness and possibilities" (1985, 736). This book is based on the premise that if we want students to learn, we must show them how. Teachers engaged in nonfiction inquiry choose their own topic of study, research it, craft a final report, and present their findings. In my staff development work, I encourage teachers to follow the gradual-release-of-responsibility instructional model (Pearson and Gallagher 1983), explicitly presenting learning strategies and then gradually handing over responsibility while modeling and guiding. (This model is discussed further in Chapter 5.)

Thoughts to Guide Our Practice

• • • • • • • • • Much of the basic premise of this book comes from the work of Donald Graves. Graves speaks eloquently about teachers being learners first, demonstrating their own learning and commitment and thereby showing students that learning is important enough for adults to do. He also stresses the importance of student ownership of learning. When students choose their topics and projects, engagement soars. And lastly, inquiry-based learning cannot flourish without time to practice and opportunities to share, both of which Graves advocates in his workshop model for reading and writing.

In the course of our work on nonfiction inquiry, my teacher colleagues and I have discovered a few things we keep in mind to guide our practice. The following notions are not etched in stone. However, they have worked for us, and this book is written with them in mind.

- *Teachers can demonstrate how to engage in nonfiction inquiry by going through the process themselves.* Teaching students about nonfiction reading, writing, and research requires teachers to show the process researchers go through as well as describe it. The teachers in this book do research projects along with their students. By engaging in research and writing a report of their own, teachers show themselves to be learners. Focus lessons on the stages of the process can be explicitly modeled. An added bonus is that teachers learn something new themselves.

- *Teachers need to share their passion and curiosity about inquiry and research.* Teachers can model their love of inquiry and share the questions they have.

- *Research begins with a question.* Humans engage in authentic research only when they are driven to find something out. Classrooms that value wonder and curiosity breed young researchers who are compelled to answer questions.

- *Research projects take time*—a great deal of it; time to think, to choose topics, to build background knowledge, to ask questions, to read, to research, to collect information, to reflect, to write, and ultimately to present findings. And it is worth every bit of time it takes.

- *To write nonfiction, read nonfiction.* Teachers can provide instruction in specific strategies for reading nonfiction. They can immerse young writers in examples of well-written nonfiction, using reference books as sources of information, not as models for writing.

- *Writers write best about things they know about, care about, and wonder about.* Encouraging young writers to discover, explore, and ask questions about their passions is a primary responsibility of the nonfiction teacher.

- *Writers need to own their topics and projects.* The obvious way to bring this about is to allow students to pursue any topic they choose. If the curriculum requires a certain topic (Africa, for example), that topic can be the umbrella under which a writer is allowed to write about a particular interest. Topics are limited only by the imagination. The writer makes project decisions with the teacher's ongoing support and input.

- *Writers need opportunities to share their products.* Celebration is in order when a research project has been completed. Writers need time to share their insights. Other members of the class can learn from these reports.

- *Nonfiction inquiry must be authentic whenever possible.* Authenticity reigns supreme in nonfiction inquiry. Topics are chosen based on sincere questions and interest. Research involves real-world pursuits such as Web searches, interviews, and surveys. Professionals serve as mentors. Writing is modeled through authentic nonfiction text from magazines, trade books, billboards. If we adhere to this ideal of authenticity, we deliver added value throughout students' lives.

A Road Map of This Book

This book has three parts. The first part, *Conditions for Successful Inquiry,* which includes chapters on passion, wonder, topic selection, resources, and modeling, lays a foundation for inquiry, suggests necessary tools and resources for inquiry-based classrooms, and sets the tone for inquiry-based learning. The middle part, *The Nitty-Gritty,* which contains chapters on reading nonfiction, secondary research, primary research, and organization, describes the messy activities of reading for information, gathering information, and sorting, sifting, and synthesizing information. The final part, *Putting It All Together,* which features chapters on crafting strategies, reporting genres, project management, and presentations and assessment, focuses on the late phases of inquiry in which researchers synthesize their ideas and gain new insight. Feel free, however, to jump to any chapter that meets a certain need at a certain time.

Conditions for Successful Inquiry

2

Honoring Passion

I never had to think much about clothing my son, Alex, because he always
dressed in the style of his current obsession—a pirate at age two, a cowboy at four, and a medieval knight in armor on the day he marched off to
kindergarten.

When he turned eight, we took him to see Andrew Lloyd Webber's
Phantom of the Opera. Subsequently, he took to dressing in a black satin cape
and a white plastic half mask. Strains of the libretto blared incessantly from
his bedroom, and he soon memorized every word and note. Spring break
that year found us at an Arizona dude ranch. Kids in chaps, boots, and ten-
gallon hats swarmed the place. On a sunrise horseback ride, Alex, in
Phantom garb, sang the score as we ambled through the desert. The adults
were charmed; he had a booming voice and a strong command of the language. The other kids, however, raised noticeable eyebrows. Later that
morning, we witnessed our little boy scrambling up a mountain with a dozen
kids in pursuit taunting him with shouts of "Opera Boy, Opera Boy, sing for
us, sing for us!" We rescued him, as good parents would, and later tried to
help him understand the real world. I advised him that he better save both
the singing and the costumes for his own house. "But I love the music and
the story," he protested.

"They'll make fun of you, like today," I told him. "If you want to get
along and have friends, you have to act more *normal.*"

He later fell in love with the stories and language of Shakespeare, mem-
orizing speech after speech and delivering them with a passion I'd never seen
in a child of ten. The historic plays soon led to an interest in history, the
swashbuckling parts of course. The potential for ridicule really worried me. As
he climbed aboard a plane for camp one year, I kissed his forehead and offered
these final words of advice: "Remember, no Shakespeare down there, Alex."

Today, these words stick like a knife in my heart. I am a reading and writing teacher, and prose, poetry, and music are paramount in my life. Yet I told my child not to imagine; I told my child not to sing; I told my child not to speak the words of Shakespeare. I surrendered my son's passion to the culture of conformity. I made this mistake as a parent. We can't make this mistake as teachers. Teachers, schools, and districts that stamp out cookie-cutter kids are selling them short.

Passion is at the heart of inquiry. Interest and curiosity breed engagement. We must honor kids' passion and celebrate their individuality. Exploring passions, interests, and questions brings the world into focus and opens the door for the broadest interpretation of ideas. Solutions to big questions rarely emerge from cloned thoughts.

When teachers share their passion and investigate compelling questions, kids climb aboard. Nonfiction reading, research, and writing stoke the inquiry engine as it chugs toward solutions to big questions. With teachers as tour guides, learners can follow the passion path to its final destination, a new insight into the world.

Share Your Passion

Passion is contagious. Teachers who share their passions develop learners who want to explore theirs. Leslie Blauman, an intermediate classroom teacher, devours nonfiction. Yet most students in her classroom were subsisting—barely—on a diet of fiction. It dawned on Leslie that although she read nonfiction daily at home, most of the books she featured in her classroom were fiction. She immediately began to supplement her classroom collection with a wide range of nonfiction text. When Leslie promoted nonfiction and extolled its many virtues, kids picked it up.

Ben, a fifth grader, hungered for a new genre. Thanks to Leslie, he has now tasted something new, and his nonfiction appetite continues to grow. We all learned an important lesson when Ben handed Leslie the note shown in Figure 2.1.

Intermediate teacher Nancy Burton also understands this contagious passion. Several years ago, after relishing Barry Lopez's *Arctic Dreams* (1986), a book written for adults, Nancy decided to guide her students through an Arctic study. She adapted Lopez's book for fourth, fifth, and sixth graders. Nancy's love for the topic shone through in her adaptation, her knowledge of the subject, and her desire to know more. Her enthusiasm spread. The kids knew that any teacher who would rewrite a four-hundred-page book must really love what the book has to say. Kids caught the bug and explored a wide range of frigid topics, ultimately choosing one that captured their imagination.

Ed, an economist who bought his first stock with money from a childhood paper route, paid a visit to Judy Davis's Manhattan New School fifth-grade class. Kids were flipping through the newspaper reading various sections. Grady, sitting alone toward the back of the room, stared quizzically at

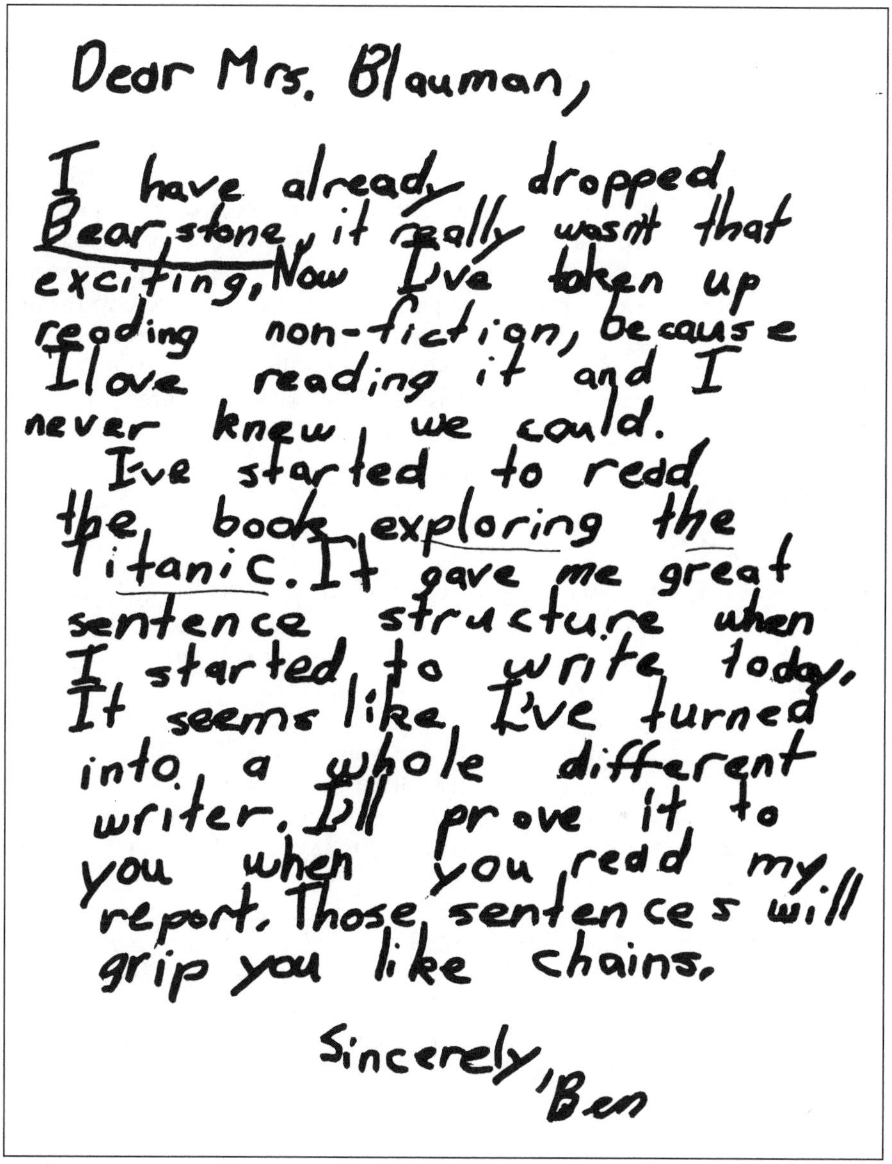

Dear Mrs. Blauman,

I have already dropped Bearstone, it really wasn't that exciting, Now I've taken up reading non-fiction, because I love reading it and I never knew we could.

I've started to read the book exploring the Titanic. It gave me great sentence structure when I started to write today. It seems like I've turned into a whole different writer. I'll prove it to you when you read my report. Those sentences will grip you like chains.

Sincerely,
Ben

Figure 2.1 *Ben extolls the virtues of nonfiction.*

the stock page. Ed crouched on the floor next to him. Grady wanted information on Nike, because he loved his shoes and Michael Jordan, in that order. However, stock-page literacy eluded him. Ed began to teach him. Soon eleven kids circled Grady and this visitor, all turned to the stock page, firing questions about the market. Judy later remarked that the stock page had never held such allure. Grady's interest combined with Ed's passion elevated the stock page right up there with the sports page, for half an hour anyway.

Some kids find their passions early on and explore them every day. You know the type, the fourth grader whose sketchpad bursts with every known breed of horse, the seventh grader who heads straight to the balance beam immediately after school each day.

Teachers need to help the reticent souls find and develop their passion. Sayab, a fourth grader in Nancy Burton's room, struggled to find his passion. Nancy encouraged him. In his search, he ventured down a series of exploratory paths, including prealgebra and short-story writing. A book about pre-Revolutionary America piqued his interest, and he decided to research that time period further. Sayab wrote in his notebook, "During this trip down the passion path, I learned that it is no easy task to find your true passion. It is a long hard search through yourself. I learned through this journey. I found worlds I had not known before. It is a great fabulous thing to truly know your passion."

Curators and Collections

● ● ● ● ● ● ● ● ● ● In 1993, my husband and I traveled to Tibet, the rooftop of the world. It is a country of a remarkably spiritual and peaceful people who continue to be oppressed by the Chinese giant next door. The experience changed my life, and I now have a commitment to Tibet and the Tibetans that only grows deeper and stronger. Tibet has become one of my great passions. Kids and teachers with whom I work know that Tibet will probably pop up somewhere in my conversation or instruction.

I simply can't ignore information on Tibet, whether it be geographic, historic, religious, artistic, musical, literary, cultural, or economic. I have a laundry basket filled with things Tibetan. Whenever I read a new article about Tibet, see a new photograph, come across an unfamiliar book, or find a tape of Tibetan music, I add it to my collection. It is a museum and a library in miniature. The more information I gather, the more I learn about Tibet, and the more passionate I become about this extraordinary country.

When I begin a collaborative nonfiction study with a classroom teacher, I talk to the kids about the role of a museum curator. Dr. Gwen Chanzit, a curator of contemporary art at the Denver Art Museum, told me in 1996:

> In one sense, a curator is a caretaker or keeper. Museum curators are scholarly specialists who study, identify, and organize objects to further the three primary functions of a museum: to collect, preserve, and interpret objects. As experts in a field, curators collect, authenticate, research, publish, and display objects, helping make collections accessible and meaningful to others.

I explain to the kids that we can become curators of our research projects. We can be passionate collectors of ideas and artifacts that help us enhance our understanding of a topic. We can develop collections around topics and act as custodians of those collections. We can make these collections our own as we ask questions, research sources, interpret information, and exhibit our final product through publication and presentation.

I let the kids know that I am the curator of my own private collection on Tibet. Whenever I launch a nonfiction research project in a classroom, whatever the topic, I share my Tibetan curatorial collection. I want kids to see how passionate I am about a certain topic and how much my collection means to me. Sharing one's passion during the germinal stages of research models a love of learning and a desire to know more that is at the heart of nonfiction inquiry.

When teachers launch a curriculum-based area of study, they can begin by collecting related resources (text sets) to share with students in an effort to build background knowledge and develop enthusiasm. If the teacher chooses interesting examples to include in the text set, students stand a good chance of getting fired up about the topic. (See Chapter 8 for more about text sets.)

Building a Community of Learners

• • • • • • • • • As kids begin to explore topics they care about as a precursor to in-depth research, their classmates can be terrific resources. What one student wants to know, another may already know. Teachers can take a number of practical actions to encourage this learning community. A bulletin board entitled Just So You Know is useful for keeping track of what individual class members are curating: "Just so you know, Mrs. Harvey needs information on Tibet." "Just so you know, Alicia has information on JFK." An alternative, which middle school kids seem to prefer, is a straightforward chart divided into two columns, one entitled Information Needed, the other headed Information Available.

Leslie Blauman displays a three-column wall chart headed Name, Topic, and Resource. Students enter their name and topic, and members of the school community are encouraged to post sticky notes with resource suggestions. For example, when Amy was investigating her passion, animal medicine, Nathan placed a sticky note with his veterinarian dad's phone number in the resource column. When Douglas was exploring the Hubble telescope, Katy volunteered an Internet address for a NASA Web page. Postings like these keep the information churning and help build a strong sense of community.

At the Stanley British Primary School in Denver, every child and adult in the school community possesses an area of expertise (AOE). These AOEs range from a first grader's knowledge about cheetahs to a custodian's expertise in quilting. AOEs are displayed prominently in the school's corridors, so school community members know where to go for specific information. People in the school, adults and students alike, are expected to set aside some time each year to teach their AOE.

Kids and teachers who assume the role of curator soon realize that passion requires ever greater amounts of information. The more they know, the more they want to know. Storage space evaporates as kids collect mounds of information providing a truly rich base for writing. A strong sense of community emerges as individuals, aware of others' interests, passions, and expertise, contribute to one another's learning.

The Nonfiction Writer's Notebook

• • • • • • • • • Many writers keep notebooks in which they record their day-to-day thinking. Don Murray, a writer and writing teacher, believes that keeping a notebook, or daybook as he refers to it, is one of the habits that distinguishes those who write from those who don't. "The daybook is a record of my intellectual life, what I'm thinking and what I'm thinking about writing" (1985, 68). Betty Osbourne suggests that writers who keep notebooks "learn not only to honor what they see, but to look in the first place" (Hindley 1996, 13). Nonfiction writers must be keen observers of the world who remember "to look in the first place."

The nonfiction writer's notebook is perhaps the most important tool for young researchers engaged in inquiry. My colleagues and I have found that first exploring passions and interests in the nonfiction notebook often leads to big research questions and compelling writing.

AKA Wonder Books

Mary Urtz, who stared up at me from those lifeless reports on countries of the world, teaches fourth grade now. Mary and her students use notebooks to support nonfiction inquiry. These *wonder books,* as her kids call them, give students daily opportunities to explore passions, thoughts, and questions in writing. Her students keep these notebooks throughout their study of nonfiction.

Mary introduces notebooks by reading true-to-life narratives in which the author or main character records and reflects on her or his thinking in a notebook, journal, or diary. She has used the following picture books to launch nonfiction notebook writing in her classroom:

- Byrd Baylor's *I'm in Charge of Celebrations* (1986), in which the main character cherishes the southwestern environment, celebrates nature, and writes about personal celebrations.
- Mary Ann Fraser's *Sanctuary* (1994), the true story of two naturalists who explored and photographed the wild Oregon coast at the turn of the century. Their handwritten notebook entries and compelling photographs of seabirds and mammals convinced lawmakers to preserve the area as the first wildlife sanctuary in the United States.
- Virginia Wright-Frierson's *A Desert Scrapbook* (1996), which offers an artist's view of the Sonoran Desert. It includes sketches, watercolors, and notes about the Arizona ecosystem.

When beginning nonfiction inquiry, Mary's young writers use these wonder books to write about their passions and interests. Ultimately, these notebooks may contain:

- Statements of prior knowledge and passion.
- Questions and wonderings.
- Current thoughts.
- Topic lists.
- Project ideas.
- Drawings, diagrams, and doodles.
- Character and scene sketches.
- Quotes from books, teachers, other kids.
- Poems and rhymes.
- Observations.
- Interviews.
- Notes from print research.
- Notes from electronic research.
- Notes on field research.
- Bibliographic information.
- Reminders about the craft of writing.
- Models of beautiful language.
- Lists of nonfiction conventions.
- Photographs, pictures, and postcards.
- Early drafts.

A Focus Lesson

After launching the concept of nonfiction notebooks, Mary shares her own interests as a model. "Here are some things I know well, care a lot about, and still want to explore further," she tells her class, listing these interests on a page of large spiral-bound chart paper. (Bound chart paper appeals to Mary because it becomes a permanent record of class activity. She keeps the flipchart where the kids can go back to it and reread pages when they need to.) Her list includes:

- Dogs and cats (their behavior mostly).
- Running.
- Families during Westward Expansion—especially pioneers traveling to Colorado.

Mary continues, "I love dogs and cats. It's so amazing how the cat streaks into the kitchen from out of nowhere when I crank up the electric can open-er. And if I happen to pick up the dog's leash, forget about it. He bounds around the house like a banshee. You know my passion for running. I could write pages about that. And I'm really interested in the brave pioneer women and children who came to Colorado by covered wagon. I'd like to learn more about all of these things.

"Now it's your turn. Think about those things you know and care about and might want to explore further. Try to think of at least three interests and list them in your wonder books." Mary asks for "at least three" in the belief that one will almost certainly emerge, even from the most reticent kids; three or more is a welcome bonus. (Jordan came up with twenty-two! See Figure 2.2.)

Figure 2.2 *Jordan's list of interests.*

The next day Mary rates the items on her list in terms of the following criteria:

- Is she passionate about it? Does she at least enjoy it?
- Does she know a lot about it?
- Could she teach someone about it?
- Does she want to learn more about it?

She eventually chooses to write about running, and does so in her notebook. After writing rapidly for several minutes, she shares what she has written with the students. Then she encourages kids to evaluate their topic list using the above criteria, putting stars next to topics about which they answer yes to one of the questions. "If a topic has more than two stars, that might be a place to start," she suggests.

Jesse categorizes those things he enjoys, knows about, and wants to learn more about (see Figure 2.3). Star Wars surfaces in each category and emerges as a good candidate for further exploration.

Figure 2.3 *Categorizing things students enjoy, know well, and want to learn more about.*

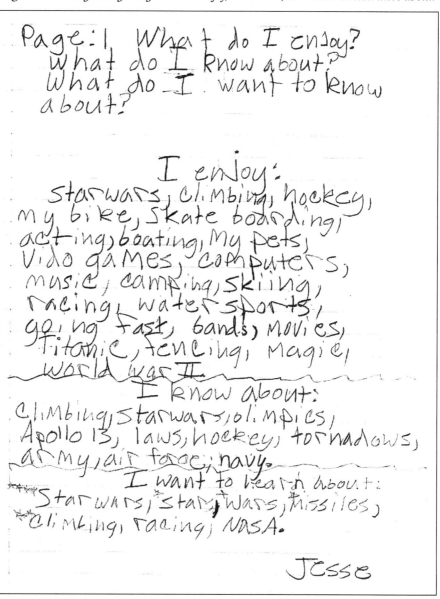

Page:1 What do I enjoy?
What do I know about?
What do I want to know about?

I enjoy:
starwars, climbing, hockey, my bike, skate boarding, acting, boating, My pets, Vido games, computers, music, camping, skiing, racing, water sports, going fast, bands, Movies, Titanic, fencing, Magic, world war II

I know about:
Climbing, starwars, olimpics, Apollo 13, laws, hockey, tornadows, army, air force, navy.

I want to learn about:
Star wars, stam wars, missiles, climbing, racing, NASA.

                                              Jesse

After selecting an interest, most kids follow Mary's lead and write as much as they can on the subject. Jade's passion for dance is obvious:

> I dance because I can express myself without words. I think that dancing is a gift. It's not something easy where anyone can just get out there and do it. My nanny Sharon influenced me. She would always talk about dancing and her experiences when she was a little girl. So I joined a dance studio. A person whom I look up to is Mikhail Baryshnikof, a Russian dancer who sneaked into America to dance freely.

Colin's knowledge of paleontology and Earth's early geology is striking. From the looks of his notebook entry, he appears to have enough background knowledge to develop some good research questions if he decides to explore this topic further:

> There are three kinds of dinosaurs, carnivores, herbivores, and omnivores, meat eaters, plant eaters and both. Our continents were different before dinosaur times. First, we only had one continent. It was called Pangaea. In later years, it split into two continents, Laurasia and Gondwana which split into our seven continents North America, South America, Europe, Australia, Asia, Antarctica and Africa. My favorite dinosaurs are Triceratops and Veloceraptor. I love to see old dinosaur bones, because I can almost see a living dinosaur when I look at a skeleton.

When kids finish writing, they share in pairs and learn about their partner's interest. Topics can be contagious. Ashley listens to Jade's notes on ballet and decides to write about dancing in her wonder book because she, too, is a dancer.

The students continue to write about their passions and interests every day. In most cases, they write expansively, because they are so interested in their topics. When they've written all they care to on one topic, they move on to another.

Amie shared Mary's love of dogs. After exhausting her prior knowledge about dogs, Amie picked up a picture book and came across some new information on dogs (see Figure 2.4), which she then shared with her teacher, aware of their mutual interest.

Writing in these wonder books and sharing the entries with one another helped shape a community of learners in Mary's classroom early in the year. The kids knew where the class expertise lay and viewed one another as important resources in the quest for knowledge. They learned from each other.

Passion goes a long way toward uncovering topics that ask burning questions and prompting successful research and writing. Adar, a fifth grader in Judy Davis's class, chose to investigate classic complaints about New York City. "I've lived in New York all my life," he wrote. "I hear people complaining all the time. I really know about this. Complaints about noise, dog-do, lit-

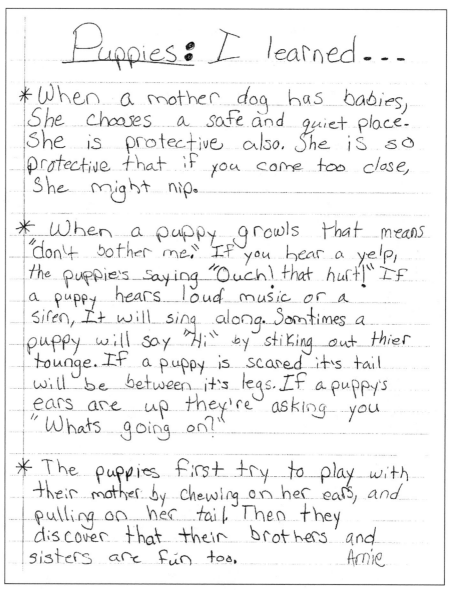

Figure 2.4 *Some information Amie gleaned from beginning research.*

ter, constant construction, high prices, scary subway stories and air pollution at its smelly worst. I'm passionate about New York. After all, I'm a New Yorker. I'm interested in finding out more, about the feelings, opinions and motivations of other New Yorkers." Adar's passion and curiosity about his topic made research and writing joyful.

Sharing passion builds community. I'm reminded of second grader Troy, who was in my class the first year I taught. He scanned the rows of desks in our classroom, searching for my nightly resting spot. When I told him I slept in a small house near a city park, his jaw dropped. He had assumed I lived at school. In a funny way, Troy taught me that I needed to share a little more of myself with the class. When teachers share their thoughts and their passions, students will pick up on it and do the same.

Some people are uncomfortable sharing their personal lives. Not to worry. Nonfiction inquiry allows us to share our interests and demonstrate our passion for learning without having to reveal the inner secrets of our soul.

In *On Writing Well*, William Zinsser's guide to nonfiction writing, he states, "Motivation is at the heart of writing. . . . Go where your interest lies or your affection or your passion" (1990, 58). Nonfiction inquiry flourishes in classrooms where teachers and kids share and explore passions and join together in a community of learners. Teachers who lead kids in the direction of their passion will not regret it.

3

Questions that Compel

It is said that as a young boy Albert Einstein had trouble getting to sleep at night. His mother would kiss his forehead, murmur "Sleep tight," and switch off the light. Later, just before she was about to turn in for the night herself, she would crack the door to check on him, only to find him lying on his back, eyes wide, staring at the ceiling. One particularly late night, she came in and sat down at the foot of his bed.

"Why can't you sleep?" she asked him.

"I'm thinking," he answered.

"About what?"

"I'm wondering where the light goes."

"What light?" his mother asked.

"When you switch off the lamp each night, where does the light go?"

If his mother was anything like me, she probably said, "Jeez, where do you think it goes? It goes out, Albert, the light goes out! Now go to sleep." Nevertheless, this story intrigues me. That Einstein's curiosity prompted him to solve one of the greatest mysteries of our physical universe serves as an important lesson. Curiosity comes in all forms. Kids have a natural sense of wonder. They wonder about all sorts of things—*nothing* is too trivial. And knowledge expands because of what kids wonder.

Kids need to be helped to build on their natural sense of wonder. Now when a student asks me something I can't answer or a question I'm tempted to deem superfluous, I think of young Albert's insomnia and answer, "Let's see if we can find out."

Valuing Questions

Questions are the door to human wonder. Mine them with a pick ax. All kids have questions. Middle school kids are often too embarrassed to ask them. I knew a sixth-grade girl who was so afraid of asking questions that her perceptive teacher checked with her after class each day to see whether she had any. But clandestine meetings in the corridor are not the answer.

We can learn a lesson from kindergartners and preschoolers. They bubble over with questions. Inhibition is a foreign concept. On our son Alex's first day of kindergarten, the principal came in to welcome the fresh new faces and ask if there were any questions. Almost every hand in the class shot up. He called on Alex, who, very sincerely, asked why kids couldn't come to school barefoot. The adults bit their lips to muffle their chuckles, and the bewildered school head mumbled something about safety and continued on his way. He missed the point. It is as important to have the question and ask it as it is to wear shoes in school. Kids need to know there are no stupid questions.

Teachers can fertilize the ground so that questions grow in abundance. Leslie Blauman sends a letter to her incoming fourth graders two weeks before the start of school each year. She writes about herself, mentioning her family life, a favorite book, her special interests, and some things she wonders about. She invites kids to come in the first day ready to share an interest and a question. Leslie sets a tone that values wonder before kids ever set foot in the classroom.

Nurturing Wonder and Promoting Questioning

Schools can strive to be safe havens for inquiry. We need to convince kids that we value their questions and celebrate them for asking. This may be difficult. In many schools asking questions takes a backseat to answering them. The following activities establish an environment that nurtures wonder and promotes active questioning instead of passive answering:

- *Holding classwide discussions.* Build in time each day for discussions about real issues, real events, and real people that increase background knowledge, arouse curiosity, and foster questioning.
- *Reading aloud.* Highlight your own questions as you read out loud and thus encourage kids to think of and verbalize their own questions. Read-alouds stimulate wonder. The conversation that occurs before, during, and after reading aloud broadens knowledge and fosters questioning.
- *Coding text.* Have students mark text with sticky notes to keep track of questions that pop up while they are reading, either entering a question mark as a symbolic prompt or writing their question out in full.
- *Identifying burning questions.* Ask students to record things they wonder on a designated bulletin board. Then have class members and school personnel check out the question board and provide information if they are able.
- *Playing question games.* Play question games for a few minutes each day. In one such game, students take turns asking questions about anything they wonder. This is a useful way to honor the myriad questions stu-

dents have and satisfy them quickly. Questions that can't be answered by anyone in the room, including the teacher, or that lead to other questions can be recorded for further research by the entire class. Question cards from games like Brainquest and Trivial Pursuit appeal to kids as well. You can share these questions while kids are putting things away and cleaning up, speeding up transitions in the process.

- *Instituting a question of the day.* Each day, challenge a different student to come up with a sincere question about a class unit or subject under study. After the student asks the question, class members and teachers attempt to answer it as best they can. This helps clear up any misconceptions.

- *Charting questions on a question web.* Create a question web by placing a question in a circle at the center of a web. Have students research the question and write answers on the arms that extend from the circled question. The central question produces many answers, showing students that questions frequently have more than one answer. Sometimes the teacher chooses the question; sometimes the students do.

- *Reading newspaper and magazine columns.* One of Denver's major dailies, the *Rocky Mountain News,* features a column entitled Reader's Wacky Questions. The column solicits readers' questions and researches answers. (One year our class discovered that neckties evolved from medieval scarves.) You can also encourage your students to submit unusual questions to local newspapers; they might be published.

- *Reading question books.* Books such as *How Come?* (Wollard 1993) deal with a wide array of interesting questions. *Who Put the Butter in Butterfly?* (Feldman 1989) answers questions about word etymology. *Where Fish Go in Winter and Answers to Other Great Mysteries* (Koss 1987) poses questions such as, Why does popcorn pop? and then answers them in the form of a poem. *Tintin's Travel Diaries* is a series of books on different countries. Each volume focuses on a specific country. One page asks a question, and the following page contains a diary entry that answers it. The Tibetan volume (De Bruycker and Noblet 1995) has a special appeal for me!

Sincere Questions: Can You Really Trust a Tiger?

A group of third-grade teachers invited my colleague Liz Stedem to come in, model some nonfiction writing strategies, and fire up their young writers about research. It was animal report time; these third graders were to choose a favorite animal, research subtopics such as habitat and food sources, and report on what they found out.

Liz didn't object to animals per se as a topic, but she knew that compelling research comes from curiosity and a desire to know more. True research is more than merely reporting information. True research answers sincere questions to which researchers don't know the answers. Liz had an idea, and more important, a sincere question.

She sat in a rocking chair with the kids swarmed in front of her. "So are you ready to think about animals today?" Liz asked. A gaggle of heads bobbed up and down. "Me too. I'll be doing my own animal research and writing along with you. I've been thinking about investigating tigers; I'll tell you why. I was in Las Vegas last weekend, and I saw an amazing show with snow-white tigers. After the show was over, the animal trainers answered questions from people in the audience. One woman asked where the tigers stayed at night, and the trainers explained that the tigers lived on their property, sometimes wandering around inside their house!" Dozens of saucer-size eyes and anvil-laden jaws grew even wider.

"You know what? I haven't been able to stop thinking about this. I mean, I just keep wondering, can you really trust a tiger to wander freely around your house, even if it is highly trained? Tigers interest me, but unless I have a burning question about them, doing research and writing about them seems a little silly. I can easily look up stuff in the encyclopedia. Why just rewrite the information? I'm going to research my own question about tiger behavior and find out about that," Liz said as she wrote the question Can tigers be trusted? in her notebook.

Liz sent the kids out to pore over the many nonfiction animal books scattered throughout the room. (See the "Well-Crafted Nonfiction Books About Animals" bibliography.) She encouraged them to jot down anything they sincerely wondered as they immersed themselves in the topic of animals. Logan, a snake lover, came across a picture of what looked like a thread-size worm less than a quarter of an inch long. The caption "World's smallest snake" stunned him. "Mrs. Stedem, how could a snake be this small? It looks like a tiny worm. I wonder how big the biggest snake is?" he asked.

The striking picture of the tiny snake inspired Logan to wonder sincerely about snake size. Liz suggested he continue searching snake books for more information. She left him flipping through a vivid picture book in search of huge snakes.

Problem Solvers and Problem Finders

My husband's economic research firm used to look for "problem solvers" when hiring new people. They now search additionally for "problem finders," those who ask authentic, probing questions and discover problems before they materialize. Students who ask sincere questions become motivated learners who solve problems and perhaps prevent problems in the process. Traditionally, schools have focused on answers to the exclusion of questions. Sincere questions are still rare in schools.

History teacher Kate Redmond asked her eighth graders, in groups of three or four, to read the newspaper critically in search of potential problems. One group found an article that mentioned that even when schools are wired to be able to access the Internet, many teachers are inadequately trained in how to use it. The students brainstormed solutions to this potential problem, including having students teach teachers how to use the Internet and earn high school credit in the process!

We need to train young minds to ask authentic questions that uncover problems as well as solve them.

You Can't Ask a Question You Know Nothing About

• • • • • • • • • Sincere questions of substance like Can you really trust a tiger? or How do you bridge the gap between technology and teacher training? emerge from the curiosity of a learner who knows enough about the topic to ask a thoughtful question. Authentic, beefy questions arise from knowing about something and wanting to know more. I overflow with Tibetan questions, because I have so much prior information on the subject. I'd be hard-pressed, however, to ask a decent question about Colorado water conservation, because I know so little about it.

Carol Newman, a school librarian in Boulder, Colorado, told me, "Kids need time to explore topics before we ask them to formulate definitive research questions. Often they don't know which questions to ask early in the research process, because they don't know enough. They can investigate topics, build background knowledge, and learn as they research, becoming more knowledgeable and more curious, gathering important questions along the way. I have seen kids go to great lengths to find answers to questions that compel them."

K-W-L Charts

Deep inquiry involves taking what you know, exploring it in depth, wondering about it, determining what else you want to know, formulating research questions, finding information, and forming new ideas. A three-column chart, commonly called a *K-W-L chart*, headed What I Know, What I Want to Know, and What I Learned has great potential for students investigating research topics (Ogle 1986). But K-W-Ls can be easily misused.

Many teachers are aware that prior knowledge precedes independent practice. K-W-L charts are an increasingly popular way to help students activate their background knowledge before delving into a new topic; they have become so popular that in some classrooms kids are asked to fill out a K-W-L chart every time they read an unfamiliar story, write an essay, or begin a new unit. "Don't forget to fill in your K-W-L first," teachers remind students. Watch out when the K-W-L chart becomes just more busywork.

K-W-L charts are highly effective tools to support nonfiction inquiry and clarify thinking when teachers not only activate but *build* their students' background knowledge by reading about and exploring a subject and then modeling K-W-L chart development in front of the class. K-W-L charts serve independent inquiry well, because students typically investigate topics they already know something about. Constructing a K-W-L is most useful when kids use what they already know from the first column to determine what they want to know in the second column and, finally, recognize what they've learned in the third column.

Xander's K-W-L chart about the history of American bluegrass music (see Figure 3.1) shows a plethora of background knowledge, some thoughtful, sincere questions, and the beginning of some key learning. Expose students to K-W-L charts and encourage their judicious use.

Categorizing Questions

Staff developer Anne Goudvis understands the importance of building prior knowledge. In collaboration with the school librarian and a classroom teacher, Anne initiated an exploration of the Civil War period with a group of fifth graders by selecting some Civil War picture books to read and discuss. Anne

Figure 3.1 *A well-conceived K-W-L chart.*

What I know	What I want to know	What I learned
It is a mountain music with a twangy sound. There is a difference between blue grass and country. Banjos and guitars are involved. It seems like a happy form of music. I'm sure I could get really interested in it. I know of one band called New Grass Revival	Because I'm so interested in history in general, I really want to know about the history of blue grass music. I want to know the fundamentals. I want to know where the limited blue grass I've heard fits in. I want to know about all of the instruments involved and what roles they play. I want to know who the definitive blue grass musicians are. I want to develope expertise in blue grass music	I learned that blue grass is an improvisationally based instrumental music. I learned that the mandolin is a big part of Blue grass. I learned that unlike any other form of music, blue grass didn't evolve, but was rather invented by one person, Bill Munrue. I learned that its mountainous origins were fewer than I expected. I learned that I wanted to be a professional mandolin player.

believed the books, a striking collection of interesting narrative nonfiction and historical fiction, would serve as a springboard, perhaps leading to a compelling question for further discussion or research. Anne hoped to guide these students to analyze questions, categorize them, and decide which best lent themselves to further exploration.

Because she suspected *Aunt Harriet's Underground Railroad in the Sky* (Ringold 1992) would spawn many questions, Anne chose to read aloud this surrealistic fantasy about contemporary siblings who are transported to the era of Harriet Tubman and the Underground Railroad.

"Anything you wonder?" she asked her listeners as she closed the book. Did they ever. Anne recorded their questions on chart paper and pointed out that the questions fell into different categories. She explained that although all questions are important, some make better research questions than others. A lively discussion ensued as the class considered various classifications. Ultimately, they decided that their questions fell into the following categories:

- Questions that could be answered in the text. *Example: Where were they going to find freedom?*
- Questions to clarify confusion. *Example: What is meant by the "cost of freedom"?*
- Questions whose answers could be inferred from the text. *Example: How come slaves were not treated as human beings?*
- Questions that might be answered from someone's background knowledge. *Example: When did this story take place?*
- Questions that require further research in order to be answered. *Example: Why didn't the Constitution protect slaves?*

Then they used codes to indicate which questions on the chart fell into which category: *T* for answered in the text, *C* for words or ideas that caused confusion, *I* for inferred answers, *BK* for answers from background knowledge, and *R* for answers that required further research. Individual background knowledge varies from topic to topic. Some readers may be able to answer questions from background knowledge while others can answer those same questions only by doing further research.

As kids discovered, easily answered questions did not lend themselves to further inquiry. However, further research could coalesce around unanswered questions. And the bigger, more puzzling questions usually emerged as the most suitable ones for in-depth inquiry.

Mini-Research Projects

Short-term research projects give kids the opportunity to indulge their curiosity, ask some questions, and find some answers. Mini-research projects allow students to scan sources to answer specific questions and satisfy curiosity rather than enter into deep, long-term explorations complete with culminating reports.

Early one year, Norton Moore and I launched a nonfiction mini-research project in his third-grade classroom. With the kids gathered around me on the floor, I explained that humans are naturally curious and driven to find things out. I pointed out that my passion for Tibet stimulates my curiosity, and I shared various print resources from my Tibetan curatorial collection, including picture books and articles on Buddhism, the Dalai Lama, sand mandalas, Mt. Everest, the Himalayas, avalanches, mountain climbing, and Tibetan daily life. I read a headline from the morning paper about a freak fall blizzard and subsequent avalanche in Tibet. Avalanches occur frequently in Colorado, and Colorado kids are often touched by news of snow slides. I explained that as a backcountry skier I needed more information on these powerful forces of nature for my personal safety. I settled on two questions I hoped to solve: How do avalanches happen? What should I do if I am trapped in an avalanche?

Thumbing through my collection, I pulled out Stephen Kramer's remarkable book *Avalanche* (1992) and turned to the table of contents to help find needed information. Avalanche safety and avalanche causes appeared as headings. I flipped to those pages and read them out loud. "There's your answer!" a voice cried out as I read. I found both answers quickly and recorded them in my notebook, having satisfied my curiosity about avalanches for now.

I mentioned that sometimes we answer our questions easily and move on to another topic. Other times, we need to conduct further research to find a solution. Sometimes we may even discover more questions. I followed up the next day with a question on the origins of Tibetan Buddhism. This search took three sources before finding an even partly satisfactory answer.

At the conclusion of this focus lesson, Norton and I suggested that kids record some burning questions and search sources in the room, ask an expert, head to the library, or get on-line in order to find solutions. Within a few days, most questions, a sample of which follows, were answered, at least partially.

- When did people first use horses?
- How do camels store water?
- Why do birds desert their eggs if people touch them?
- Which jet is fastest?
- Why do we get goose bumps?

Introducing nonfiction inquiry through mini-research engages kids without overwhelming them. These mini-investigations are an effective way to begin teaching kids about research. Later on when they tackle long-term research projects, they are more familiar with both the process and the terminology. Kids are curious. Mini-research projects value wonder and satisfy curiosity. Through these efforts, kids ask questions, search for information and find answers.

Last spring, I visited Manhattan's P.S. 234, a social studies focus school. The fourth and fifth grades were wrapping up an in-depth study of the Pilgrims. They had read, researched, and written reams about this time period and its historical impact. The teachers sensed that if they had done their jobs well, even deeper questions would emanate from the Pilgrim study. And sure enough, kids acquired new information that led to more thoughtful questions. Near the end of the project, a student asked why people move today. An interested research team interviewed people who had moved and discovered that people today move for much the same reasons as they have throughout history—to search for a better economic opportunity, to guarantee freedom from repression, and to be near loved ones. These students learned a powerful lesson about history's tendency to repeat itself from a question that lingered beyond the project.

Learners are naturally curious. Teachers who invite kids to identify an interest and ask questions about it are rewarded with classrooms filled with excitement, enthusiasm, and wonder. Classrooms like these give students the courage to wonder and take risks that lead to deeper explorations, longer journeys, and more valuable insights. Teachers and schools that celebrate curiosity and value wonder provide the foundation needed for lasting learning to take place. Live the questions. Value the questions. They are the doors to understanding.

4

Topics that Resonate:
Let the Writer Choose

My best questions emanate from those things I know and care most about. Writer and educator Lucy Calkins says, "Living like a nonfiction writer means watching for surprise and perplexity and mystery. It means knowing that even the subjects we know very well can be endlessly new to us" (1995, 438). When I am intrigued or perplexed by something, I begin collecting information and curating this new idea, recording my thoughts and questions in my notebook. The more information I collect, the greater my desire to find out about the idea.

Topics for inquiry emerge from the learner's interest and desire to know more. Some teachers encourage students to explore any topic of interest. Other teachers prefer to have their students study something in common, generating a community of learners who stretch toward greater understanding of a mutual idea, culture, event, or period. Either way, it's important to let the students choose.

Independent Inquiry

Nonfiction reading, research, and reporting is hard work. For students to maximize their inquiry experience, they should choose a topic they care about, know something about, and wonder about. Topics that surface from passion and wonder have the best chance of engaging students over the long haul. Choosing appropriate topics for further research takes time and thought on the part of both teachers and kids.

Librarian Carol Newman collaborates with classroom teachers on nonfiction inquiry. She reminds teachers to build in plenty of time for exploring interests, developing questions, and choosing topics. As kids explore interesting ideas, new questions arise and new topics emerge. Juanita, eager to learn about her dad's childhood in Mexico, initially decided to research Mexican holidays. However, early on she came across a captivating picture book, *Day of the Dead* (Hoyt-Goldsmith 1994), that captured her imagination and piqued her curiosity. A richer more focused topic emerged as Juanita expanded her study and explored a wider variety of sources.

Mary Urtz's and Leslie Blauman's students may choose any topic under the sun for further research. They spend the first three or four weeks of the year writing about their interests and passions in nonfiction notebooks (see Chapter 2). The more students explore interests through writing, the more questions they have and the more they want to know. By the time Mary and Leslie set a deadline, many students have already settled on a topic and developed some possible research questions.

Most students select topics they know something about but about which they want to learn more. Some students select topics they know a great deal about but not everything.

Dinosaurs were one of Colin's great passions. Like many fourth graders before him, this kid was a dinosaur nut! He knew the characteristics of almost every breed. Mary asked him if he wondered anything about dinosaurs. Colin acknowledged that he was curious about extinction. Rather than merely reporting on each dinosaur's behavior, sustenance, and habitat, Colin decided to investigate and evaluate the various theories of extinction, a more sophisticated inquiry than a mere recounting of facts about dinosaurs. Colin could tackle such a high-level topic because of his prior knowledge of dinosaurs.

Nudging Kids to Make a Choice

Some students struggle with topic selection. On the eve of the topic deadline, Thomas had not come up with a single idea for research. His mother rang Mary first thing in the morning and described a family in turmoil. Thomas had been up all night fraught with anxiety over his eleventh-hour missing topic. His mom's voice cracked as she wondered how he would ever organize sources, take notes, or write a report if he couldn't even think of a topic. School was not easy for Thomas. Thomas's mother believed that independent inquiry demanded too much of him. She suggested that Mary simply assign Thomas a topic so he could get started. Mary felt bad for Thomas and promised to talk with him that morning. The last thing Thomas needed was to be losing sleep.

Before kids entered the room, Mary pulled out Thomas's wonder book. The twisted spiral wire extended at least six inches beyond the half-torn cover. Writing was conspicuously absent. But precise drawings of NFL team logos covered the lined pages. Mary approached Thomas during writing time and asked how things were going.

"Lousy," Thomas answered.

"Why?"

"I can't think of a topic for this research project."

"What interests you, Thomas?" Mary asked.

"Nothin'," Thomas answered.

"Tell me about these drawings," Mary nudged.

"Oh those, those are nothin'," Thomas said, as he slid his notebook back into his desk.

"It looks like football stuff to me," Mary commented.

"Yeah, I guess," Thomas acknowledged.

"Can I see them?"

Thomas reached into his desk and handed the tattered wonder book to Mary.

"Wow, these are great. How many team helmets did you draw in here?" Mary asked.

"All of 'em," Thomas answered.

"No kidding. Did you copy them from somewhere?"

"No, I know the logo of every team in the NFL," Thomas said.

"Really! Which is your favorite?"

"The Broncos, of course."

"Thomas, these are really terrific drawings," Mary told him. She continued to draw Thomas out on the subject of football. Thomas not only knew the logos, but also the standings, schedules, and player statistics of most teams in the league. Thomas was an expert on the NFL and football in general, even though he had begun this conference by saying he had no interests. When Mary suggested that Thomas write about football in his wonder book and list a few questions he had, he was pleasantly surprised. He didn't associate football with school.

Mary pulled out several beautifully illustrated picture books and wondered whether Thomas might want to write and illustrate a picture book on some aspect of football as his research project. Thomas pulled a *Sports Illustrated* from his desk. John Elway graced the cover. Mary left Thomas reading about his idol. She hadn't actually assigned a topic. But she had explored Thomas's background knowledge and nudged him in a direction that matched his interests.

Thomas's struggle was far from over, of course. Reading, note taking, and writing challenged him throughout his inquiry. But finding an engaging topic represents a major step forward for kids like Thomas. Independent inquiry allows for the widest range of exploration. Choosing freely from an unlimited spectrum of topics gives kids the best shot at finding a subject that appeals to them.

Young writers need to know that selecting a topic is challenging. When I meet professional writers, I often ask them what they find most difficult about writing. The answer is almost always the same: thinking of something to write about. My students are relieved when I share this with them, because they too struggle to come up with ideas to write about.

Umbrella Topics

• • • • • • • • •   Nonfiction inquiry also lends itself to specific content areas. Many school districts mandate curriculum. In this context, a specific science or social studies unit can become an umbrella for an array of related topics. Teachers can teach content within a schema that incorporates the whole class, and students can choose a specific topic underneath this umbrella that allows them to explore a personal interest.

The Vast Umbrella of American History

The fifth-grade social studies curriculum in Lorraine Becker's school focuses on American History from the Revolution to the twentieth century. Two hundred and twenty-five years in one hundred and eighty days . . . whew! Lorraine decided to focus on the most significant historical periods: the American Revolution, the Civil War, World War II, and postwar twentieth century.

In September, Lorraine told her students they would be doing a year-end American History research project and encouraged them to think about a topic of interest as they studied American History over the course of the year. Their assignment over spring break would be to identify their topic.

After spring break, Lorraine made copies of the class topic list so that each student knew whom to ask for related information. Here is the final list:

- The legacy of Martin Luther King.
- Jackie Robinson and the great experiment.
- The Challenger disaster.
- Women's right to vote.
- The history of quilting.
- Revolutionary War clothing.
- The Minute Men and their contributions.
- Life of children during WWII.
- Boy soldiers in the Civil War.
- Nurses in WWII.
- The surprise attack on Pearl Harbor.
- Food in WWII.
- Letters home from Civil War soldiers.
- WWII bombs.
- The Ku Klux Klan.
- The expedition of Lewis and Clark.
- WWII battleships.

These rich, diverse topics bubbled to the surface because students had been thinking about their questions and passions throughout the year as they expanded their knowledge of events and eras in U.S. history. The topics originated in real things the kids wondered about: the plight of children during war; the food eaten and clothing worn by other generations; bombs; battleships; significant people. With an umbrella the size of American history, every student could find a topic of personal interest.

Australia from A to Z

One spring, third-grade teacher Kathy Marquet invited me to lend a hand with her class's annual Australian-animal reports. The previous year's reports had been uninspired. She knew her kids could do better. I remembered Liz Stedem's lesson on sincere questions. I wondered whether Kathy's students had any authentic questions. What about the students for whom animals held little interest? How could we help them write well about a topic they didn't care much about and therefore might not wonder much about?

I decided we needed to encourage a wider range of topics. How would Kathy feel about such a drastic change? "Could we use the larger umbrella of Australia for our topic?" I asked. Kathy looked at me quizzically. I elaborated: "Look, some kids love animals. They should pick one and write about it. But Australia is a big place. The range of topics is vast."

"Tough to manage. Every kid could be writing about a different topic." She raised her eyebrows sky-high.

I knew that management might be more difficult at first, but we could work on that. "Writers write best about things they care and wonder about. Encouraging a wider range of topics just might stimulate their interest and punch up the writing. What do you think?"

"Well, since we're in this together, why not?"

The next day, with Kathy, the rest of her teaching team, and the kids gathered round, I read from a photographic alphabet book called *A Is for Australia*. Things Australian, from A to Z, filled the pages. As I read, I thought out loud of topics that sparked my interest and piqued my curiosity, writing them down in my notebook. Later, I transferred them to a chart so everyone could watch me identify my top three choices:

- Australian pearls.
- Aboriginal art. (3)
- Box jellyfish/stingers. (1)
- How to care for cockatiels.
- The Great Barrier Reef. (2)
- The Sydney Opera House.
- Marsupials.

Thus began this class's wild and woolly process of choosing topics for nonfiction inquiry. The Australian sky was the limit. Kathy surrounded them with books, magazines, CD-ROMs, videos, and filmstrips to stimulate their thinking and increase their knowledge. As students came up with possible topics, we listed them on a class chart. Ideas burst like popcorn. The list grew longer every day. Eventually everyone was able to find a topic that grabbed him or her and learn a lot about Australia in the process.

Wondering and Asking

• • • • • • • • • For the Australian study in Kathy Marquet's room, I chose the poisonous box jellyfish. Did you wonder why?

Well, while my family was on a rain forest tour of northeastern Australia, our Land Rover stopped at a deserted powdered-sugar beach on the northern coast of Queensland. I had never seen a more pristine ribbon of sand or a more inviting turquoise sea. My daughter, Jessica, ten at the time, bounded across the beach, her hands clasped in a steeple above her head, ready to dive into the surf. A uniformed forest ranger appeared out of nowhere: "No swimming. Stay at least fifteen feet from the shore. It's stinger season . . . box jellyfish, the most poisonous creature on earth," he was explaining as I caught up with her.

The most poisonous creature on earth? I had never even heard of a box jellyfish. No wonder the beach was empty. We had to sit and swelter at the edge of that sparkling water and refrain from even dipping our toes. Needless to say, box jellyfish were not my passion, but I sure wanted to learn more about them.

My mind was alive with questions. Where did they come from? Did they live anywhere else? Could they really kill you? I put a two-column transparency on the overhead projector and scribbled down those things I knew and then jotted down related questions. (I suggested that the students try this double-entry format for their own investigations. Nicholas's entries about kangaroos are shown in Figure 4.1.)

Box Jellyfish

What I know	*What I wonder*
They are the most poisonous creature on earth.	How long does it take to die from a sting?
They sting.	How do they sting?
Their tentacles are very long, because the ranger told us to stay over 15 feet from shore.	How long are the tentacles?
	Are they the biggest jellyfish?
They are a type of jellyfish.	Are they good for anything?

My questions propelled my study. I searched for information, collecting books, articles, and pictures of the venomous creature and recording important ideas and questions in my notebook. The students soon began to share anything they came across that I might add to my collection. Their fascination with box jellyfish grew along with mine. Our questions fueled our inquiry, and our passion for the topic intensified.

A variation on this focus lesson uses a two-column format headed What I Learned and What I Wonder. After we had completed the Australian inquiry, I read these same third graders Kathryn Lasky's striking book *Monarchs* (1993), the story of the monarch butterfly's journey from egg to adulthood. The climax of the book is the massive black-and-orange migration from Canada to Michoacan, Mexico, each winter. Millions of monarchs fly there for a seasonal respite. (So many people travel to Michoacan to see this phenomenon that local residents have been able to replace logging—and the resulting deforestation—with tourism as a means of support.)

To demonstrate how we learn from nonfiction reading, I projected a portion of the text on the overhead, giving each student a copy. As we read

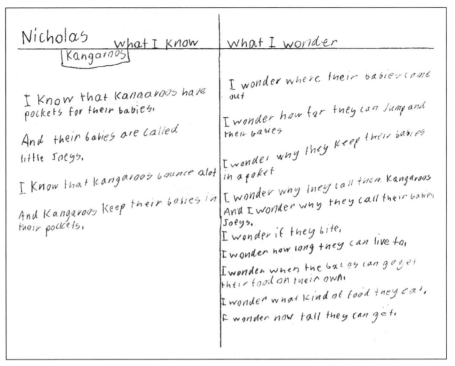

Figure 4.1 *Nicholas shows what he knows and what he wonders.*

through it, I had the kids raise their hand whenever they learned something new. I marked these new ideas with an *L*. I hinted that when they were surprised by something, it might mean they were learning something new. Then we read the passage again, and they raised their hand whenever they wondered something. I coded these sentences with a question mark. Later, while we discussed what we had learned and wondered, I entered this information and these questions on a two-column transparency headed What I Learned and What I Wonder. (Amanda's version of this chart is shown in Figure 4.2.)

After several more days of guided practice, the kids tried this independently, filling in their own learn/wonder charts on self-selected topics. David was reading *Exploring the Titanic* (Ballard 1988). His questions and learning are shown in Figure 4.3. Kathy had wondered whether David would be able to stick with this particularly challenging piece of text, but his passion for the topic stretched him to be able to do so.

Topic Roadblocks

• • • • • • • • • • Topics can be too broad, too narrow, or too difficult. Bruce, a fourth grader in Leslie Blauman's class, chose the Rocky Mountains for his inquiry. One visit to the library overwhelmed him with information and convinced him to

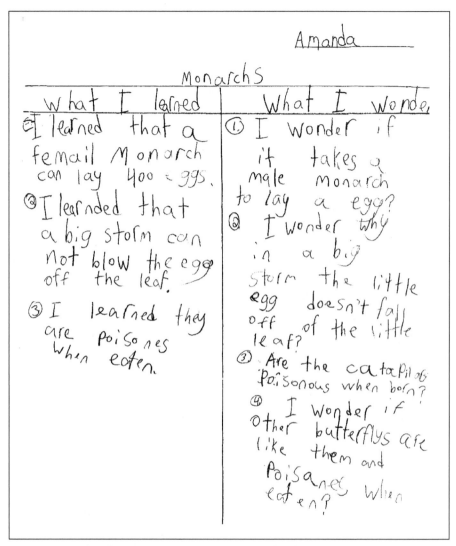

Figure 4.2 *After listening to her teacher read out loud, Amanda learned new information and had new questions.*

limit his focus to Colorado's "fourteeners" (peaks over 14,000 feet). Erin was interested in the evolution of earrings. The school library had little information, and she didn't find much at the public library either. She decided her topic was too narrow. Although there was a wealth of information on Peter's topic, virtual reality, most of it was aimed at high school students and Peter couldn't read it. His classmates suggested that he interview the managers of a nearby arcade, but Peter still felt he would be short on material. The kids all agreed that virtual reality was here to stay, and Peter decided to explore it later when he could digest the necessary information.

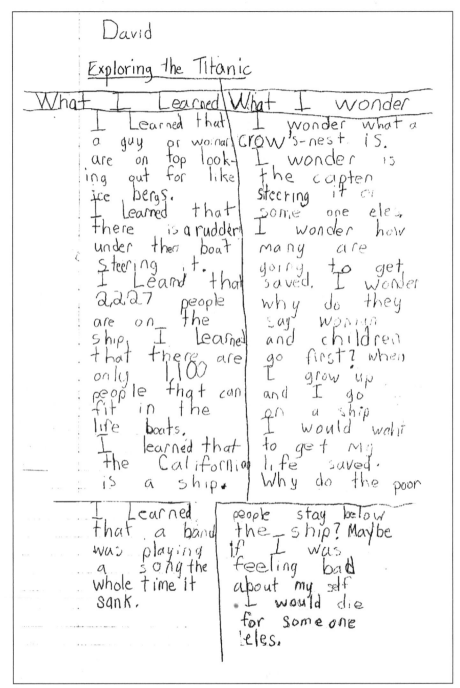

Figure 4.3 *David's notebook entry shows his independent learning and related questions about his passion, the Titanic.*

Leslie Blauman posts her students' selected topics and encourages everyone to evaluate the choices. These classwide discussions nudge kids to reconsider their choice if it appears too broad, too narrow, or too difficult. Leslie points out that kids may need to do some more reading and research before selecting a topic. The more kids know about a subject, the easier it is to pare it down to a manageable state.

When talking with students about the topic they have chosen, Leslie watches for obstacles that may trip up their research process, particularly the level of difficulty of available resources. She also verifies their interest in the topic, since she is convinced that the quality of the writing depends on the passion with which the subject is pursued. Choosing comfortable, manageable, and compelling topics starts young researchers off on the right foot.

Can You Ever Assign a Topic?

In some schools, teachers routinely assign topics, denying students the opportunity to learn how to choose their own. O. Henry said, "Write what you like. There's no other rule." Writers write best about topics they choose.

Sure, you can occasionally assign topics. Activities in school should reflect those in the world, and professional writers are sometimes told what to write about. However, if our goal is to improve the quality of writing and research, self-selected topics should predominate. Donald Graves suggests that about 80 percent of a student's yearly writing topics should be self-selected, the remainder assigned. Selecting from an array of subtopics under an umbrella topic often satisfies the teacher's need to have the student write about a content area and the student's need to choose a topic of interest.

5

Authentic Resources

As Beverly Kobrin, publisher of *The Kobrin Letter*, a quarterly publication that reviews nonfiction books for children, once said, "Life is nonfiction." Teachers can set up classrooms that encourage kids to live a rich nonfiction life, a life of passion, wonder, and excitement. Inquiry-based classrooms should sing nonfiction. The walls, the halls, the print, the shelves, and the furnishings can invite further exploration. Kids can't resist classrooms jammed with real things from the real world. When teachers pay attention to what's going on in the world and fill their classrooms with resources and tools that have a real purpose, deeper, more complete understanding results. Classroom resources and a supportive climate put the pedal to the metal in the drive toward understanding.

A Climate that Promotes Inquiry

Denver kindergarten teacher Sue Kempton maintains a classroom that looks like the Denver Zoo, complete with a working beehive. The bees fly in and out of a tube through the window to the outdoors, where they collect pollen and bring it back to the hive to produce honey. Sue's kindergartners keep a daily log of hive activity. Intermediate students who wander in for announcements or buddy readings can hardly drag themselves away.

First-grade teacher Debbie Miller teaches science and social studies through a jobs curriculum: students are assigned real jobs such as geologist, archaeologist, mathematician, historian, reporter, comedian, poet, surveyor, zoologist. They learn to view the world through a different lens and begin to make important new discoveries.

It's not fair to restrict these wonderful activities to five- and six-year-olds. Adolescents would revel in these explorations. Stimulating classrooms like

42

Debbie's and Sue's spark enthusiasm and curiosity at all levels. Engagement follows naturally.

Comfortable classrooms foster inquiry. Teachers need only hearken to the libraries of their youth. Rooms lit by soft lamps, containing overstuffed couches, area rugs, bulging bookshelves, framed pictures, fresh flowers, promote reading, thinking, and discussion. Clusters of small tables lend themselves to the easy exchange of ideas. When kids engage in inquiry, busy conversation is the norm. I search far and wide for inexpensive furnishings to soften the classroom and frequently hit the jackpot at garage sales.

Conveniently placed resources and equipment keep unnecessary teacher interruptions to a minimum. Baskets of nonfiction books placed on each table assure that kids always have something to read; no unnecessary scrambling around in a harried search for text. A relaxed environment eases daily tension and contributes to thorough inquiry.

Don't Forget the Halls and Walls

Walls can teach. In classrooms that value inquiry, teacher- and student-created charts summarizing research reminders and strategy guidelines hang throughout the room. Topics, questions, sign-up sheets, and kids' work cover the walls. The information is topical and useful. Teachers no longer need worry about coming up with cute bulletin boards.

Halls offer the open space environmentalists dream of. Use the halls to your advantage. Shelley Harwayne considers corridors rich with life an essential ingredient of inquiry-based education. Halls can house student-led classes, club sign-up sheets, announcements, presentations, kids' work, popular Web sites. Halls come alive when we see the tracks of the students who inhabit them. Hospitals are sterile; schools are not. Let's not confuse the two.

Classroom Correspondents

Classroom correspondents who keep everyone informed about goings on in the community are central to inquiry-based classrooms. Literary correspondents stay in touch with the bookstores and libraries through newsletters or occasional phone calls and report upcoming author signings and storytelling sessions. Broadcast correspondents follow radio and TV schedules and enter the day and time of important programs on a weekly chart. Film and drama correspondents report on films and theatrical productions of interest. Everyone tells everyone else about good books, magazine articles, films, plays, and TV programs read or seen, either through oral announcements or written reviews.

Take Note of Real Events

Classrooms engaged in nonfiction inquiry celebrate real events, real issues, real people, and real stories. They invite a veteran in to share experiences on Veterans Day. They study the electoral process during a national election year. They follow a breaking news story. Replicating real situations fosters inquiry and enhances understanding.

To help students get a sense of their place in history, some teachers encourage kids to chronicle public and personal events in a scrapbook or on a time line. Birdie, a seventh grader, highlighted sixteen events, half public and half personal, from her birth in 1983 through the fall of 1994. Taking a scrapbook, she headed to the library and copied old newspaper headlines and magazine covers that marked important public events during her young life, including the space shuttle Challenger disaster, the Gulf War, and the arrival of the Colorado Rockies in baseball-starved Denver. Personal artifacts included her first lost tooth, a blue ribbon for diving, and a picture of her first day of kindergarten. Exploring public events alongside personal milestones helped her understand the relationship between her life and world affairs in the eighties and nineties.

Resources to Support Nonfiction Inquiry

• • • • • • • • • Classrooms that foster nonfiction inquiry should bubble over with information. The big test for me is whether resources have an application outside the classroom. Those on the following list do. We can make these resources available and teach their use. Many of them are free or can be acquired at little cost.

- *Maps, globes, and atlases*—of the neighborhood, city, state, country, world, and sky. I love maps! Accessible maps of the neighborhood, city, state, country, and world should be standard issue in every classroom where inquiry is valued. Kids need a sense of where they are in the world in order to understand it and write about it. Post these maps in plain view for kids to see easily. Neighborhood aerial maps available at county geographic information departments are great resources. They are inexpensive, and kids can put their initials on their own residence. GIDs also provide hand-drafted plat maps of neighborhood subdivisions. Young cartographers can mark these up to show local landmarks. The National Geographic Society sells a six-by-nine foot wallpaper map of the world for $55.00. Call 1-800-447-0647 for their map catalogue. Ask the Educational Services department for a variety of teacher and school discounts. The National Center of Atmospheric Research in Boulder, Colorado, publishes a map of the United States showing how it looks from the air at night; the distribution of light is a graphic indication of the distribution of the population. Don't underestimate atlases. Many different types abound. *The Rand McNally Historical Atlas of the World* contains world maps from different historical periods.
- *Phone books*—for finding and contacting resources. Have you ever thought about how much information there is in a phone book? Time zones, emergency numbers, area codes, community service numbers, etc. Teachers I work with teach the phone book: its contents, how to use it, alphabetization, yellow pages verses white pages. Researchers

need the phone book. It is a primary tool for research. (See Chapter 9 for more on the phone book.)

- *Newspapers*—for the latest information. I can't get on with my day if I haven't read the paper each morning. Several teachers I know begin the school day by reading and discussing the paper. Many national dailies have newspaper-in-education programs that provide reduced rates to schools. Students can be taught how to read the newspaper, section by section. The cumulative effect of daily newspaper reading pays major dividends in broadening a student's knowledge. *Tomorrow's Morning*, a weekly newspaper aimed at grades 4–6 is engaging and well written. *The Furry News: How to Make a Newspaper* (Leedy 1990) is a whimsical book explaining the nature of a newspaper and the steps to creating one. (See the "Models for Newspaper Writing" bibliography.)

- *Travel brochures*—for sparking interest in other places. Travel agencies, airlines, and bus and train companies are great resources for information about the world. They often discard old posters, maps, and brochures that may be perfect for your classroom and course of study. I once entered a classroom that had a life-size English Beefeater guarding the door thanks to an expired Continental Airlines advertising campaign.

- *TV Guide or a similar broadcast schedule*—for upcoming programs. The classroom broadcast correspondent can check regularly for upcoming relevant programs.

- *Almanacs*—for finding specific information. Almanacs not only list more than a million current facts, but also include all the newest flags and maps of the world, the most recent census reports, and comprehensive coverage of the year's prominent issues. These are truly amazing bundles of information. Show kids how to use the general index, and they're off on their own.

- *The Guinness Book of World Records*—for fun! What can I say? Kids love this nutty thing. Find me the kid who doesn't want to know the weight of the world's largest donut!

- *Calendars*—for information and planning. Past, present, and future calendars are all useful. Past calendars published by groups such as the Sierra Club, the World Wildlife Fund, the National Geographic Society, and the Smithsonian are loaded with information. Bookstores usually sell them in June for about 70 percent off, just in time for the new school year. (Current calendars are discussed under Inquiry Tools later in this chapter.)

- *Catalogues*—for investigating specific items. Catalogues are everywhere: music catalogues, car catalogues, fly-fishing catalogues, art catalogues, Civil War–reenactment catalogues, and on and on. They are filled to bursting with specific information.

- *Museum publications*—for scientific, historic, and artistic information. Museums and other cultural organizations publish monthly newsletters, magazines, and articles filled with nonfiction information.

- *Charts, graphs, and tables*—for visual cues and reminders. Charts, graphs, and tables are everywhere in the real world. Classrooms need to reflect this. Researchers must know how to read them. They also provide a real-world way to weave math into the content areas.

- *Books*—for information and as models of strong expository writing. Inquiry-based classrooms should brim with nonfiction trade and reference books of all types. Informational books come in every form imaginable. A particularly interesting book, *Then and Now* (Perring and Perring 1991), contains photographs of ancient ruins as they stand today with acetate overlays showing how they looked in ancient times.

- *Magazines*—for information and as models of nonfiction writing. Much of the reading adults do is from magazines. A good selection for the classroom includes major weekly periodicals such as *Time* and *Sports Illustrated* and a variety of kid's magazines. *Kids Discover,* a magazine aimed at intermediate students, features a specific scientific or historic theme each month. (See the "Nonfiction Magazines for Kids and Young Adults" bibliography.)

- *Thesauruses, dictionaries, instant spellers, style guides*—for helping kids with the craft of writing. Multiple copies of each are helpful.

- *Encyclopedias, reference books, and manuals*—for beginning print research and factual information. Manuals for VCRs and computer software and hardware are particularly useful.

- *Posters and quotations*—for reading and viewing. Historians, scientists, artists, writers, researchers, have much to say about their study and craft. The class can collect favorite pictures and quotations and display them in the classroom.

Inquiry Tools

Nonfiction tools are limited only by the imagination. Sue Kempton, the teacher with the working beehive, also has an angora rabbit in her classroom menagerie. The kids collect the shedding fur and save it for a volunteer who helps them spin it into yarn, which they then use for various class projects. Talk about authenticity!

Teachers should think about how to use authentic tools in their classroom and how to arrange their classroom so that equipment and resources are easily accessible. Tools need to be within easy reach of chubby fingers. Classroom management improves when equipment is conveniently dispersed throughout the room.

The following pages list the equipment that will benefit kids and teachers engaged in nonfiction inquiry, that will help get the job done. Don't freak out about the costs just yet. Some acquisition strategies are discussed at the end of this chapter.

- *Nonfiction notebooks.* These are the lifeblood of nonfiction inquiry, and their use leads to well-managed projects (see Chapter 2). Some teachers prefer a two-pocket folder with three-hole prongs in the center to hold notes and other papers kids amass during research projects.

- *Boxes or baskets for curatorial collections.* A box or a basket is the perfect spot for a student to store her or his nonfiction folder/notebook as well as the books, articles, and artifacts collected while exploring and researching a topic. Upright cereal box–shaped plastic containers can remain on desks or tables without being in the way. Stackable mini-laundry baskets can be piled up in a far corner of the room or remain under student tables. Of course, cardboard boxes will suffice if these baskets are too costly. Most unidentified materials find their way into the proper collection at the end of each working period. When kids find a stray book, they usually know whose it is, because they know each class member's topic of interest.

- *Nonfiction bookshelves.* Setting aside bookshelves for classroom nonfiction books improves accessibility. Shelves can be classified and labeled according to genre: biographies, histories, fine and performing arts books, zoology books, botany books, geography books, books on world cultures and religions, earth science texts, etc. History books can be further classified according to historical period, earth science books can be further categorized into geology, meteorology, astronomy, and oceanography. Habitat books can be subdivided into rain forest habitats, arctic habitats, desert habitats, etc.

- *Book baskets and text sets.* Some teachers prefer nonfiction book baskets to bookshelves. They label them by genre and place them throughout the room at convenient locations. Text sets (explained more completely in Chapter 8) provide easy access to thematic nonfiction information.

- *Index-card files.* These card files hold questions that arise while kids do research and questions they might want to consider at a later date. Kids can jot the topic on the blank side of a three-by-five card and related questions on the reverse lined side. Kids in Debbie Miller's class call these wonder boxes. Card files value student questions, support organization, and give kids an authentic reason to practice alphabetizing.

- *Calendars and planners.* Research projects proceed more efficiently when kids have a general idea of where they should be in the process. Deadlines are a fact of life; teachers can impose some around topic selection, question development, first drafts, final drafts, and presentations. Current calendars and planners allow students to plot a time line for their nonfiction study. Time management is a skill that will serve kids throughout life. A long-term inquiry is a great place to start teaching how to plan ahead.

- *The telephone.* When asked to name the most important tool of the investigative reporter, Ward Lucas, a veteran Denver television reporter, remarked, "You might think I'd say the computer. However, the telephone is clearly the most valuable tool for the reporter seeking information." If you are lucky enough to have a phone jack in your room, use it. Phones are essential tools for contacting people and gathering information. (You can turn the ringer off to avoid unwanted incoming calls that disturb the class.) More on phones in Chapter 9.

- *A classroom Rolodex.* Why look up often used phone numbers and post-office, e-mail, and Web-site addresses over and over? Most computers come with a Rolodex function. Alternatively, teachers can order a desktop Rolodex. Or kids can make their own using key rings and small hole-punched cards. Separate key rings for phone numbers, Web sites, e-mail addresses, and postal addresses make sense. Wall charts can list the addresses of popular Web sites and important phone numbers.

- *Postal supplies and individual mail boxes.* When kids do research, they get mail and faxes. Individual mail boxes help manage this barrage of responses. Necessary postal supplies include stamps, labels, envelopes, and small scales.

- *Tape recorders.* Tape recorders are invaluable when kids do interviews. They allow kids to concentrate on the interview rather than on taking notes. When kids finish the interview, they can transcribe it. Word-for-word transcriptions are time-consuming and arduous. To save time, students can transcribe only the most important parts and summarize the rest. Kids need to know that quotes, however, must be transcribed word for word. Tape recorders are also useful for taping model interviews. Or teachers can tape-record difficult text that might provide useful information for a student studying a specific topic. Having several tape recorders in the classroom is a must.

- *Cameras.* Photographs lend realism to research products. Regular thirty-five-millimeter cameras can capture important information. Polaroids come in handy when time is of the essence. The new disposable cameras are great for recording information on field trips.

- *Video cameras.* Video cameras are particularly useful when the subject is action packed. Kids can videotape interviews when conducting primary research. Some kids create final presentations on video (see Chapter 1).

- *TVs and VCRs.* Having a TV in the classroom allows you to cover breaking news, watch relevant documentaries, follow interesting stories. VCRs allow you to show pertinent movies, as well as tapes of final presentations.

- *Binoculars, compasses, telescopes, microscopes, magnifying glasses, thermometers, and barometers.* All of these instruments facilitate research both in and out of the classroom.

- *Aquariums, terrariums, cages.* Living things can be observed, recorded, studied, and written about in classrooms that promote nonfiction. Kids can record the date and observations made on an attached clipboard to contribute to an ongoing record of the life form on display.

- *Highlighters and sticky notes.* Inquiry-based teaching and learning relies on these items.

- *Clipboards.* The essential tool of a researcher, a clipboard allows him or her to take notes anywhere, anytime.
- *Computers, software, and modems.* Kids in classrooms that are lucky enough to have these resources can travel the globe without ever leaving their chair.
- *Overhead projectors, transparencies, and erasable markers.* Overhead projectors are among my dearest instructional friends; they are reasonably low tech and offer a clear way to demonstrate instruction. Some teachers I know run two overheads side by side, showing text on one and noting responses on the other. Another teacher shines the overhead text on a white board and responds to the text on the board. Either option may be preferable to moving transparencies on and off the overhead projector in a vain effort to show them simultaneously.
- *Other instructional aids.* Plastic laminating material, poster paper, and oversized spiral-bound charts are tools for modeling inquiry strategies. Kids need regular exposure to enlarged text for instructional purposes. High school teacher Cris Tovani writes her favorite poems, speeches, quotations, or excerpts on sheets of large poster paper, laminates them, and hangs them up in the classroom. Students mark the text with washable markers, which allows Cris to roll up the text at the lesson's conclusion and save it for further use. I sometimes use spiral-bound chart paper (approximately nineteen inches by fifteen inches) as an alternative to overhead projection. I sit with the chart across my lap, the kids on the floor in front of me. I write text large enough for the kids in back to see when I hold it up. And I never forget to write frequently in my own nonfiction notebook, the most authentic and natural way for teachers to write and model writing.
- *The research corner.* To jump-start individual and class research projects, some teachers set up a research corner, a spot in the room laden with tools and print that promote inquiry. The location is often determined by the phone jack or the bookshelves. A number of the resources and tools listed here might find a home in the research corner. Posters that depict and quote famous researchers, class charts having to do with inquiry, and student work can adorn the corner's walls.

Procuring Resources Without Going Bust

• • • • • • • • • Teachers may sigh at these extensive lists of resources and tools. How many classroom budgets can support all this equipment? Sadly, not many. These days of diminishing educational funds demand a creative response to resource acquisition. Use your budget for the things you need most, then scheme to get the rest.

Books, magazines, and newspapers must lead the list. An inquiry-based classroom can't have too much reading material. Garage sales, tag sales, schools, libraries, and churches often give books and magazines away or sell them at little cost. The Denver Public Library allows teachers to check out as many as ninety books at a time for classroom use and to renew them for up to six weeks. Ask your own public libraries about their checkout policies. And teachers can develop a substantial classroom library of trade and reference books with the money it costs to purchase a class set of textbooks or basal readers. Having a plethora of trade books available guarantees young readers an opportunity to read interesting text at an appropriate reading level.

Many recommended print resources—catalogues, brochures, posters, and newsletters—are free. Teachers and kids can contact travel agents, museums, etc., in an effort to secure useful resources at no cost. And keep your mind open and a list of resources in your pocket when you browse garage sales—and browse a lot of them. We all remember the game, poster, or book that we later kicked ourselves for passing over.

Teachers and kids in inquiry-based classrooms consume a seemingly endless supply of sticky notes, note cards, and spiral notebooks. Many teachers place these supplies on the annual supply list, along with clipboards, and dole them out during the year as needed.

Last, but most important, teachers can add grant writing to their job description. Grants can cover the cost of many of the resources mentioned above. A teacher I know received a grant to cover the cost of a variety of nonfiction magazine subscriptions for her seventh-grade class. Another received a grant for a dozen miniature tape recorders to support fourth graders engaged in primary research. Classrooms around the country brim with computers and software supplied by corporate grants. An article by Denise Schnitzer titled "Navigating the Net for Grant Money" (1996) features a lengthy list of potential funders' Web sites. Log on and take a peek.

Believe it or not, the world is filled with ways to get money into your classrooms. Corporations, small businesses, and public/private partnerships such as Denver's Public Education and Business Coalition provide educational grants of all types. Regularly check your school district's public relations office, the main offices of corporations and foundations, the State Department of Education, and your local education associations for grant and scholarship information. And above all peruse the bulletin boards in the teachers lounge for grant and scholarship announcements. With a little creativity and determination, resourceful teachers find what they need.

The resource and equipment lists in this chapter are by no means exhaustive. No one is better at thinking of additions than the teacher in the classroom. When adding to the list, think about the real world. Classrooms stocked with real-world resources ring with authenticity. We need to establish an exciting, rich, safe environment for inquiry, foster a comfortable climate, and make resources and tools accessible.

6

Showing Kids How

Elizabeth glanced up at me, oblivious to the wad of brightly colored tissue paper and rubber stamps stuck in a wet clump in front of her. A felled bottle of Elmer's Glue lay there, a thick white puddle oozing out, its orange hat kicked under the table. My "How's it goin' Elizabeth?" rang hollow as I tore the stamps apart and peeled away tiny bits of tissue.

Elizabeth, a six-year-old with Down's syndrome, was fully mainstreamed into Kathy's kindergarten class. Working in Kathy's room offered me the chance to watch Elizabeth over the course of a year. I wondered how much Elizabeth gleaned from this experience and what her presence brought to other kids in the class. These thoughts made me uncomfortable, but the questions haunted me.

Three soft piano notes floated through the air. A hush filled the room as kids responded to the signal and headed to the sharing circle to join Kathy. Elizabeth noticed the kids moving toward their teacher and left her seat to join them. En route, she spied her baby doll lying face down on a nearby table. Veering left in a motherly detour, she scooped up her baby, cuddled it in her arms, and cradled it against her shoulder. Clearly, the group was out, the doll was in. Elizabeth eyed the playhouse crib at the back of the room and shuffled over, hugging her doll and cooing as she went.

Gently, she laid her baby on the floor beside the crib. She smoothed the sheets and tucked in the blankets, murmuring, "Fluff up your pillow, tuck you in." Elizabeth rarely spoke, and these tender expressions were the clearest words I'd ever heard her speak. She patted her doll's head and whispered something in its ear. Eventually, she tucked the doll into bed and planted a loving kiss on its forehead. I nudged her in the direction of the others, who were bunched up on the floor listening to their teacher read a picture book. She wandered up front looking over her shoulder several times to check on the baby.

4

PART ONE Conditions for Successful Inquiry

The power of modeling loomed large in Elizabeth's life. Her family had recently expanded to include a new baby. Daily, Elizabeth watched her mom with this newborn. Her mother's tender care came shining through. Elizabeth was learning every day by watching others. At the 1994 conference of the Colorado Council of the International Reading Association, I heard Frank Smith, the noted educational researcher and writer, say, "We learn from the company we keep." Elizabeth kept the company of a loving mom and a classroom filled with blooming kindergartners. Just as she modeled her mother's maternal behavior, she also learned from her classmates.

I learned from Elizabeth's company. She may miss the first line or two of a story or make a mess of the Elmer's Glue, but watching her taught me worlds about expectations, sensitivity, and diversity. She belonged here, where she could model kids' behavior and they could learn from her. As the read-aloud concluded, three kids followed her to the playhouse. Guess who played mommy? Elizabeth, of course. She knew how! Her presence in this kindergarten classroom led to a richer, more thoughtful learning environment for all who dwelled in it.

Inquiry-based learning allows teachers to engage in authentic research and model the research process. Teachers, experts in the field, mentors, other students, and rich text are all useful models for students engaged in inquiry. If we want students to learn, we need to show them how.

The Gradual Release of Responsibility

• • • • • • • • • My colleagues and I encourage teachers to deliver instruction through the gradual release of responsibility (Pearson and Gallagher 1983). Staff developer Laura Benson visualizes gradual release in terms of learning to ride a bike. First, the child watches an adult ride a bike, which parallels the teacher's doing the activity alone while the students watch. Next, the child rides the bike with training wheels, a metaphor for guided practice in pairs or small groups. And finally, the happy five-year-old sheds the training wheels and cruises down the street, illustrating how children perform the task independently and apply it in new situations.

Teachers engaged in nonfiction inquiry explicitly teach the steps of the research process, model their use, and gradually release responsibility for learning. Fielding and Pearson (1994) explain that explicit instruction involves four phases: the teacher explains and models a strategy; the teacher gradually gives students more responsibility for completing the task during guided practice; the students engage in independent practice accompanied by feedback; and the students apply the strategy in real reading situations. This kind of explicit instruction gives students the best shot at understanding and remembering what they learn.

The Teacher's Role

In my work as a staff developer, I come in contact with inner-city teachers, suburban teachers, veteran teachers, rookie teachers, special education teachers, librarians, administrators, and other staff developers. I listen to what they say, and common themes emerge: "I hate to write. I've never been any good at it. I just can't do it." More than a few report negative experiences with early writing practices. They remember red marks on their papers, negative comments in the margins, hours spent staring at blank pages. Few cite any writing instruction before high school; many can't remember any before college.

In American education, we have traditionally asked students to write without showing them how. We've assigned reports with a list of expectations, yet we've frequently ignored the steps in the research process, and we've rarely taught the craft of writing.

This is confounding. A coach wouldn't ask a young athlete to dribble a soccer ball without teaching footwork. A master chef wouldn't ask an aspiring gourmet to make an omelet without first demonstrating how to crack an egg. Yet students frequently read, write, and attempt research without having been taught the techniques of how to do these things.

While attending a summer institute, I heard Donald Graves say, "The teacher is the chief learner in the classroom." Teachers cannot be experts at everything, but they can be expert learners, professional learners if you will. They can show their students how they learn. By engaging in inquiry themselves, they can reveal their expertise:

- Teachers can model their enthusiasm and wonder by sharing their passions and questions. Enthusiasm and wonder are contagious. Teachers can share their passions, ask sincere questions, and show students how they search for answers.

- Teachers can model the research process and demonstrate the importance of engaging in nonfiction inquiry. Modeling is a key ingredient of instruction. By going through the inquiry process themselves, teachers demonstrate the importance of learning.

- When reading aloud or discussing ideas, teachers can show and articulate their thinking.

- Teachers can share the learning struggle. Reading, researching, organizing, and writing are not easy. Teachers can admit that this is hard work and share the struggle with kids.

- Teachers can read to improve writing. The writers we read are our best writing teachers. Teachers can demonstrate how they read as writers, notice good writing, and share strong nonfiction writing models, encouraging kids to do the same.

- Teachers can acknowledge that they don't know all the answers but are willing to go to great lengths to find out. Kids need to know that no one is an expert on everything. However, teachers can stress the joy of the search.

- Teachers can foster a safe haven for inquiry by taking risks themselves. A teacher's willingness to take risks can assure kids that their heads will not be separated from their shoulders if they try something new.

- Teachers can expose students to experts and mentors who provide information and/or guidance. Teachers can't possibly have all the answers. We need to help kids find the people who can help out in certain situations.
- Teachers can encourage kids to watch and learn from one another. Students are frequently their own best models.

In *What a Writer Needs,* Ralph Fletcher explains, "Writing teachers draw upon three distinct areas of expertise. We must know our students. We must know how to teach. And we must know something about writing itself" (1993, 2). This also rings true for the reading and research strategies addressed in nonfiction inquiry.

Learning from Experts and Mentors

• • • • • • • • • • There is no substitute for learning from a master. Watching and doing provide the best opportunity for internalized learning. A teacher I know displays a poster-size copy of this ancient Chinese proverb in his room:

Tell me, I forget.
Show me, I remember.
Involve me, I understand.

It is a daily visual reminder of the importance of watching and doing in the art of teaching and learning.

The Search for Expertise

Elementary teachers are generalists by nature; we teach across the disciplines. For this reason, we must ferret out specialists for our students to interview, e-mail, listen to, read, follow, and watch. We must know our students' needs, passions, and interests in order to point them in the right direction in the search for expertise. We can begin our search in the classroom and move on from there.

- *Student experts in the room.* Teachers in classrooms that stress community and practice inquiry know their students' expertise and rely on students for information. Wall charts and bulletin boards can advertise classroom experts and their expertise. These charts grow each day as students continue to learn throughout the year.
- *Experts in the school.* Experts abound in schools. The area-of-expertise concept referred to in Chapter 2 is a useful way to sort them out. Kids can distribute questionnaires (see Appendix 1) to staff, faculty, and other students to find out their area of expertise. Teachers can post this information in a public place, informing the entire school community of the special interests of every member, and encourage students to take advantage of these experts. And, of course, the school library pro-

vides a wealth of information, which the school librarian can help students access.

- *Visitors to the school.* Be aware of visitors to the school and invite them to meet interested students. Schools are rife with assembly speakers, artists-in-residence, guest musicians, science and health practitioners, and parents, any of whom might provide special expertise. Check in the office for schoolwide events. Encourage teachers to announce upcoming classroom visitors at faculty meetings. Invite interested students to meet these visiting experts. Spread the word around the school—who, what, when, where.

- *Experts outside the school.* The phone and phone book are invaluable in the search for experts. (Focus lessons on how to teach the phone book are included in Chapter 9.) The Internet provides direct access to a broad horizon of expertise in almost anything imaginable. Teachers can show kids how to do a keyword search, or perhaps just type in a Web address: www.Tibet.com sent me straight to the Tibetan government's home page where a vast array of Tibetan expertise lay ready for the taking. Other useful community resources for locating experts include libraries, educational institutions, cultural institutions, religious institutions, political offices, medical facilities, corporations, banks, small businesses, courthouses, radio and TV stations, professional firms, newspapers, and publishing companies. The chamber of commerce publishes lists and phone numbers of regional professional organizations, business associations, and nonprofit groups. The convention and visitor's bureau has information on local cultural institutions. Some branches of the American Association of Retired People (AARP) provide lists of senior volunteers and their areas of expertise. Local branches of the International Reading Association and the National Council of Teachers of English may provide lists of local authors, as do statewide authors associations. The education departments of cultural institutions often have lists of professionals with a specific area of expertise. *The Kid's Address Book* (Levine 1994) contains over two thousand addresses of entertainers, athletes, clubs and organizations for kids, self-help groups, publishing companies, corporations, U.S. state houses, U.S. government agencies, and international government offices. This is a terrific resource for contacting professionals or finding interesting information. *Free (and Almost Free) Adventures for Teenagers* (Grand 1995) offers two hundred ways for teens to learn about history, language, fine arts, music, theater, literature, law, science, and more. Summer and year-round internships and mentorships in every field are offered at little or no cost. Application and deadline information is included. Numerous opportunities to develop a deeper understanding of one's chosen field are suggested.

- *Community events.* Pay attention to community activities. Weekend entertainment sections in newspapers tell of upcoming events and distinguished visitors headed your way. Check out readings, lectures, book signings, television specials, dramatic productions, and films. Someone in your class may be interested. Remind class correspondents to inform the class of any special activities. Libraries and bookstores are wonderful resources for putting kids in contact with writers. In Denver, two wonderful bookstores, The Tattered Cover and The Bookies, publish regular newsletters with the schedules of visiting authors, illustrators, and storytellers. This is a common practice among bookstores everywhere. Public libraries sponsor special literacy events.

Mentors and Mentorships

The practice of mentoring dates back to the time of Homer. In his epic poem *The Odyssey*, the goddess Athena disguises herself as a sage old sea captain known as Mentor and provides guidance and encouragement to Odysseus's son Telemachus during his father's lengthy absence after the Trojan War. Traditionally, mentoring involves guidance in life skills as well as on-the-job training. Unlike the expert who agrees to a short one-time meeting, mentors often commit to the long haul, helping steer mentorees through uncharted waters.

Teachers can help connect students with people who might be willing to serve as mentors. And we needn't get caught in the trap that mentors must be much older or laden with advanced degrees. I know an eighth-grade paleontology nut who mentored a fifth grader interested in the Cretaceous period. A cafeteria worker who traced his ancestry to a notorious seventeenth-century slave ship mentored a seventh-grade girl fascinated by the Civil War. Help foster these relationships. Kids can arrange lunch meetings, coffee or juice before school, or an after-school rendezvous with these possible mentors.

Our schools and communities are alive with potential mentors. We need only find them:

- *Parents.* Schools bemoan the lack of parental involvement while at the same time underusing their expertise. Communication may improve if parents and teachers know more about one another's interests and pursuits. Students can develop and distribute parent resource forms (see Appendix 2) that inform the school community of a parent's special interests or talents. Take a moment at back-to-school night to welcome parents and speak about the idea of parents as student mentors. In my experience, most parents want their involvement in schools to impact kids directly.

- *Relatives and special friends.* Time is always a factor. Grandparents are frequently not as busy as parents. And godparents are often searching for ways to get involved. Don't forget about them. Encourage kids to send mentor resource forms to relatives and other special friends.

- *High school students.* Interested high school students make outstanding mentors for intermediate and middle school students. Contact your local high schools and speak to the specific department chair about this possibility.

- *Professionals in educational and cultural institutions.* Don't hesitate to contact museum and theater staffs and high school and college faculties in your search for mentors. A surprising number of professionals can't resist the opportunity to mentor an enthusiastic younger student.

Telementoring

On-line mentoring is becoming increasingly common. Mentoring students via e-mail is a practical alternative when logistical problems make face-to-face mentoring difficult.

Rory Wagner, an earth science teacher at New Trier High School, was preparing his geology class for a research project. Like many of the teachers in this book, Rory gave his students great latitude in selecting a topic. Their choices, ranging from avalanches to volcanoes, seemed unrealistic, given their and their teacher's limited knowledge of certain topics, the seven weeks they had to complete their projects, and the available resources. Wagner knew that a geology mentor might help his students clarify their topic choice and collect and analyze otherwise unobtainable data. Class researchers exchanged e-mail with a graduate student in geology over the course of the project and received both intellectual and emotional support (O'Neill, Wagner, and Gomez 1996). This on-line attention does not guarantee a superior project, of course, but telementors can guide students through missteps and confusions that would otherwise interfere with progress.

Although it isn't my general practice to supply Web addresses in this book, I do include a few particularly interesting sites now and then. I caution you, though, about the transient nature of Web sites: now you see 'em, now you don't. Anyway, teachers who are looking to establish mentoring relationships for their students may find the Web site maintained by a group of researchers associated with the Northwestern University CoVis Project very useful. You can access the CoVis mentor database by directing your Web browser to http://www.covis.nwu.edu/mentors/welcome.html.

The truth is, experts and mentors abound in every facet of life. Nobody knows better how fast grass grows than the guy who cuts it every week. Nobody knows better what trout eat than the fishermen who catch them. Nobody knows better how hard it is to craft a powerful sentence than the writer on deadline to finish a manuscript. Help kids find the right experts and mentors, people who love their craft and want to share it.

Students Learning from One Another

• • • • • • • • • The teachers with whom I work recognize the value of one kid's learning from another. Teachers can facilitate cross-class learning in a variety of ways. They might share quality student work on the overhead as a model. They might conduct a focus lesson to share classroom expertise (see the vignette from Kathy Haller's classroom, below). Or students might actually teach a lesson, as fifth-grade computer jocks Michael and Demetrius did in Carol Quinby's classroom (also see below).

A reminder: save student work to use as models. Be on the lookout for those pieces that beg to be shared, and don't forget to ask the students' permission to use them. Most kids are flattered by the request.

A Focus Lesson in Sharing Classroom Expertise

As a beginning exploration into nonfiction inquiry, Kathy Haller models how to write a "teaching manual," a quickly written little pamphlet whose purpose is to teach the reader something new. Kathy first prepares her students by immersing them in how-to books and instructional manuals. Then she chooses a topic she knows and wants to teach, relying on her background knowledge for information. Demonstrating on the overhead, she writes down the topic and lists the most important things she wants to convey:

> Snorkeling
> Equipment
> Safety—the buddy system
> Hand signals
> Salt water
> Sea life/colorful fish

After this, Kathy elaborates each major point with supporting details on a separate page of a stapled paper booklet, thus sowing the seeds of beginning paragraphing. The first page describes equipment, the second safety, and so on.

Finally, the kids choose a topic they're familiar with and follow Kathy's lead. When they're finished, they share their manuals with another student. These "teaching manuals" are another opportunity to share expertise in the classroom and help students begin to organize their thinking on paper.

Students Teaching

While visiting Carol Quinby's bilingual fifth grade one afternoon, I noticed Michael and Demetrius sharing a computer. I watched as other class members asked them question after question. The boys explained that some kids didn't know the basic commands for opening, deleting, printing, etc., and that they were frequently called on to help. I asked whether they'd be interested in teaching a computer class to their classmates. They eagerly agreed, and asked me how they might proceed. Together, we determined that they needed to identify:

- The important teaching points.
- The audience (how many, as well as how knowledgeable).
- The materials they would need.
- The time the lesson would take.
- How they would know whether they had done a good job.

The boys adapted a lesson plan Carol had used to teach a literacy strategy (see Figure 6.1). Then they printed a flyer (see Figure 6.2), asked their

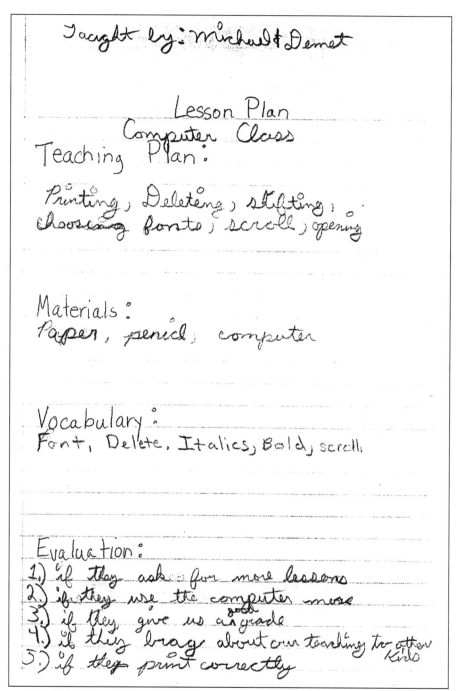

Figure 6.1 *A lesson plan designed by two fifth graders.*

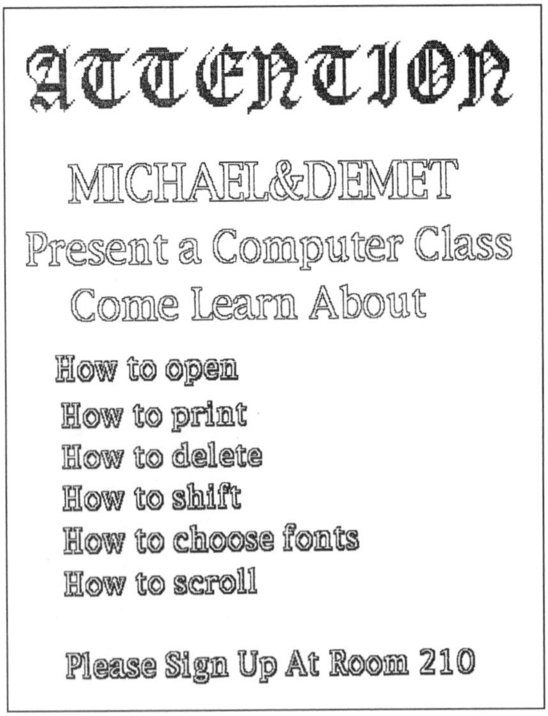

Figure 6.2 *A student-designed flyer to advertise a student-led computer class.*

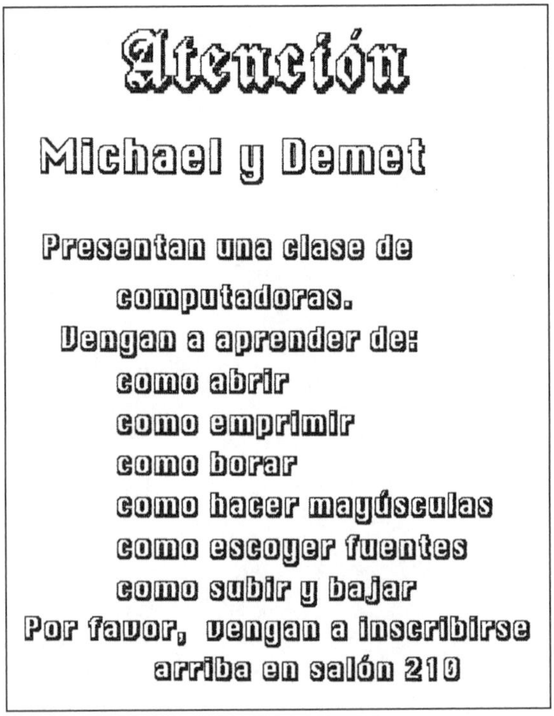

Figure 6.3 *Maribel's Spanish version of the computer flyer.*

classmate Maribel to translate the flyer into Spanish (see Figure 6.3), and distributed both versions.

The response was overwhelming. Computer novices jumped at the chance to learn these skills, and more experienced kids used the class to brush up the skills they already had. Michael and Demetrius taught the course more effectively than many technologically challenged adults might, and they made themselves available as resources when kids needed extra help.

A colleague of mine once described the typical classroom as a place in which the relatively young go to watch the relatively old work. Not the case in Kathy's or Carol's room. In rich, thoughtful classrooms like these, the relatively young work, teach, and learn *alongside* the relatively old.

Reading as a Writer: Learning from Authors

• • • • • • • • • Samuel Johnson once said, "The greatest part of a writer's time is spent reading, in order to write; a writer will turn over half a library to make one book" (*Oxford* 1979, 276). Our favorite authors can be our best teachers. We grow to know them through their books, and we learn about writing by reading their work.

Certain nonfiction authors are known for their expertise in particular content areas. Jean Fritz and Joy Hakim write compelling historical narratives. Seymour Simon regales us with facts about earth science and biology. Robert Ballard pens true adventures about the world's vast oceans. Rick Reilly churns out stories about famous sports figures. Andrea Pinkney writes about important yet often little-known characters in African American history.

Teachers can familiarize themselves with nonfiction authors and their focus and can surround young nonfiction writers with compelling texts and encourage them to read with the eye of a writer. Classrooms that promote nonfiction literacy should be filled with well-written models of expository text (see the "Well-Crafted Science Picture Books," "Well-Crafted Social Studies Picture Books," "Well-Crafted Biography Picture Books," and "Well-Crafted Nonfiction Books About Animals" bibliographies). Genres for nonfiction writing are more fully explored in Chapter 12.

Role Models

Several years ago my daughter, Jessica, and I headed to a small suburban bookstore to hear Dave Barry, the author and humorist. Our family had recently devoured *Dave Barry's Only Travel Guide You'll Ever Need* (1991). To our surprise, we found him completely alone, sitting at a table, peering out from behind one of his books. He autographed Jessica's copy of his book, and then she handed him a piece she had written emulating his style. Dave read her piece, and as he read he chuckled. His impact on Jessica continues to this day, and his work remains one of her best models for humorous nonfiction writing. When I place a Dave Barry excerpt alongside a paragraph from Jessica's piece about family driving trips, I am reminded of the power of models:

From *Dave Barry's Only Travel Guide You'll Ever Need*

And what qualifies us as a travel expert? For one thing, we frequently refer to ourselves in the plural. For another thing, we have been traveling for many years, dating back to when we were a young boy in the early 1950s and our father used to drive our entire family from New York to Florida in a car that actually got smaller with every passing mile, so that by the time we got to Georgia, the interior was the size of a standard mailbox, but not as comfortable, and the back seat hostility level between our sister and us routinely reached the point where any object placed between us would instantly burst into flame.

From *Jessica Harvey's Family Driving Trips*

Mostly, we drive in our trusty old Ford Aerostar van, which I might add is lucky, because my brother and I each have our own territory. The problems arise when *he* invades *my* space. I am minding my own business, being the perfect angel that I am, when suddenly I feel a tweak on my lovely golden locks. I jerk around to see the little Tasmanian Devil peacefully reading his book with the slightest grin on his face. My pale face turns red with fury and I take my perfect little paws and pinch him right on his thigh. Things really heat up, now. He hits me. I punch him. He practically pulls my hair out of my head, and I start bawling. This is when the car swerves off the road as my dad's faithful arm flails around the back seat groping for either one of us to give us a swat. Finally, the peace treaty is signed and everything returns to normal until boredom ignites another flare up an hour or two later.

Although it's not every day that one garners a private audience with a favorite writer, young writers can contact authors at their publishers, and the publisher will generally see that the writer gets the message. Gil, a fifth grader, became enamored with the writer T. A. Barron. After Gil wrote the letter in Figure 6.4, Mr. Barron invited him to attend a book signing at The Tattered Cover bookstore.

Teachers and students can also collect and share vignettes about important people who read and write. Elizabeth, an eighth grader at St. Anne's, participated in a writing project as the school prepared to open a new library. Midge Kral, the librarian, suggested the kids write role models, asking them to reflect on the impact of books and reading in their lives. Elizabeth's interest in politics prompted her to write the Rhodes Scholar and then senator Bill Bradley. His stunning response captures the importance of books and the value of reading in his life:

Dear Elizabeth:
Thank you for your recent letter. It is always good to hear from the daughter of a fellow Princetonian.

I commend St. Anne's Episcopal School for building a new library in honor of one of its founding sisters, Mother Irene. I hope that all the students of St. Anne's will benefit from the library and use it to share in the joy of books and literature.

For me reading is one of life's greatest joys. As a young boy growing up, I loved to read biographies; Benjamin Franklin's was one of my favorites. Throughout college, I continued to devour books, particularly political histories and literature. Books have remained an important part of my life. As a professional basketball player, I took advantage of the long flights and nights spent in hotel rooms to catch up on the latest best sellers. Now, as a U.S. Senator, I continue to read both fiction and nonfiction, in order to help me research policy issues as well as to explore the deeper questions in life.

I urge all young people to read as much as possible. From newspapers to novels, magazines to histories, reading will help you in school as well as introduce you to new ideas, places, and people. Books can evoke the full range of emotions and open your eyes to new experiences: I shed tears as I read Arthur Miller's *Death of a Salesman*, pictured myself as a proud knight as I sat engrossed in the tales of King Arthur, and found myself sitting on the banks of a river

Dear Mr. Barron,
    I just joined Mrs. Harvey's book club this year. We have read Dracula, Heartlight, Andromeda Strain & we a currently into The Ancient One.
    I am intrigued by your writing. You describe every thing so precisely. Heartlight is on of my favorite books ever. When you write every thing in imagination is there. I would really enjoy disscussing Heartlight, and The Ancient One with you seeing your perspective and feelings about them. What gave you the idea of the science & fantasy involved.
I would be honored to discuss them with you.
                        Yours Truly,

Figure 6.4 *Gil's letter to the author T. A. Barron.*

in Montana as I became a part of the Maclean family in Norman Maclean's *A River Runs Through It*. Few things can be as enriching or as enlightening as a good book for opening your mind to the world of ideas and experiences.

Again, thank you for writing. I am glad to have this chance to share my thoughts on books and reading.

Warm regards to you and your family.

In the fall of 1996, Oprah Winfrey jump-started American readers when she announced she was going to host a monthly book club on her TV show. "We need to start reading again. The happiest moments in my life are when I'm sitting down reading a good book, knowing that when I'm finished there's another good book waiting in the wings." And viewers read!

Toward the end of six months aboard the space station Mir, a CNN reporter asked astronaut Shannon Lucid what she first hoped to do upon her return. Without a moment's hesitation, she responded that she intended to head straight to the nearest bookstore. She missed books most!

Margot Hammond's column published in the *Rocky Mountain News* on President Clinton's first inauguration day reads in part:

> Extra! Extra! Read all about it. Bill Clinton reads. The fact that we are about to have a president who reads books has been big news since the election of the Arkansas governor. . . . "Clinton, An Omnivorous Reader," proclaims the *New York Times*. . . .
>
> Isn't it pathetic? Wouldn't you think that being a reader would be a minimum requirement for the leader of the free world? Apparently not. For presidential timber, we seem to admire men of action—not men of reflection. Presidents are photographed hunting, sailing, riding, fishing, not curled up reading a good book. . . .
>
> No wonder we have greeted the news that Clinton reads as a man-bites-dog story. We actually may have a president who needs to order more bookshelves for the White House. . . . Clinton has been known to devour four or five books a week and rereads Marcus Aurelius' *Meditations* every year or two. The Clintons reportedly have a private library of about 4,500 volumes. . . . (1993)

We need to encourage kids to seek out the personal learning stories of people who matter to them. Charts of role models who read and write can adorn classroom walls. When powerful people read, we pay attention. Let's look to a future in which a president who reads will not make headlines. Let's surround kids with role models: parents, teachers, coaches, and authors who read, write, and inquire.

Showing kids how we learn levels the playing field. For too many years, we simply asked students to perform without showing them how, and then expressed disappointment at the less-than-hoped-for results. If we know our kids and their interests well, we can surround them with teachers, experts, mentors, and authors who ignite their passion. Be ready to discover the surprising things kids do on their own after watching teachers, experts, and mentors apply their craft. The power of modeling in the acquisition of knowledge cannot be underestimated.

Part 2

The Nitty-Gritty

7

*Reading Nonfiction:
Learning and Understanding*

E arly one fall, I visited Cris Tovani's ninth-grade reading class at Smoky Hill High School. Cris's students had a history of reading difficulty. Few of them chose to read. Cris knew that she needed to get these kids reading if they were ever to improve.

Cris understood that proficient readers connect what they read to their own lives and that this type of reading promotes engagement and enhances understanding. In an effort to make reading relevant, she searched newspapers and magazines for articles that might capture her students' attention and help them make connections to their lives. One morning she read the following column and shared it with the class, thinking it just might grab their attention.

Wanna light up a Lucky?

Then don't go to McNichols Arena, or city hall, or the Colorado statehouse, or the Cherry Creek mall or even here, at the friendly Denver Post building.

You can't smoke at any of those places.

So go to Cherry Creek High School.

You can light 'em up at Creek and enjoy inhaling with a bunch of underage smokers at one of the school's designated smoking plazas—inside the school's Drug Free Zone.

While it's illegal for adolescents to buy cigarettes, administrators at Cherry Creek are accommodating their habits.

Yet, while it's legal for adults to smoke, they are banned from lighting up in most governmental buildings and nearly all places of business.

Common sense, it seems, has gone up in smoke.

Administrators at Creek justified the school's designated smoking areas because they keep smoking students from crossing the street to light up off campus. The jaywalking was dangerous because students might get hit by a car, they insisted.

Questions: If a 17-year-old high school student can't look both ways before crossing the street safely, could he be smoking more than tobacco?

It seems ludicrous that educators who proudly post their own school grounds as a drug-free zone simultaneously pamper nicotine-addicted teens—at the same time the federal government labels cigarettes as a dangerous product.

Meanwhile, adult smokers are being banned at facilities like Denver's Big Mac basketball and hockey arena.

The smoking bans make sense; the obliging of underage smoking at Creek does not.

I suppose that if beer is banned at Mile High Stadium or Coors Field, authorities at Cherry Creek High School will invest in a microbrewery on campus—even though it's illegal for teenagers to buy beer, just as it's illegal for them to buy cigarettes.

After all, Creek administrators who encourage teenagers to "Just Say No" to drugs can't "Just Say No" to the same teenagers and their addictions. (Green 1996)

"So, what do you think?" Cris asked her students when they finished reading the column. A wild discussion ensued. Most took the article as a personal slam. "What a jerk!" "Smoking's no big deal." "Ninety-five percent of adults smoke." "Adults just want to rag on kids. That's why they tell kids not to smoke." Comments like these poured out fast and furiously. Although they missed the author's point, the conversation engaged them and even the more reticent kids joined the fray.

Cris was pleased her students were so engaged in the conversation, but she worried about their misconceptions. She understood that merely telling them smoking is a health hazard wouldn't cut it. Moreover, it would be counterproductive to their process of inquiry. She needed to help them uncover the facts so they could draw conclusions based on objective information. They needed to do research.

When I returned the next week, the difference in tone struck me immediately. Kids were speaking in turn, confidently, without raising their voices. Drew explained that they had spent the week reading everything they could find on smoking, spending much of their time on-line. John added that his Internet research revealed that only twenty-eight percent of American adults smoke, and Samantha noted that smoking-related health risks seemed to be a bigger deal than she had previously thought.

The class was transformed since that first hysterical smoking discussion. The kids felt empowered because they had done the research. No one had harped at them about the perils of smoking; they had found out for themselves. This knowledge enhanced their understanding and, in many cases, changed thinking.

Inquiry is reading for information. If readers can't identify and synthesize important and useful information, their research efforts are futile. This chapter is packed with strategies and suggestions to help students read nonfiction. All of these strategies require explicit instruction, and young readers will need time and practice to make them their own. Don't become frustrated, and tell your students not to either; reading for information is an ongoing learning process that extends years beyond a ninth-grade inquiry project. Research is an exceptional medium in which young readers can practice reading for information.

Reading to Learn

Although most of the reading people do in life is nonfiction, most classroom reading programs focus heavily on fiction. We need to correct this imbalance by incorporating nonfiction reading and comprehension strategies into our daily regimen. The ability and propensity to read and understand nonfiction is a necessary skill for students involved in inquiry and research.

We can promote nonfiction reading in a number of ways:

- *Reading nonfiction aloud.* This is a great way to fire kids up about the genre. Teachers can read passages on a wide range of topics from magazines, books, Big Books, or newspapers, pointing out nonfiction features, building background knowledge, appreciating style and diction, and discussing content.

- *Giving nonfiction book talks.* Kids clamor for a book a teacher has recommended enthusiastically.

- *Studying the work of a particular author.* Introducing kids to wonderful nonfiction writers like Kathryn Lasky, Diane Stanley, Jean Fritz, and Stephen Kramer helps them become as familiar with them as they are with their favorite fiction writers.

- *Forming nonfiction book clubs.* Kids need opportunities to read the same nonfiction their peers are reading and talk together about what they've read.

- *Forming informational study groups around a common interest.* Studying a nonfiction topic in common using a variety of resources and texts builds community, broadens insight, and energizes inquiry.

- *Reading the newspaper.* Reading the paper lets kids find out about the world around them. It is a great way to start the day. If your schedule doesn't allow this as a whole-class activity, keep the paper in a convenient place where they can pick it up when they have a moment. (See Chapter 12 for more on newspapers in the classroom.)

- *Following magazines.* It's impossible for everyone to read every magazine out there. Ask individual students to be responsible for a certain magazine each month, combing through, reporting on what the articles are about, and noting information that may be of interest to a classmate. (Teachers can practice this among themselves as well. A different teacher or team can peruse one professional journal each month and share what they find with interested colleagues or the entire staff.)

Purposes for Reading Nonfiction

We read different genres for different reasons. We read fiction primarily for enjoyment, to connect the text with our lives, to let our imagination carry us away, to hear the sound of narrative language, and to explore age-old themes. We read nonfiction to learn. If we lose ourselves too far in the language or the mood of a nonfiction piece, meaning may be disrupted, comprehension can suffer, and learning may go up in smoke.

Third grader Eu-Shin Ahn points out that reading nonfiction is like watching the Discovery Channel. When Eu-Shin turns on the Discovery Channel, he has something else in mind than when he turns on Nickelodeon. Nickelodeon makes him laugh; the Discovery Channel makes him think. Bathroom breaks won't ruin *Happy Days* for Eu-Shin, but you won't catch him at the microwave popping corn during a Discovery Channel program. Eu-Shin grasps the similarities between reading to learn and watching to learn and reading for entertainment and watching for entertainment. If you have any TV watchers in your class, ask them how they watch different types of programs. Eu-Shin's analogy may help them distinguish the purposes for reading fiction and nonfiction.

Kids need to be taught the distinct purposes for reading different genres. Students should be cautioned, however, that these purposes overlap. Nonfiction text presented in an interesting fashion is both informative and fun to read. At its best, we learn from and enjoy both fiction and nonfiction. Some specific purposes for reading to learn include:

- *To acquire information.* Nonfiction readers read to find answers to specific questions. They also read to increase a body of information.

- *To satisfy curiosity.* Nonfiction helps us find out more about things that pique our curiosity. Whenever I see an article on Tibet, my curiosity gets the best of me; I drop everything and read.

- *To understand our world more fully.* In a broad sense, reading nonfiction can help unlock the mysteries of the surrounding world. Nonfiction gives readers a chance to learn about real things—other historic periods, the natural world, the human condition, current affairs.

- *To understand new concepts and expand vocabulary.* Reading nonfiction gives kids the opportunity to explore unfamiliar concepts and the related vocabulary.

- *To make connections to our lives and learning.* Nonfiction readers learn about the world by making connections between new information and that which is already known.

- *To write good nonfiction.* Well-written nonfiction can serve as a model for the writer. Don Murray says, "Readers don't have to be writers, but writers have to be readers" (1998). The more nonfiction kids read, the better their nonfiction writing.

- *To have fun.* Reading for information can be fun. Factual information presented in an interesting manner is rarely boring. Even dry, somewhat unfamiliar text can be enjoyable to read if the subject is of great interest.

One day while stopping by Mary Urtz's room, I noticed a wall chart headed When I Read Nonfiction. . . . Mary explained that she asks her students to take a moment now and then to complete the prompt. Here's what some of them had written:

I'm so enthusiastic, because I get to pick the topic I'm interested in.
I really want to learn something.
I have to think more and focus. I like that.
It's difficult, because there are hard words.
I learn new information.
I want to keep going and going just like the Energizer bunny.

These readers have grasped why we read nonfiction.

Narrative Versus Expository Text

In 1973, I walked into my first classroom to face a group of beaming second graders ready to conquer the world. As I attempted to stay afloat in a choppy sea of basal readers and purple dittos, a veteran fifth-grade teacher remarked that I'd better dedicate some serious time to teaching reading, because second grade was the last opportunity for kids to learn how: in third grade, they would start reading to learn. I felt as if I'd been hit by a truck.

Fortunately, my principal understood that learning to read is a lifelong process and that while it was my responsibility to take these young minds as far as they could go, I would not be relegated to the chain gang if my second graders still needed reading instruction in third grade and even later. One of reading's biggest myths is that we learn to read in the primary grades, then suddenly read to learn in the intermediate grades. Reading is not nearly so simple a process; we develop strategies to improve reading proficiency well into adulthood.

Important differences mark narrative and expository text, differences in structure, content, and purpose. The story is the earliest literary structure kids encounter. Fortunate toddlers curl up on laps everywhere and listen to Dr. Seuss. Some babies first hear *Runaway Bunny* from the womb. Increasing numbers of parents and teachers understand the value of reading aloud to kids. Day care programs and public television broadcasts like *Sesame Street* include reading aloud as a regular feature. And like it or not, we can't forget commercial TV and the strong appeal it has for young viewers. Narrative text is user-friendly. The story is familiar territory.

Expository text is often schematically unfamiliar to young readers. Textbook-variety expository text comprises unfamiliar topics, factual material, and uncommon structures. Teachers need to expose students to a variety of expository text to familiarize them with the genre and teach different strategies for comprehending it.

Strategies that Help

• • • • • • • • • • For the past ten years, Denver's Public Education and Business Coalition has sponsored a reading project focused on comprehension. The training kids receive is based largely on the work of P. David Pearson and several of his colleagues, who in the early 1980s isolated seven strategies that proficient readers use to help them understand what they read (Pearson et al. 1992). They found that thoughtful, active readers:

- Use existing knowledge to make sense of texts.
- Ask questions before, during, and after reading.
- Determine what's important in the texts they read.
- Monitor their comprehension throughout the reading process.
- Repair their comprehension once they realize it has gone awry.
- Draw inferences during and after reading.
- Synthesize information when they read.

Later, other researchers (Keene and Zimmerman 1997) added sensory imaging to this list of comprehension strategies. Let's look at each of them a little more closely.

- *Activating background knowledge.* Expository text can be dull and difficult. Readers pay more attention when they relate to the text. Knowing something about an article's content before reading it gives readers an edge. Part of the meaning breakdown that can occur when reading expository text derives from a lack of prior information. Teachers can help readers build background knowledge where little or none exists.

- *Questioning.* If confusion disrupts meaning, nonfiction readers need to stop and take stock of why and what they don't understand. Asking questions is at the heart of nonfiction inquiry and often leads to further research (see Chapter 3).

- *Determining important ideas.* Nonfiction reading to learn requires readers to identify essential information. There are many ways to help students do this, and this chapter discusses a number of them.

- *Monitoring and repairing comprehension.* Nonfiction text is often packed with unfamiliar ideas and vocabulary. Cracking these strange words and concepts is crucial to understanding, and knowing how to adjust when meaning breaks down is critical.

- *Drawing inferences.* Writers leak rather than spill information onto the page. Reading between the lines requires inferential thinking. Inferring is particularly helpful when you are searching for answers to questions that are not answered directly in the text.

- *Synthesizing information.* Reviewing, sorting, and sifting information can lead to new insights that change the way readers think.

- *Visualizing.* Sensory imaging makes reading pleasurable. When readers get pictures in their mind while reading, they are more likely to hang in with the text against difficult odds.

During reading, our thinking is peppered with connections, questions, inferences, important ideas, mind pictures, syntheses, and fix-up strategies. Using the gradual-release model of instruction (Pearson and Gallagher 1983), explained in Chapter 6, teachers can explicitly teach young readers to employ these interconnected strategies to comprehend nonfiction text. Read on to find out how.

Connecting Text to Self, Text to Text, and Text to World

Connecting prior knowledge and experience to reading deepens comprehension. To demonstrate how to activate background knowledge, teachers need to show their thinking. One way is to stop while reading aloud, explain a connection that arises in your thinking, and jot it down in the margin or on a sticky note.

Staff developer Colleen Buddy models different types of connections readers make during reading. Most connections young readers make are those between the text and their own experiences. Colleen marks these connections *T–S* (text to self). She marks connections between one text and another *T–T* (text to text). Text-to-text connections are those the reader makes between the text he is reading and what he has read elsewhere. The most sophisticated connections the reader makes are to the bigger issues and concerns of society and the world. Colleen marks these with a *T–W* (text to world).

Some connections cross these boundaries. Rudolfo, a fifth grader of Peruvian descent, was reading *Our Endangered Planet: Tropical Rain Forests* (Mutel and Rodgers 1991). He first coded a passage as a text-to-self (T–S) connection, because he was reminded of his grandparents still living in Peru. However, the plight of the rain forests struck him simultaneously, and he correctly recognized that as a text-to-world connection (T–W). So he coded the passage that way as well.

Teachers can model each of these connections independently over time, beginning with text-to-self connections, then introducing text-to-text connections, and finally bringing up text-to-world connections. Discriminating between different types of connections encourages kids to look in several directions when activating background knowledge. Kids engaged in nonfiction inquiry read pages and pages of research. Activating background knowledge when reading keeps them focused and increases deep comprehension.

A Note on Coding Text

Coding text helps readers monitor their comprehension and remember what they've read. In addition to the previously mentioned codes indicating connections, others might include:

* for interesting
BK for background knowledge
? for a question
C for confused
I for important
L for learning something new

W for wondering something
S for surprising information

These are only suggestions; the possibilities are endless. However, if all the teachers in your school use the same ones, kids won't have to reinvent the wheel each year. By the same token, this shouldn't stop you from developing additional codes for specific purposes. Kids enjoy experimenting with codes and choosing those that best fit their purposes. Fifth grader Alex chose different codes for fiction and nonfiction and listed them in his notebook (see Figure 7.1). (Several of his fiction codes—*D* for disagree and *F* for feel, for example—can also apply to nonfiction.)

Figure 7.1 *Alex's codes for fiction and nonfiction.*

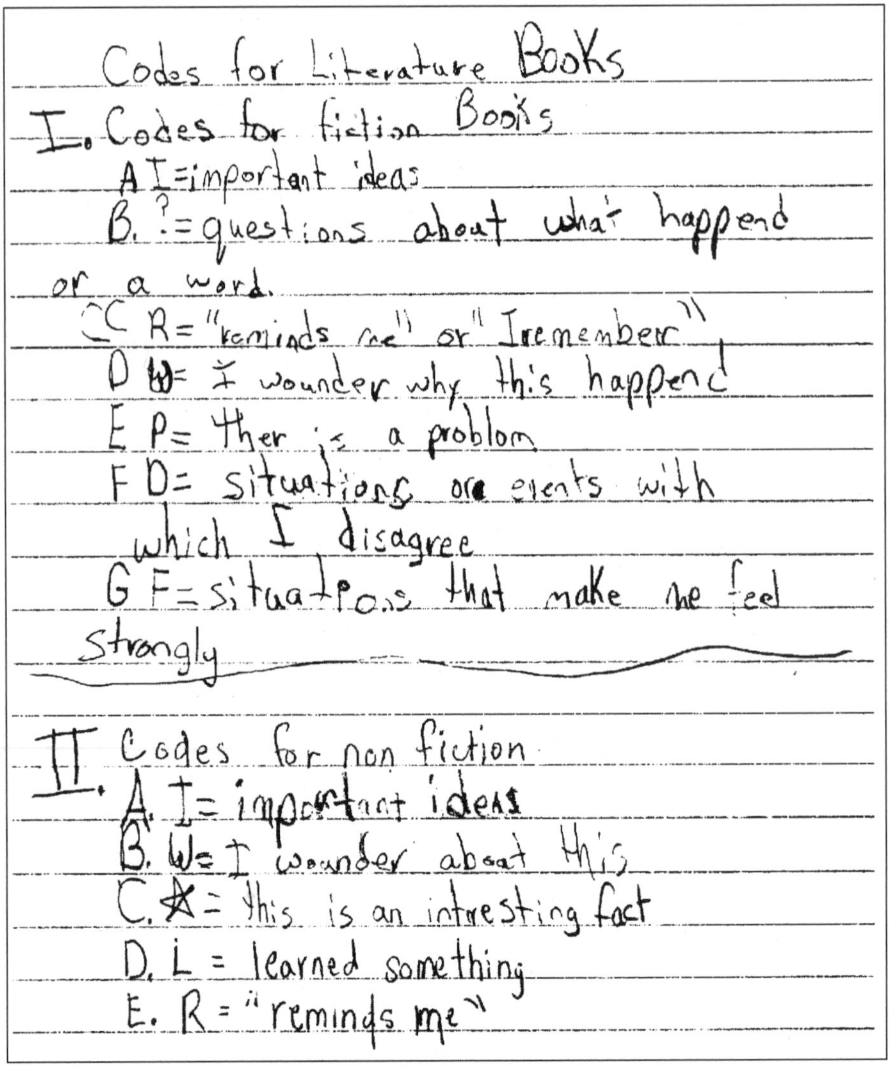

Codes for Literature Books
I. Codes for fiction Books
A I=important ideas
B. ?=questions about what happend or a word.
C R="reminds me" or "I remember"
D W= I wounder why this happend
E P= Ther is a problom
F D= situations or events with which I disagree
G F=situatpons that make me feel strongly

II. Codes for non fiction
A. I= important ideas
B. W= I wounder about this
C. ★= this is an intresting fact
D. L = learned something
E. R= "reminds me"

Determining Importance

Not long ago, my parents sent a footlocker jammed with mementos from my past. Photographs, scrapbooks, my high school diploma, celebrity autographs, and stuffed animals cascaded over the side when I lifted the lid. A few college textbooks found their way into this bastion of memorabilia. As I opened a tome on modern European history, a blast of yellow blinded me. Paragraph after paragraph was shaded neon yellow in a remarkably unsuccessful attempt to highlight the important parts. I can only imagine my confused nineteen-year-old head when I went back to this textbook to cram for a test.

No one ever taught me how to determine what was important in text. I was simply asked to highlight the important parts. Asking someone to highlight what's important is easy. Choosing *what* to highlight is the challenge, and it takes more than a simple command. When I mention this paradox to teachers in nonfiction workshops, heads nod in agreement. Apparently I'm not the only mad highlighter out there.

So how do we help kids determine what's important in their nonfiction reading without creating highlighting monsters? Mary Urtz tells her students: "Decision making is involved in determining importance in text. For example, when you highlight, you need to read the text, think about it, and make decisions about what you need to remember in order to learn. You can't remember everything." The following strategies help readers determine important ideas in nonfiction text and remember them.

Marking Text

I rarely read without a pencil in my hand. Highlighting, jotting notes in the margin, underlining sentences, and circling key words is second nature to me. Unfortunately kids in schools rarely have this luxury, since their textbooks need to be returned in unblemished condition.

However, you can give your students photocopies of short pieces that they can mark up, and newspapers and old magazines are ripe for a reader's pencil.

If possible, students should be given a paperback or two each year that is theirs to keep and in which they can mark things to their heart's content. This may be the first book some of these kids have ever owned. Some teachers I know put a class set of a paperback book on their supply list. Others apply for grants to purchase books or distribute the freebies they get from publishers' book clubs.

To help a group of fifth graders understand highlighting, I recount the story of my yellow textbook and tell them we're going to practice highlighting to guarantee that they aren't similarly blinded by yellow in the coming years.

A book called *The Unhuggables* (Waldrop et al. 1988) lends itself to highlighting instruction. These short, funny, well-written pieces about animals you wouldn't want to cuddle appeal to most intermediate and middle school kids. I display an article on cockroaches on the overhead and give each student a copy, along with a highlighter and a clipboard.

I read the first paragraph out loud and highlight the sentence that calls cockroaches truly amazing creatures. I point out that often the first and last lines in a paragraph of expository text carry essential thoughts.

Next I ask them to suggest what they think is important in the second paragraph. Chelsea asks if it's necessary to highlight entire sentences or will just a couple words do? I applaud her question, and we agree to highlight only words and phrases.

Robert approaches the overhead to highlight the part in the third paragraph comparing cockroaches to dimes, but reconsiders and decides that flat cockroaches are only an interesting detail. All agree that the last sentence in the final paragraph contains the most important idea.

When we've finished, the article looks like this:

> Cockroaches are really yucky. They look disgusting, they crawl over food left out in kitchens and people have a very hard time getting rid of them. But, like them or not, <u>cockroaches are truly amazing creatures.</u>
>
> <u>Few animals are better equipped for life on earth</u> than they are. They <u>can live almost everywhere,</u> <u>eat almost anything,</u> and <u>survive</u> for weeks <u>on almost nothing.</u> They can withstand heat waves and cold spells. And in tests, they survive radiation a hundred times stronger that what it takes to kill a human.
>
> When cockroaches scatter, they scurry away on long, strong legs at nearly one foot per second. At the same time they flatten themselves as thin as a dime and squeeze safely through cracks and crevices. <u>Cockroaches are so successful at staying alive that they have survived for more than 350 million years</u>—since before the age of dinosaurs.

When students highlight they should keep the following guidelines in mind:

- Look carefully at the first and last line of each paragraph.
- Highlight only necessary words and phrases.
- Don't get thrown off by interesting details.
- Try not to highlight more than half of a paragraph.

Overviewing

Overviewing is a form of skimming and scanning the text before reading. Reading comprehension theorist Jan Dole (1997) suggests focus lessons on the following to help students overview the text:

- Noting text length and structure.
- Noting important headings and subheadings.
- Determining what to read and in what order.
- Determining what to pay careful attention to.
- Determining what to ignore.
- Deciding to skip text because it contains no relevant information.

- Activating prior knowledge.
- Deciding if the text is worth careful reading or can be skimmed instead.

A careful overview saves precious time. The ability to overview means kids don't have to read everything when doing research. Teachers can model overviewing in their own inquiry studies.

Identifying Nonfiction Features

When I walk into a nonfiction reading workshop, I know it. My eyes catch the striking illustrations, the realistic photographs, the bold headings, and the telling subtitles. These features of nonfiction alert the reader to important information. I grew up ignoring these features, believing that readers need only attend to standard text. To this day, I need to force myself to pay attention to these signposts. Let's look at some of them in more detail.

- *Fonts and special effects.* Titles, headings, boldface print, color print, italics, bullets, captions, labels, and the like signal importance in text. Different font and special effects are red flags that wave *This is important. Read carefully.*

- *Textual cues* (see Appendix 3). Nonfiction writing often includes verbal cues that signal importance: *for example, for instance, in fact, in conclusion, most important, but, therefore, on the other hand,* and *such as.* These words and phrases, like stop signs, warn readers to halt and pay attention. Proficient adult readers automatically attend to these textual cues. Young readers don't; they need to have them pointed out. As students come across these signal words, they can add them to a classroom chart of textual cues that guide readers through difficult expository text.

- *Illustrations and photographs.* Illustrations play a prominent role in enhancing reader comprehension. Nonfiction trade books and magazines brim with colorful pictures and photographs that kidnap young readers and carry them deeper into meaning.

- *Graphics.* Diagrams, cutaways, cross sections, overlays, distribution maps, word bubbles, tables, charts, graphs, and framed text graphically inform nonfiction readers of important information.

- *Text organizers.* Don't assume that kids understand standard elements of text like an index, a preface, the table of contents, a glossary, and an appendix. Knowing about these text organizers saves precious time, and a nonfiction inquiry presents an authentic opportunity to teach students how to use them. To avoid tedium and frustration show students how to use an index by first checking the reference that devotes the largest number of pages to a topic (e.g., glaciers, 14–17).

Using Nonfiction Big Books with Older Kids

Big Books are wonderful models for introducing and familiarizing students with nonfiction text conventions. Although often thought of as primary-grade tools, these captivating books can be used at all grade levels to ensure that everyone sees examples of textual cues, organizers, fonts, special effects, graphics, and informative illustrations.

To introduce nonfiction features to a group of sixth graders, I used *Tree Habitats* (Seifert 1994), a nonfiction Big Book chock full of nonfiction conventions. With the class on the floor in front of me, I opened the book and asked what they noticed. Most were struck by the book's sheer size and the huge illustrations. I remarked that nonfiction text is often enhanced by realistic, colorful illustrations. I continued by pointing out some of the typical features of nonfiction and explained that all of these features signal importance.

After flipping through *Tree Habitats,* I suggested that the kids break into smaller groups of five or six students each. I handed out a different nonfiction Big Book to each small group. They closely examined their Big Book and recorded examples of nonfiction elements. The group with a Big Book called *Land Habitats* (Phinney 1994) produced the list shown in Figure 7.2.

Pairs of students can do the same thing with standard-size books. After reporting findings to the class, students can create an ongoing chart of the many different nonfiction features and their purposes. Teachers can add important features the kids might overlook.

A word of caution here. Although these nonfiction conventions occur frequently in nonfiction text, they don't always. Biographies, historic events, scientific discoveries, and the like are often recounted in narrative form. No bold print in sight. This may confuse readers who assume these books are fiction merely from the look of them. Reading a variety of different nonfiction formats aloud will help kids differentiate between them.

Analyzing Expository Text Structure

The sequential narrative framework—beginning, middle, end—and the literary elements of setting, plot, character, problem, and resolution are recognizable to anyone who has heard a fairy tale or seen a movie. Expository text is framed around different structures, and these structures crop up both in trade books and in textbooks. Understanding the expository text structures gives readers a better shot at determining important information when reading nonfiction.

At a nonfiction reading workshop led by Jan Dole, we explored some of the most common expository text structures by building sentences around the term *goose bumps.*

- Cause and effect. *Goose bumps make me shiver. When the temperature drops below 45 degrees, my skin crinkles into goose bumps.*
- Problem and solution. *Goose bumps make me shiver. But they disappear as soon as I cover up with a jacket or sweater.*
- Question and answer. *What happens to people when they shiver? They get goose bumps.*
- Comparison and contrast. *Some people get goose bumps from fear. Others get goose bumps when they are touched emotionally.*

Land Habitats

WHAT DO YOU NOTICE ABOUT NONFICTION?

Nonfiction material is organized much differently than fiction material. The way a genre is organized is called, "text structure." Examine the books on your table and jot down anything you notice about the text structure of the book.

1. Information has arrows pointing to the animal/lots of facts.
2. Title for every page.
3. Has captions and maps on every page.
4. Has headings on all the pages
5. Has a table of contents.
6. Has a glossary and a Index
7. Pictures look real
8. Filled with photo graphs
9. Has authors and illustration and diagrams
10. Has summary of the book on the back.

Based on your observations of the text structure write down any notions you may have about nonfiction. Asks lots of questions.

Raquel   Geno   It almost looks 3-D.
Stephanie   Stephen   Bold print means important.
Luz   Ronnie   Gives lots of information. (Tovani '95)
Denise   Great colorful pictures help to understand. Answers questions.

Figure 7.2 *A group of sixth graders list nonfiction features.*

- Description. *Goose bumps make me shiver. I get little bumps on my skin. They look like sesame seeds.*
- Sequence. *Goose bumps make me shiver. First I get cold. Then I shake all over.*

These examples are typical of the way expository text is structured. The text in standardized tests and traditional textbooks frequently falls into one or another of these text structures. If students know what to look for in terms of text structure, they grasp the meaning more easily.

Teachers and students can practice analyzing text structure, creating examples, and identifying patterns. After we have talked about and worked with text structures extensively, my colleagues and I encourage kids to identify expository text structures while reading in small groups and pairs. Grappling with nonfiction text structure and coming to understand it helps readers determine essential ideas.

Reading Out Loud, Rereading Important Parts, and Retelling

Much to my chagrin, my daughter, Jessica, would rather come down with poison ivy than read nonfiction. For a mom who reads at red lights, this is tough to handle. After years of treating all reading like a trip to the dentist, Jessica turned on to Holden Caulfield in the eighth grade. Life changed for her after reading J. D. Salinger's *Catcher in the Rye* (1951). Reading fiction now ranks near a trip to the Gap on her priority list. But she continues to avoid nonfiction like the plague, which is a problem, because so much of middle school reading is nonfiction in its most deadly form, the dread textbook.

One evening while passing Jessica's room, I heard her talking on the phone when she was supposed to be doing her homework. Frustrated after a long day, I burst into her room, only to see her lying on the bed, a textbook in her lap, no phone in sight.

"Who were you talking to?" I demanded.

"No one. I was reading. Reading out loud to myself helps me focus and remember important things. The reading seems more like a story that way. I also remember better if I reread the hard parts and then tell myself what I've read when I finish."

Jessica had developed some important strategies for digesting new information and storing it. Vocalization (or subvocalization, if talking out loud isn't possible) is a great strategy to help easily distracted readers stay on target when reading difficult expository text. Rereading and retelling are terrific ways to help one remember unfamiliar information.

Sorting Out Confusion and Expanding Vocabulary

Carol Quinby launched her bilingual fifth-grade class on a study of explorers and the nature of fifteenth- and sixteenth-century exploration. She began this study with a whole-class investigation of Christopher Columbus. The students in Carol's class included monolingual English and Spanish speakers, students who were completely bilingual, and those who were anywhere in between. Everyone, however, seemed to have some background knowledge about Columbus.

During this Columbus investigation, Carol read Jane Yolen's *Encounter* (1992), a fictionalized account of Christopher Columbus's arrival in the New World from the viewpoint of the gentle natives of San Salvador. At the end of the story, Yolen includes an author's note in which she tells what is actually known about Columbus's encounter with the Taino tribe. To build background knowledge, Carol first read the author's note out loud. She hadn't read more than a sentence or two when several kids shot their hands up with questions, primarily related to unfamiliar vocabulary. Carol realized she needed to provide more support for text comprehension, so she made a transparency of the author's note to analyze with the class.

The next day, the kids, clipboards and pencils in hand, sat on the floor around the overhead projector as Carol handed them copies of the author's note. She began, *"Encounter* was written by Jane Yolen. This author's note indicates what she learned about Columbus and the Taino before writing this story, the research she did. As I read the first paragraph from the transparency, raise your hand when I come to a word or concept you don't understand."

Carol read out loud from the transparency while the class followed the text. Fernando raised his hand, "Landfall," he said when Carol called on him. "I thought it meant that the land fell off, but that doesn't make any sense."

"Does anyone know what *landfall* means?" Carol inquired. Blanca raised her hand and suggested that it might mean the place where sailors first saw land. "Why do you think that?" Carol asked. Blanca explained that it made sense when she read the sentence over. Carol asked if others agreed; they did and marked the meaning of *landfall* on their copy. Carol told the class that rereading the text as Blanca had done is an important strategy for clarifying meaning before heading to the dictionary.

They continued reading. *Taino* was quickly recognized as a tribe, the uppercase *T* an important clue. Juan knew that an *iguana* was a reptile, having seen many back home in Juarez. When a dictionary was needed, one student searched for the word while the class kept reading. (The student reported the definition as soon as he or she had found it.)

Students practiced reading on, rereading, and reading surrounding sentences to crack the meaning of words and concepts they didn't understand. Practicing these fix-up strategies in authentic situations gave kids the opportunity to measure their effectiveness. After completing several paragraphs under Carol's direction, they finished the passage with a partner. As they read, they recorded unknown words on a three-column Have a Go vocabulary form (see Appendix 4). (Blanca's annotated copy is shown in Figure 7.3.) The kids soon discovered that although they needed a dictionary for a few words, most could be cracked by using context, background knowledge, or a partner's help.

Pulling out text and demonstrating how to untangle confusion goes a long way toward increasing comprehension. Readers need to be taught how to repair meaning when it is disrupted. Strange vocabulary can trip even the most fluent reader. Knowing how to extract meaning from unfamiliar words is critical to determining importance in text. Carol knows that the most effective way to crack strange words is through context. Her lesson masterfully shows how to help kids access meaning without giving up on the text or heading off to the dictionary every few words.

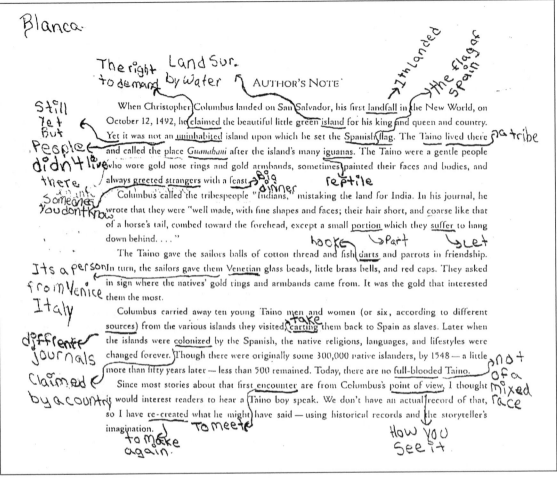

Figure 7.3 *Using context to crack unfamiliar vocabulary.*

Distilling Important Ideas from Interesting Details

In the past decade, numerous compelling, well-written nonfiction trade books have emerged as important sources for information. Before this, most nonfiction text in schools was of the reference variety, informational but frequently dry, dull, and lacking in literary quality. In many schools, trade books have supplemented and in some cases replaced traditional science and social studies textbooks.

Though sometimes boring and lifeless, textbooks are arranged in a predictable format. Information is presented in a logical and sequential fashion; important concepts are stressed. Paragraphs begin with a topic sentence, continue with a group of supporting sentences, and end with a sentence that restates the topic and captures the main idea. Each paragraph elaborates one main idea. Nonfiction features that signal importance abound.

Teachers can make copies of textbook pages and distribute them to students, teaching the art of textbook reading on the overhead. The truth is, determining the important information in a textbook is not nearly as big a problem as staying awake while reading it.

Ironically, identifying important information in exciting, well-written expository text can be troublesome, because compelling details may grab the imagination and lead readers astray. (Robert experienced this when reading about dime-thin cockroaches.) The most important ideas in well-written nonfiction are often deeply embedded in rich detail. Digging out the essence can present a challenge. Distinguishing what's important from what's interesting can mean walking a pretty thin line. Sometimes the interesting ideas are the most important, but not always.

While working on my box jellyfish inquiry in Kathy Marquet's classroom, I demonstrated how I distill what's important from what's interesting. I began by reading aloud from a *National Geographic* article on box jellyfish (Hamner 1994):

> Shimmering in the glow of the flood lamps along the pier, two large ghostly shapes undulated just beneath the surface of the dark sea. Webs of long, almost invisibly thin tentacles swept out behind their box-shaped translucent bodies. We had spotted our quarry: Chironex fleckeri, the infamous box jellyfish found near the waters of Australia and Southeastern Asia. . . . Known also as marine stingers or sea wasps, box jellyfish have killed at least 65 people in the past century. . . . [They are] without question the most venomous animal on earth. No other animal's venom can kill a human in four minutes or less. . . . "A large box jellyfish has enough venom to kill 60 adults and the pain of its sting is instant and unbearable," says physician Peter Fenner. . . .

Next I recorded the parts that most caught my interest in the What's Interesting? column on a transparency. Then I talked with the kids about what seemed most important; I decided to pay attention to those things that surprised me and those things I needed to remember. After a lively discussion, I chose three facts to enter in the What's Important? column.

Box Jellyfish

What's Interesting?	What's Important?
"large ghostly shapes undulated in the dark sea"	Known as stingers or sea wasps
"webs of long, thin tentacles"	Live along north Australian coast
"cubic phantoms cast long deadly shadow over Australian coast"	Most poisonous animal on earth.
Most venomous animal on earth. Can kill human in four minutes or less. Enough venom to kill 60 humans. 65 people killed this century.	Death is painful and instant.

I pointed out that quite often the interest column is longer than the important column. Kids have little difficulty recalling compelling details, but big important ideas often elude them. Practicing sifting, sorting, and separating out important ideas from interesting details helps readers determine the essence of an authentic nonfiction piece.

Reading and Inferring to Answer a Specific Question

Answers are not always dressed and waiting on a silver platter. Authentic nonfiction demands that readers think.

When she was thirteen, staff developer Anne Goudvis visited the ruins of Pompeii and the Pompeii Museum in southern Italy. A concrete cast of a sleeping dog, a victim of the volcanic Vesuvius explosion and subsequent destruction of Pompeii, caught her attention, and its image stayed with her for years. The dog was peacefully at rest. Why hadn't this dog run away or been burned beyond recognition in this natural disaster?

Several years ago, Anne encountered a book called *The Secrets of Vesuvius* (Bisel 1990). Much to her amazement, while flipping through the pages, she saw a photograph of this very dog. She read the book for the specific purpose of finding out how in the world this dog could have remained intact. While reading, she realized that her question was not going to be answered directly; she had to infer the answer. She decided to use the book to show a fifth-grade class how we read to find an answer to a specific question.

Anne put a copy of the first two pages of *The Secrets of Vesuvius* on a transparency while students perused copies at their tables. She began by asking if they had ever had a burning question they hoped to answer while reading. A number of kids nodded, but many seemed confused. As she held up the book, she described her childhood encounter with the concrete dog and explained that she still wondered how it survived in-tact.

"What do you think I said when I came to this picture in the book?" Anne asked, showing them the photograph.

"What a coincidence, because you saw it in a museum when you were thirteen and then later in a book," DJ offered.

"That's for sure. I knew the dog had been caught in the volcano, but I couldn't figure out how. I didn't see anything about lava in the caption. I still wonder how this dog remained in-tact." Anne answered.

"Why wouldn't it burn up?" asked Caitlin.

"You would think that lava would scorch that dog," Andy said.

"So how could the dog survive in this shape?" Breanna asked.

"We need to read it," Jamison chimed in.

"We will, but we need to remember something. This is a different kind of reading. Right now I'm not reading for fun or to find all kinds of information. I'm reading to learn something specific. I want to find out about that dog. Let's think about the questions we need to answer in order to know how this dog remained in-tact after undergoing a volcanic explosion," Anne suggested.

After some discussion, the kids decided that the most puzzling questions were, *Why didn't the dog burn up?* and *Why didn't it run away from the flowing lava?*

Anne explained that the text might not directly answer what happened to the dog, but she planned to search for clues that could help her infer the answer. She defined an inference as an educated guess that comes from blending new information from the text with one's prior knowledge in order to make a judgment. "Inferring allows readers to make reading discoveries. Read along with me and stop me when you think we've found some information, a key word maybe, that helps answer our questions. Don't forget to use what you already know to help unlock the answers," Anne added.

As Anne read a sentence in the first paragraph that described how hot gas raced down the slopes of Vesuvius at speeds of up to seventy miles per hour, Andy shot his hand into the air. "A dog couldn't run that fast. He couldn't get away. That dog would have been luckier to be born a cheetah!" he joked.

Anne asked Andy which key words had helped him make this inference. "Blast, racing, seventy miles per hour. Oh yeah, that whole sentence that starts with *eventually* was helpful too." Anne underlined the sentence and circled Andy's key words (see Figure 7.4).

The kids returned to their table groups to answer the second question. Anne reminded them to underline important sentences and circle key words

Figure 7.4 *Highlighting and circling key words to infer answers to specific questions.*

WHY DID VESUVIUS ERUPT?

Far below the earth's surface, gigantic plates of the earth's crust are constantly moving. Where these plates meet, one piece may rub against another, causing an earthquake. But if one plate pushes itself under another, it will melt and become liquid rock or magma. The super-hot liquid rock creates gas and steam, building pressure until it blasts through weak places in the earth's surface. These weak spots are the world's volcanoes.

How did they find out about the dog?
Why didn't the dog go to ashes?
Why didn't the dog run away?

When Vesuvius erupted, ash and gas came spewing out of the summit, forced straight up into the air by the pressure and heat of the (blast) Eventually, this cloud cooled, and some of it collapsed, sending ash and hot gas (racing) down the slopes at speeds of up to seventy miles (110 kilometres) per hour, ripping the roofs off houses and overturning ships in the bay. These surges were followed by thick and glowing avalanches of fiery ash, rock and pumice — (hot magma) that has cooled so quickly that it is still full of volcanic gases, like a hard foamy sponge.

This ★ is why the dog couldn't of got away.

Vesuvius had not actually erupted for hundreds of years before A.D. 79, and the people of the area believed the volcano was extinct. But they could remember an earthquake seventeen years earlier that had caused much damage to the town. And in the days before the volcano erupted,

occasional rumblings and ground tremors were felt, creating the odd crack in a wall, or causing a statue to tumble off its stand. And other strange things happened: wells and springs mysteriously dried up, flocks of birds flew away, and animals were exceptionally restless.

We know now that the dry wells were caused by the increasing heat and pressure that were building deep in the earth, and that (animals) are always more sensitive than humans to changes in the earth and the atmosphere. But, I wondered, were the people in Herculaneum aware that something was about to happen? Before the mountain actually erupted, did it occur to anyone that it might be a good idea to leave town? How many waited until the streets were so crowded that escape was almost impossible? Were they spooked by the tremors, their suddenly dry wells, or the to help unlock the answer. Well into the piece, these young readers found that living things were suffocated by ash, and that lava flowed only near the top of the explosion; thus they could infer that the dog wouldn't have burned up but rather succumbed to asphyxiation.

These fifth graders read for the purpose of answering a specific question using skimming, scanning, underlining, and circling key words as aids. They inferred answers to their questions by merging their prior knowledge with new information acquired in the text. Reading to learn places demands on the reader to find information.

Support for Struggling Readers

This book does not assume that all readers are proficient. The reading strategies and activities described here support struggling readers as well as proficient ones. All readers, those who struggle and those who don't, need to be taught the strategies that proficient readers naturally use to construct meaning from text.

Because inquiry-based learning is tailored to individual need, learners of every shape and size can commit to a topic, wonder about it, find out information, and report on it. The reading workshop (see Chapter 13) allows all readers to participate in the research process at their own pace, choosing appropriate text at their own level. Inquiry-based classrooms breed readers who come to one another's aid. Managing the many different reading levels in a research-oriented classroom, however, can be a challenge. The following techniques can support less proficient readers as they move through the demanding research process.

- *Using teacher-made tapes and books on tape.* When a young reader comes upon text that is interesting and informative but too difficult to read, teachers can record it on tape for her or him. Teachers can also ask older students and more proficient readers to record difficult text for struggling readers. And books on tape are a boon to any classroom that values inquiry.

- *Concentrating on primary research.* Readers who struggle with textual decoding are frequently excellent listeners. The tape recorder is a lifesaver. Struggling readers are as effective as proficient readers at conducting interviews. Field research allows strugglers to jump into the fray. And effective note taking includes shortcuts that serve these kids well (see Chapter 10).

- *Coding text.* Coding or marking the text, as discussed earlier in this chapter, is of particular help to struggling readers as a way to articulate their thinking. My colleagues and I encourage strugglers to code *confusion* and we help them monitor their comprehension, so they recognize when meaning has broken down for them rather than just going on.

- *Graphic organizers.* Maps, webs, and diagrams provide readers with a visual display of main ideas. Many struggling readers have difficulty categorizing content and pulling important ideas from text. Combining new concepts with old ones in a graphic representation helps them construct meaning. (Graphic organizers are discussed in more detail in Chapter 10.)

- *Working in pairs.* Kids engaged in nonfiction inquiry need plenty of opportunities to share and discuss material. Inquiry is rarely carried out in isolation. Paired reading can support struggling readers when they encounter difficult text.

- *Research teams.* Nonfiction inquiry lends itself to collaborative teams (see Chapter 13). A less proficient reader on an inquiry research team might act as photographer, oral historian, surveyor, interviewer. Certain jobs in the research cycle place less emphasis on the act of reading.

- *Using CD-ROMs and the Internet.* Bard Williams, author of *The Internet for Teachers* (1995), notes that Internet research caters to different learners in different ways. Kids who struggle in traditional classrooms may shine on the Internet. Some Web pages are graphically striking and shorter on text. CD-ROMs often have a voice component. For some struggling readers, new technology brings new motivation in the reading quest.

- *Using word processors.* For kids who struggle with writing and spelling, you can't beat a keyboard. Encourage kids to use computers when writing.

While nonfiction inquiry breeds successful learning for a wide range of readers, my colleagues and I always aim to increase reading proficiency with every student. Listening to tapes and listening as teachers and partners read gets information to less proficient readers: it doesn't replace the need they have to be able to read text. Teachers must set aside extended periods of time in which less proficient readers can practice reading text. The many compelling nonfiction books in inquiry-based classrooms let struggling readers choose text at an appropriate reading level.

Further discussion of reading instruction for less proficient readers steps outside the boundaries of this book. For more information on reading comprehension strategy instruction, check out *Mosaic of Thought: Teaching Reading Comprehension in a Reader's Workshop* (1997) by Ellin Keene and Susan Zimmermann. And Barbara J. Walker's gem of a book *Supporting Struggling Readers* (1992) is a wonderful resource for teaching students with reading difficulties. Check it out if you are searching for some practical strategies to support less proficient readers in their quest to make reading complete.

Reading nonfiction takes readers outside of their own realm and expands horizons. It teaches us about other people, other cultures, and other points of view. And as Cris Tovani's class can attest, reading nonfiction enhances understanding and even changes thinking.

8

Zeroing In: Observation and Secondary Research

Teachers were particularly touched by the space shuttle Challenger disaster on January 28, 1986. Along with six other brave men and women, Christa MacAuliffe, one of our own, gave her life that day. "I touch the future, I teach," she said shortly before her own future was abruptly suspended. My initial feeling of disbelief and then horror lingers even now, a decade later. The image of that infamous white wisp of smoke trailing downward toward the sea is in my brain forever.

The search for the cause of this tragic event taught an enduring lesson. William Graham, the head of NASA, appointed Nobel prize–winning physicist Richard Feynman to the twelve-person commission investigating the shuttle explosion. Feynman's first inclination was to refuse. "Anyone could do it. They can get somebody else," he told his wife.

"No," she said. "If you don't do it, there will be twelve people, all in a group, going around from place to place together. But if you join the commission, there will be eleven people—all in a group going around from place to place together—while the twelfth one runs around all over the place, checking all kinds of unusual things. There probably won't be anything, but if there is, you'll find it. There isn't anyone else who can do that like you can" (Feynman 1988, 117). Feynman couldn't disagree.

He threw himself into the shuttle investigation, inspecting the evidence, talking to numerous experts, asking questions, collecting data, observing, and taking notes, all the while using his own imagination as his compass. It didn't take the consummate researcher long to conclude that rubber O rings, which expand to make a seal in normal temperatures, remain stagnant in cold weather. The temperature at launch time was a mere twenty-eight degrees, twenty-five degrees colder than any previous launch. At a shuttle commission hearing, Richard Feynman simply dropped an O ring into a glass of ice water to demonstrate that O rings do not expand at or below thirty-two degrees.

As a young boy, Feynman spent countless hours examining gadgets, viewing paramecia through microscopes, and observing insects through magnifying lenses. Discovering the problem and figuring out the solution captivated him. This "puzzle drive" (Feynman 1985, 9) caused him to crack safes, decipher Mayan hieroglyphics, learn Portuguese, master painting on velvet, work on the Manhattan Project, and join the shuttle commission.

Whether cracking safes or studying O rings, Richard Feynman read his world carefully. He scrutinized his surroundings. People like Feynman thrive in the research arena. Serious researchers observe their world intently, think for themselves, ask probing questions, and forge ahead toward solutions and new insights. Research is the engine that drives us toward understanding. True research is compelling, because it attempts to answer difficult questions and enhance understanding. The search for solutions fuels our inquiry. Research helps us know our subject, a necessary precursor to nonfiction writing.

The Research Cycle

More times than I care to admit, I have walked eagerly into an upper elementary classroom only to face groans and frowns when I am introduced as the person who's come to help the class with research. "I hate research" is a common refrain in middle school and usually stems from past experience with traditional encyclopedia-style school reports. We need to convince kids that authentic research is engaging, and we can start by helping to demystify it.

Susan Oakes, library media specialist at Ponderosa Elementary, says, "We do research to find things out. We do it every day, not just once a semester for report writing. We do research when we buy a new car, pick out a pet, go to the grocery, or look for a job. Kids need to know this. They should see adults conducting research in their daily lives. Research gives us the information we need to make choices."

Susan wants kids to know that research is not an abstract, boring endeavor reserved solely for school. Research is a viable process that involves a number of steps that may lead to new insight that can help us make decisions and take action. Pursuing nonfiction inquiry involves finding out about a topic by doing authentic research. When kids recognize that research is purposeful and addresses sincere questions, the frowns and groans begin to disappear.

The teachers I work with guide their students through a research cycle with the following steps: *questioning, planning, gathering, sorting and sifting, synthesizing, evaluating,* and *reporting*. The goal of this cycle is to achieve insight at the conclusion of the project (McKenzie 1995).

Careful Observation

To pursue inquiry, researchers need to observe their world closely. In his youth, Richard Feynman took apart radios, studied them, and put them back together. Aware of this, a neighbor asked him to fix his radio, which was making an annoying blasting sound. Young Richard listened to the noise and stared at the radio. "What are you doin', standing around, staring like that? I heard you fixed radios. I knew you were too young!" the skeptical neighbor cried.

"I'm thinking. I'm thinking," Richard shot back as he rearranged some wires, thereby eliminating the cacophonous blare. Richard repaired radios by observing them closely, thinking, and then acting (Feynman 1985).

"The writer's first act is to listen and observe the details of living" (Graves 1994, 36). Closely observing one's world is central to research. Questions spring from observations, and solutions spring from investigation. Nobel prize–winning writer Toni Morrison once commented, "I type at my desk, but I write all over the house." We can train students to be good observers.

In our work with teachers and students, my colleagues and I have come up with some characteristics common to successful researchers. We determined these by reading about famous researchers like Feynman and noting some of their special qualities. Teachers can discuss these attributes and display them in the classroom. (The list is by no means exhaustive. You and your students will undoubtedly add others.)

- Researchers observe their world closely.
- Researchers *always* have their antennas up.
- Researchers are curious and ask questions.
- Researchers are driven to figure things out.
- Researchers think about where to find important information.
- Researchers investigate different situations and scenarios.
- Researchers listen to others, yet think for themselves.
- Researchers make connections between their lives and their questions.

Don Murray says, "I am never bored, because I am constantly observing my world, catching, out of the corner of my eye, the revealing detail, hearing what is not said, entering into the skin of others" (1992, 14). Writers' notebooks are the perfect tool for recording observations, making connections, and jotting down thoughts while we observe the world around us. Amie records daily observations in her wonder book (see Figure 8.1). The act of writing these down promotes reflective thinking and allows Amie to begin to live like a writer.

Techniques that Encourage Observant Behavior

- *Notebooks.* Have the kids carry notebooks whenever and wherever possible when doing research, so that they can record surprising things, confounding things, connections to their project, and things they want to remember.
- *Field trips.* Have the kids jot down observations and thoughts when they take field trips.
- *Sensory awareness walks.* Encourage the kids to head outside to various blocks, neighborhoods, or playgrounds and record sights, sounds, and smells in their notebooks. Encourage them to wander around the school yard and record some things they never noticed before. They

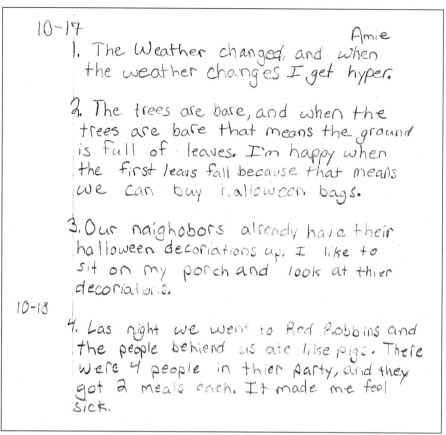

10-17
Amie
1. The Weather changed, and when the weather changes I get hyper.

2. The trees are bare, and when the trees are bare that means the ground is full of leaves. I'm happy when the first leavs fall because that means we can buy halloween bags.

3. Our naighobors already have their halloween decoriations up, I like to sit on my porch and look at thier decoriations.

10-18
4. Las night we went to Red Robbins and the people behiend us ate like pigs. There were 4 people in thier party, and they got 2 meals each. It made me feel sick.

Figure 8.1 *Amie's wonder book record of her daily observations.*

can share these observations in pairs or small groups, noting and comparing surprising revelations on a chart for classroom display.

- *Nature walks.* Have the kids get out and walk or hike in a natural setting. Jack McKenna, a sixth-grade science teacher in the Denver area, regularly takes his students to nearby Cherry Creek and has them observe the changes that take place from visit to visit.

- *Observation solos.* Have the kids participate in an activity similar to the Outward Bound *solo,* in which individuals spend extended periods of time alone in the wild with their journals. Jack McKenna asks kids to spend an hour or two alone in contemplation at Cherry Creek every so often and to record their feelings, thoughts, and observations.

- *People watching.* Have the kids visit spots where large crowds congregate—shopping malls, train stations, airports—to watch people and record their observations.

- *Guessing games.* Have the kids choose an adult or another student in the school (whom they don't identify) to watch closely, observing behavior, characteristics, etc. Later, they share these observations with their class-mates, who attempt to guess the observee's identity. (Encourage them to be sensitive to others' feelings.)

- *Character sketches.* Have the kids watch someone carefully for weekend homework, writing down their observations as a character sketch. Josh incorporated this assignment into his fall Sunday-afternoon-football ritual:

> The person I saw was a short, muscular, big thighed, silver streaking running back. When he ran his feet danced across the astro-turf. His calf muscles were larger than my arms. When he looked at the camera, his eyes glistened. When he dislodged his helmet, steam drifted off. His teammates respected him and idolized him. He never dropped the ball and was sly with the linebackers. During this game, he caught three passes and made two touchdowns. Who else? Barry Sanders!

Being observant keeps us interested and inquisitive. Activities like these help kids slow down, read the world, and prepare for the close examination they must give their inquiry topics. Developing these observation skills builds a solid foundation for further research.

Let's take a look at how teachers get kids fired up about the research process. Focusing on passions, interests, background knowledge, and related questions reaps big rewards.

Let Kids in on the Search

My friend and fellow staff developer Chryse Hutchins is an inveterate gardener. Flowers are her great passion, and she is rarely seen without a glorious basket of multicolored fresh-cut flowers dangling from one arm. She brings floral arrangements to parties, workshops, classrooms, and friends' homes. I marvel at the way my house masquerades as an English garden after a visit from Chryse.

One morning a friend of Chryse's showed her a picture of a new breed of dahlia. The Optic Illusion dahlia was a deep, pinkish purple flower about the size of a man's fist with white petals laced throughout. It was the most beautiful flower Chryse had ever seen, and she began a search to locate this remarkable tuber and add it to her ever expanding garden.

She hopped in her car and dashed off to her regular supplier. She ruffled through the bins in search of the elusive dahlia with no luck. She visited several familiar floral distributors to no avail. Using the yellow pages, she made "cold calls" to florists and nurseries she'd never heard of and soon exhausted the possibilities. Next Chryse phoned the education department of the Denver Botanic Gardens. They knew the Optic Illusion dahlia and gave her a phone number for Swan Island Dahlia, a nursery that grew them. Chryse called and requested a catalogue, which arrived several days later. Chryse pored over it, placed an order, and awaited delivery.

Later that week Chryse headed off to Samuels Elementary, where she planned to launch a group of fourth graders in nonfiction inquiry. She arrived in class armed with the catalogue and began by recounting her dahlia search. She knew from past experience that kids pay attention when you share your personal stories. "I research things in my life every day. Research is about being curious. It begins with a question of some sort," she told the kids. "When I'm curious about something, I need to find out more about it. I won't stop until I've found what I'm looking for or at least until I have exhausted all possibilities."

Chryse's passion permeated her instruction. By the end of the fifteen-minute demonstration, the kids knew this lady was a flower nut. Enthusiasm spread as the colorful catalogue traveled from lap to lap. Chryse pulled out a three-by-five index card and wrote *Optic Illusion dahlia* on the unlined side and a few related questions on the flip side. She handed each student a card and suggested they do the same with a topic of their own. "These questions can start the research journey. They may lead to more curiosity about the topic, sending you further down the research path. Or you may be satisfied with the first answers you find and go on to something else. You can take these cards with you to the class bookshelves, the library, the phone, the computer, wherever you plan to search," Chryse told them.

Allison, an enthusiastic swim-team member, wondered about the exact length of an Olympic swimming pool. One trip to the library answered her query. Although easy to answer, this question was important to Allison, a swimmer gauging her distance. Katie's card listed three questions about UFOs concerning authenticity, materials, and sightings. Chances were these questions would require further research and discussion—unless Katie parked herself on the Boulder Mall, where answers to questions like these flow like water!

Chryse's search for the Optic Illusion dahlia demonstrates how researchers slog about to find answers. The search often leads down dead-end alleys, and we have to turn around and seek a different path. Passion strengthens commitment. Caring deeply for one's topic helps researchers persevere. Today, Chryse's Optic Illusion dahlias stand six feet tall in her glorious garden, a testimony to her never-say-die attitude.

Early Research: Activating Prior Knowledge and Formulating Questions

As in Chryse's dahlia quest, early research efforts often spring from a personal reservoir of background knowledge. Questions worthy of further pursuit emerge from prior study, experience, and interest. Some teachers model a three-column chart headed Topic/Experts/Reading, which lists the topic and some people and text resources that might provide valuable information. Students can create a similar chart in their nonfiction notebooks.

As researchers mine their background knowledge, questions pop up that defy answers. Jade, Mary Urtz's fourth-grade ballerina who dreams of dancing *Swan Lake* with the American Ballet Theater, came up with numerous questions because of the information she already had in her head. She recorded some in her notebook:

> Why is there no talking in ballet dances?
> When were toe shoes invented?
> How is ballet similar to gymnastics?
> How come some football players take ballet?
> How come many dancers also take piano lessons?

Her drive to answer these questions prompted a quick trip to the library to check out a book on ballet. She found that football players take ballet to learn moves that strengthen their legs so they can jump higher and run faster. She remained nose deep in the book, searching for answers to other things she wondered about.

Jimmy used a form headed Question/Answer (see Figure 8.2) to address some general questions he had concerning the atmosphere, in an effort to narrow his focus so he could begin to conduct manageable research. As they had with Jade, meaningful questions for further research sprang from Jimmy's background knowledge.

Accessing Information: Secondary Sources

• • • • • • • • • Researchers need to know where and how to access information. After dipping into the reservoir of prior knowledge and formulating questions, researchers go beyond their own sphere and seek information of two types: *primary source information* and *secondary source information*. Primary research involves going directly to an original source by way of personal interviews, surveys, letters, primary documents, etc. (see Chapter 9).

Secondary research is information gleaned from material *based on* or *written about* a primary source. Secondary information is readily available in most classrooms and libraries and on the Internet. Typical secondary sources include books, magazines, CD-ROMs, videos, audiotapes, filmstrips, films, and the World Wide Web. (Chapter 5 suggests a wide array of print materials that provide access to secondary information.)

Teaching students how to gather secondary information is critical to the inquiry process. Secondary information builds our knowledge base. Checking out a book or flipping through an encyclopedia can be the most effective way to glean information quickly. Secondary research often precedes primary research, providing the information needed to ask the right questions of primary sources when the time comes.

Classroom Text Sets

Students can begin the search for secondary information in their own classroom libraries. Classrooms that brim with trade books, reference books, magazines, and newspapers nurture young researchers in their quest. Bookshelves and book baskets labeled according to genre seem to provide

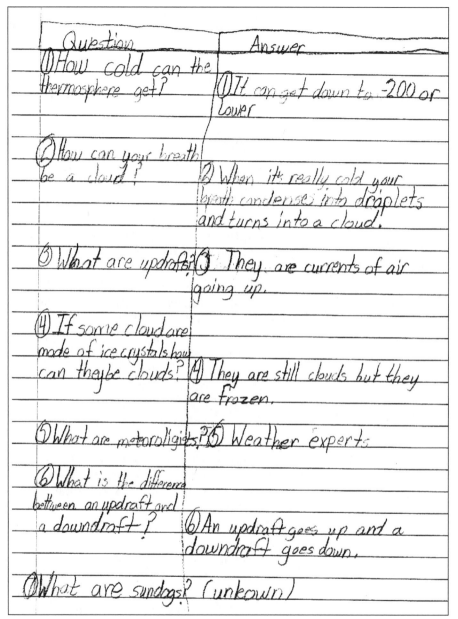

Question	Answer
① How cold can the thermosphere get?	① It can get down to -200 or lower
② How can your breath be a cloud?	② When it's really cold your breath condenses into droplets and turns into a cloud.
③ What are updrafts?	③ They are currents of air going up.
④ If some cloud are made of ice crystals how can they be clouds?	④ They are still clouds but they are frozen.
⑤ What are meteroligists?	⑤ Weather experts
⑥ What is the difference between an updraft and a downdraft?	⑥ An updraft goes up and a downdraft goes down.
⑦ What are sundogs?	(unkown)

Figure 8.2 *Jimmy's two-column question/answer form.*

the easiest access for young researchers. Text sets—collections of published materials grouped around a subject, interest, or theme—are important secondary sources in inquiry-based classrooms. Students as well as teachers can contribute to these collections, which may include examples from a number of genres. Text sets can be built around:

- *A unit in the curriculum.* Text sets lend themselves to unit studies. If the class is studying the Civil War, teachers and students can compile text sets around different aspects of the period: a military text set, a Lincoln text set, a text set focused on slavery. Kids can easily put their fingers on Civil War information.

- *A topic of individual study.* My Tibetan curatorial collection is a text set of Tibetan and Himalayan culture. Kids develop their own text sets or curatorial collections around their inquiry topics and share them with interested classmates.

- *Short expository pieces.* Since so much of what kids will read in their lifetime is in newspapers, magazines, manuals, brochures, and computer printouts, they need opportunities to read this kind of text. Teachers can clip and laminate interesting short pieces for this purpose.

- *A topic with general and lasting appeal.* Baskets of text grouped around global subjects of interest such as the environment can occupy a permanent place in a classroom. Often, movies like *Twister* or *Jurassic Park* popularize a subject like tornadoes or dinosaurs.

- *A nonfiction author.* These text sets contain examples of the author's work as well as biographical information about the author.

- *The craft of writing nonfiction.* These text sets can include style guides and books on writing instruction by authors such as William Zinsser and E. B. White. They are a good place to go for specific answers to questions about nonfiction writing.

- *A specific artist or artistic period.* Along with copies of artwork, these text sets can include sketchpads, matte board, and markers for kids' own artistic impulses. These can be replenished every month or so.

- *Music.* These text sets can include books about composers and various musical genres, sheet music, tape players and audiotapes, CD players and CDs, and small instruments such as harmonicas and recorders. A different genre and composer can be featured each month.

- *Sports.* These might include sports magazines, sports newspapers, and trade books about famous sports figures. Seasonal sports can be featured: soccer and football in fall, basketball in winter, baseball in spring. (Women's sports should receive equal time.)

- *Social issues.* Text sets grouped around issues like sibling rivalry, being different, and divorce can be particularly helpful for kids at times.

Secondary Sources in the Library

Going to the library is as American as eating a Big Mac. We have a responsibility to teach students how to use the library. Much secondary research depends on understanding how a library works. Knowing how to access information and knowing what to do with it are important life skills. School libraries are great places to become immersed in print and practice finding specific information. Teachers and librarians can let kids in on the magic of libraries by telling them stories about how libraries fit into their own lives. In addition, they can advocate for the public library. The first field trip of the year might be a trip to the public library to procure a library card for each student.

School libraries brim with nonfiction books of all kinds, and knowledgeable librarians can often fill specific requests from teachers and kids. Don't overlook picture books with kids of all ages. Nonfiction picture books fire kids up, especially if text quality matches the compelling photographs and illustrations. There's nothing like a photograph of the jaws of a great white shark clamping down on the front end of a surfboard to spark kids' interest in sharks. Interesting, authentic nonfiction fuels kids' curiosity, enticing them to dig deeper and do further research.

Advanced computers with CD-ROM capability and Internet links are found in school libraries with increasing frequency. As these tools become available, teachers need to familiarize themselves with software programs and Internet operation. Librarians can provide much-needed support for teachers as they wade into the vast technology ocean.

One particularly useful resource to hone library research skills is Randall McCutcheon's delightful book *Can You Find It? Library Scavenger Hunts to Sharpen Your Research Skills* (1989). The book is peppered with cartoons and jokes to spur kids on in their attempt to sharpen their independent research skills. Written primarily for high school kids, this book can be adapted to any age group. Middle school kids, in particular, love it.

What About the Encyclopedia?

As a child, I loved to read the encyclopedia—the illustrations of the solar system, the acetate overlays of the human muscular structure, the color-splashed pages of flags of the world. Our family routinely uses the encyclopedia to find answers to specific questions. Our library would be sadly lacking without those white, green, and gold *World Books.*

Encyclopedia is not a four-letter word. Print research can begin with the encyclopedia. Traditionally, the problem with the encyclopedia is that research begins and *ends* there. Big mistake! The encyclopedia gives a general overview of a topic. It's a decent place to *start* the research process. Kids can get their minds around encyclopedic information and sometimes answer specific questions quickly. Certain topics are well served by the encyclopedia, particularly those that lack time sensitivity: the dimensions of the Statue of Liberty, Greek mythology, the state capital.

The limitation of published encyclopedias, of course, is that things change. For example, only recent editions recognize the many positive contributions of Native Americans in the development of the American West. And how many moons did Jupiter have when you were in third grade? Go ahead and start your research with the encyclopedia. Just don't forget to move on from there.

Bibliographic Information and Publication Dates

As kids pore over numerous books and articles that might provide information for their research projects, teachers and librarians can teach some basic bibliographic skills. They can show where to find the bibliographic information and follow up by asking kids to write the source of their information (title and author) at the top of their note pages. Students can also reserve a notebook page on which to record the bibliographic information of each source they use: title, author, year of copyright, publisher, and city of publication (see Figure 8.3). Teachers can stress the proper bibliographic form in middle school.

It's important to note publication dates. Gregory, a fourth grader in Mary Urtz's room, chose a *National Geographic* with a cover story on the space shuttle (Gore 1981). The article was entitled "When the Shuttle Finally Flies." "Mrs. Urtz, what's wrong with this cover story? The space shuttle has already flown, many times. I know, I've seen it land on TV," Gregory protested. He had failed to notice the 1981 publication date.

Figure 8.3 *Allison's bibliography of the Summer Olympics.*

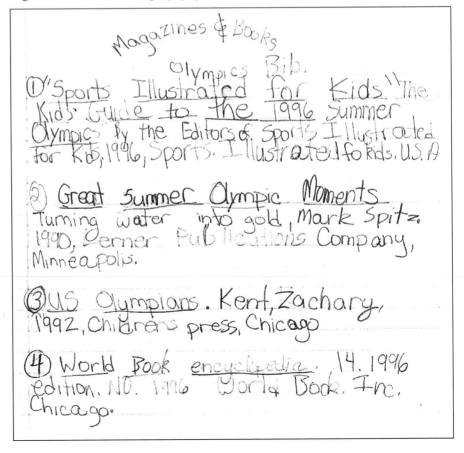

Mary pointed out the antiquated date and explained that although the information might be interesting, it was untimely and inaccurate. The class engaged in a lively discussion of publication dates, concluding that historical topics had a better chance of being accurate in less current publications than scientific topics did. From then on Gregory checked publication dates when reading.

Teachers and Librarians Working Together

• • • • • • • • • I can't count the number of times I've walked by a school library that is completely devoid of kids. Libraries should be the beating heart of the school, not mausoleums for dusty books. Most school libraries overflow with resources. Libraries are research havens. Far too frequently in schools, kids come to the library only when their teachers drop them off. Kids need regular access to school libraries. Nonfiction inquiry is the perfect opportunity for teachers and librarians to collaborate in the best interest of kids.

I arrive at Heatherwood Elementary and ask directions to the school library. A hand waves me across the hall to an open space full of kids. It looks like a library bursting with books of every shape and size, but it sounds like a classroom. Kids fill the tables that are scattered throughout. They pore over books, hunch over writing folders, flip through note cards, and study computer screens. A quiet buzz fills the room. You could *not* hear a pin drop in this library. Teachers and librarians mull about from table to table, conferring with kids.

Library media specialist Carol Newman welcomes me to this place where librarian and teacher collaborate on planning and instruction. Teacher Debbie Deem does not drop kids off and take a break. She joins the librarian to teach students about nonfiction inquiry. Her fifth-grade students come to the library for about an hour each day over the course of several weeks to read, do research, and work on organizational strategies. They return to the classroom to craft their pieces. The teacher and the librarian deliver instruction together.

This collaborative effort was born out of a Public Education and Business Coalition initiative designed to integrate the school library into the daily teaching and learning activity of the school and to strengthen the partnership between librarians and teachers. This partnership serves literacy development in unique ways. Kids spend a lot of time in the library, and they learn how to use it. Teachers spend a lot of time around books, periodicals, software, and hardware they might never otherwise see. Librarians teach literacy strategies. And libraries come to life! This collaboration enriches nonfiction inquiry. Teachers, librarians, and kids working together is a partnership that works.

The Information Revolution

• • • • • • • • • The past decade has seen a revolution in the way we access and disseminate information. Late-twentieth-century technology has changed the landscape of research forever. The October 1995 issue of *National Geographic* features a startling photograph of Microsoft founder Bill Gates perched atop a 333,000-sheet stack of eight-and-a-half-by-eleven-inch paper reaching over fifty-five feet high into the canopy of a Pacific Northwest rain forest. Mr. Gates, wearing climbing gear, smiles for the camera and holds one CD-ROM in the palm of his hand. He is quoted in the caption, "This CD-ROM can hold more information than all the paper below me" (Swerdlow 1995, 16). A picture *is* worth a thousand words.

Surfing the Net

The Internet eliminates the barriers of space and time. We can now circumnavigate the globe without leaving our den or classroom, researching reports, communicating with mentors, making travel plans, or buying cars. Access to the Internet enhances our ability to collect both secondary and primary information. Using the Internet, we can answer specific questions, exchange information, retrieve information, disseminate information, and have a lot of fun doing it.

In his practical book *The Internet for Teachers,* Bard Williams defines the Internet this way: "The Internet is a collection of networks that are tied together so that many users can share their vast resources" (1995, 9). Wired classrooms take advantage of this network, allowing kids and teachers access to instantaneous information. Williams values classroom Internet use for the many opportunities it affords for collaborative learning, communication, and authentic knowledge integration.

He notes that Internet research caters to different learners in different ways. Kids who struggle in traditional classrooms may shine on the Internet. In addition, he points out that the Internet is a culturally, racially, physically, and sexually blind medium that allows for the broadest exchange of ideas.

Using the Internet to conduct secondary research is a natural. A quick confession: I was so intimidated by on-line exploration that even though I received a daily barrage of free Internet time in the snail mail, I could never bring myself to install it. After much haranguing from my family, I finally inserted the installation disk, and now wild yahoos couldn't drag me away.

Bard Williams's book provides useful and practical tips for classroom Internet use and offers a powerful antidote for first-time net surfer intimidation. An additional resource, Kevin Crotchett's *A Teacher's Project Guide to the Internet* (1996), takes the reader through the Internet one step at a time and includes a disk that provides direct access through your browser to any of the author's recommended Web sites.

When to Jump On-Line

The exploding Internet technology with its lightspeed pace forces us to reframe our thinking. Although excited by the enormous potential on-line technology holds for research, technology specialist Jamie McKenzie cautions young researchers to use the Internet only when it is the source most likely to produce desired information. Gathering, sifting, and sorting on the net can be highly inefficient because of the sheer mass of information. McKenzie warns of the dangers of "info glut," an insidious condition that preys on net surfers (1996, 30). At times, traditional secondary research may prove more practical than Internet research.

Librarian Evelyn Scott recalls the day "a group of six kids came in searching for the dimensions of the Empire State Building. Three of them asked to use the Internet. I recommended the print encyclopedia as a first resource, but they wouldn't hear of it and raced off to the computer. The others used the *World Book*. The encyclopedia group found their information and headed back to class before the first group had even completed scrolling though Empire State Building entries." Of course, browsing the Web is new and fun, and kids should do it. But we must guide them to explore a variety of resources before choosing one.

The Internet brings the world to the classroom. Yet lengthy Internet searches can be cumbersome and time-consuming and often fail to yield sought-after information. Eighth-grade social studies teacher Helen Bennis and her students brainstormed situations when the Internet offers the best tool for research and posted these on a classroom chart.

Use the Internet for Research When . . .
- The information needs to be current.
- The information is difficult to find in print.
- The information comes in primary-document form.
- The researcher has exhausted other possibilities.
- Immediate conversations with professionals are needed.
- Information provided by distant adults and peers will enhance the project.
- The researcher wants to share information with others.
- The researcher has a great deal of time to delve and explore.

Getting On-Line for Current Information

One afternoon, I watched three fourth graders deliver a Hyper Studio video presentation on the Hubble space telescope as a culmination to a research project. Hyper Studio, a popular software program, allows students to incorporate photographs, graphics, illustrations, voice-overs, and movies. These fourth graders' slick presentation included a movie of the Hubble launch and a number of striking graphics and illustrations. I can tell you one thing, it was a far cry from my fifth-grade Smokey the Bear fire prevention poster.

After their presentation, I interviewed these boys about their research process. Luke explained that they started with some questions, including why the Hubble was made and what NASA expected to find in space. Tony noted that they read trade books and reference books and browsed through CD-ROM encyclopedias to gather information, but couldn't find much because the sources were out of date. Talking with their teacher, they concluded that they needed more recent information, so they turned to the newspaper. Here they found their most compelling question. "The paper said there might be life on Europa, a moon of Jupiter that the

Hubble photographed. We wondered if life could really exist somewhere else in our solar system," Luke stated.

"We wanted more facts so we went to the Internet, where the information was more recent and complete than the newspaper. NASA was getting regular updates and pictures from Europa and putting them on the net. We checked several times a week for new information. We couldn't have gotten so much current information so quickly anywhere else," Chris explained.

"And what about life on Europa?" I asked.

"Yeah, we think so. Maybe not now, but a long time ago," they smiled.

Challenges to Internet Research

With all great opportunities come great challenges. The advent of the Internet is no exception. Here are some challenges to Internet use:

- *Accessibility.* Unfortunately, equipment in classrooms and schools has not kept up with the flurry of worldwide technological advances. Don't fret. More schools and classrooms are coming on-line, and as they do, the World Wide Web will become an increasingly important research tool.

- *Difficult searches.* Some searches take forever and come up empty. Others are successful in nanoseconds. Seeking the advice of an expert can be a lifesaver. Most classrooms have at least one or two super-surfers who can help guide novices through difficult searches. Kids need to learn to choose "just right" key words, those neither too specific nor too broad. Kids need practice to narrow searches effectively. Schools that build in supervised time for kids to fool around on-line will reap big payoffs later. Net surfers improve their search abilities by searching, and kids need time to explore the Internet to develop Internet literacy.

- *Validity.* Kids need to know that quality control for cyberspace information is in short supply. A good rule of thumb is to double-check any information that strains the imagination. Teachers and librarians can post Web addresses of legitimate sites, and kids can count on the accuracy of known institutional Web sites such as NASA or the Smithsonian.

- *Supervision.* The Internet is full of inappropriate and even dangerous information for preadolescents and adolescents. Many teachers have classroom net surfers sign contracts formalizing their commitment to stay away from inappropriate sites. But in the end, close supervision by an adult remains the best safeguard.

- *Distraction.* The vast amount of information on the Internet holds much allure for net surfers. It's easy to get off-track when searching. It's not uncommon for me to come across a fascinating, unrelated Web page and forget the clock for an hour or two while I read about the most recent ascent of Mount Everest. Kids are no different. We need to help them stay on target and save further exploration for those built-in practice times mentioned above.

- *Transient Web sites.* Web sites come and go like Rocky Mountain rain. It is useful for kids to keep track of favorite Web sites, but remind them not to be too disappointed when they find their favorite site gone. Vanishing Web sites are the nature of the beast.

- *Typing errors.* Hit the wrong key and bye-bye cyberspace. When typing a Web address, one extra space or one misplaced period constitutes a fatal error. Teachers can prepare kids for this possibility and encourage them to exercise caution and pay attention when keyboarding on-line.

- *Cyberspace gridlock.* Jammed lines and busy signals are often the rule, not the exception. Any adult who's ever tried to get on-line during prime time has experienced this frustration. Also, the crowded Internet can freeze up just when the researcher is on the verge of answering her question. Patience is truly a virtue when surfing the net, and teachers can model this.

Despite these challenges, the Internet contributes to authentic, adventuresome research in inquiry-based classrooms. If users maintain a healthy dose of caution, jumping on-line can be one of the most effective ways to access needed information. And it's frequently the most fun.

Bard Williams says, "Get ready to adjust your sails. The winds of the communication age are blowing. It is up to us to grab the video-game generation by the brains and use the Internet to give them something to think about" (1995, 21).

Research Guidelines

As kids engage in research, they learn important strategies for finding accurate information. To keep them from having to reinvent the wheel, an ongoing research-guidelines chart should be given a prominent place in the classroom. These guidelines will vary from class to class, but here are a few that crop up time and again:

- Choose the source that will best serve your needs, and start there.
- Skim and scan material before attempting to read it word for word.
- Mark important information with sticky notes for later reference.
- Ensure accuracy by rechecking information before recording it.
- Record bibliographic information in notebooks.
- Use what you already know to help understand new information.
- Use encyclopedias to begin research, not to model writing.
- Pay attention to publication dates.
- Look to CD-ROMs for live presentations.
- Check newspapers and weekly magazines for up-to-date information.
- Get on-line for up-to-the-minute information.

- Scientific topics often require current information.
- Historic topics may require less-current information.

Kids can add guidelines as the class uncovers them during the research process.

Students who understand how to access information have tremendous advantages over those who do not. The next century's educational have-nots will come from the ranks of the informationally illiterate. Susan Oakes, Ponderosa librarian, feels it's time to add another R to the three Rs: reading, 'riting, 'rithmetic, and *research*.

9

Primary Research:
Going Directly to the Source

Several years ago, sixth grader Hector Vilas and I climbed the porch steps of a tan, suburban-style ranch house in Denver's University Park neighborhood and rang the rusty doorbell. A fifty-something, slightly hunched man with a shaggy goatee opened the door and greeted us with a wide smile: "Welcome, please step inside." A few days before, Hector had contacted the University of Denver history department to get information on the French Revolution, his topic for a long-term research project. Dr. Eric Arnold, resident expert on eighteenth-century France, had agreed to be interviewed and had invited Hector to his home. I helped Hector design an interview guide, and off we went.

We entered a dimly lit room where classical music was playing in the background. Embers smoldered in the fireplace. Floor-to-ceiling oak bookshelves bursting with books of every color, shape, and size covered the walls: an entire wall of different Louies, four shelves of Robespierre, assorted biographies of die-hard revolutionaries, and leather-bound volumes with French titles embossed in gold. This man was passionate about French history.

Hector's eyes roamed from one bookshelf to the next in awed silence. He clutched his pencil, notebook, and interview questions tightly in his fists. Dr. Arnold broke the quiet by asking Hector what he had learned about the Revolution so far. Hector handed Dr. Arnold about twenty pages of notes on the subject, the product of forty hours of research. Dr. Arnold skimmed through the pages. "My friend, you could easily write a lengthy report on every topic you've mentioned here. I've studied the French Revolution for more than twenty-five years, and I still continue to learn from it. Although your information is compelling, I'm afraid your topic is far too broad." Hector's smile disappeared. All of that work, down the drain.

"Then what should I write about?" Hector asked sheepishly.

"Hector, let me tell you a story. When I started my doctoral dissertation, I asked my professor what I should write about. He answered 'That's your choice. My interest is mine and yours is yours. They may be the same; they may not. Write about what interests you.' What interests you, Hector?"

Hector thought for a moment. "The people, the people of the French Revolution," he answered.

"Which people?" Dr. Arnold asked.

"Maximilien Robespierre!" Hector shouted, finding his smile once again.

"One of my very favorites! Let's sit down and I will tell you what I know of Monsieur Robespierre." As Dr. Arnold regaled us with tales of Robespierre's life, Hector stuffed the predetermined questions into his pocket. We took copious notes as Dr. Arnold rattled off fascinating information about Robespierre. Hector asked genuine questions as they arose. Forty-five minutes later, the professor concluded by recommending several books Hector would probably want to read.

"Now, come downstairs for a big surprise!" he beckoned. We followed him into a finished basement. Antique muskets, daggers, prints, and etchings covered the walls. Hector's jaw dropped in amazement. Dr. Arnold led Hector to a corner and pointed to a print on the wall. "This is an original drawing of Robespierre rendered three days before he went to the guillotine. I paid a dollar for it in Paris twenty years ago. This collection goes back thirty years." Dr. Arnold's house was the by-product of his consuming passion, and he was the curator of his own private collection.

An hour went by before I could pry Hector away. We said our thank-yous and bid our farewells. As we hopped in the car, Hector commented, "You know, maybe I'd like to be a history professor when I grow up." If he does become one, the credit surely goes to Dr. Arnold.

Mark Twain once said, "War talk by someone who's been to the war is always interesting. Moon talk by someone who's never been to the moon is always dull."

Hector's interview with Dr. Arnold did not go altogether as planned, but good interviews often reveal surprising information. Hector discovered that his topic was too broad and that the questions he had designed were therefore irrelevant. He was momentarily at a dead end. But with Dr. Arnold's help, he was able to redirect his research and conduct a successful interview on a new topic.

In addition, Hector learned important lessons about preliminary research. Although too broad, Hector's original topic, the French Revolution, and his hours of dedicated research gave him the background knowledge necessary to understand the larger topic as a whole. Hector could not write about Robespierre without understanding eighteenth-century French culture and how it brought about a revolution. This foundation allowed him to zero in on a compelling topic. Broad-based preliminary research is not a waste of time.

Searching for primary information requires flexibility. Primary research throws kids into the middle of the fray. It brings research to life. (Hector will no doubt remember his afternoon with Dr. Arnold forever.) Here are some methods for gathering primary information:

- *Personal interviews.* Students can conduct interviews with people who have expertise or a special interest in the topic they are studying.

- *Focus-group interviews.* Students can arrange to meet with a small group of people all at once, asking questions and generating a discussion on a particular topic or issue.

- *Surveys.* Students can develop surveys to gain objective information from a larger sample of the population.

- *Field research.* Students can head into the world to observe and investigate topics. Museums house original letters, papers, newspapers, and documents that fascinate and give a feel for the times in which they were written. The public library is home to primary sources like transcribed interviews, autobiographies, letters, diaries, and journals.

- *Internet research.* Chat rooms and bulletin boards where people talk about common interests abound on-line. Primary documents of all types can be found on the World Wide Web—speeches, essays, videos. The Library of Congress houses many of our nation's most important original documents, and now we can access many of them at WWW.loc.gov (the Library's Web address) without leaving our classroom. This is a truly great Web site for inquiry-based classrooms.

- *E-mail.* Students can conduct on-line interviews with specialists and other interested people and develop relationships with them. Telementoring (see Chapter 6) is a powerful way to learn more about a specific topic from a knowledgeable person.

- *CD-ROMs, videotapes, and audiotapes.* Primary source audio- and videotapes are increasingly available. Check with your local stores. CD-ROMS are particularly useful when searching for famous speeches and news coverage of important events.

- *Workshops, conferences, or institutes.* Groups of every size put these on to inform the public about a specific interest or topic. If logistically possible, kids can attend these lectures and presentations. Otherwise, they can write and request materials and summaries. Universities, cultural institutions, libraries, professional organizations, education associations, and the local chamber of commerce can tell you about upcoming conferences and workshops at the state or local level.

- *Classes.* Universities, school districts, and cultural institutions offer ongoing classes on numerous topics. As a volunteer tour guide at the Denver Museum of Natural History during an exhibit of artifacts from the time of Ramses II, I took an Ancient Egyptology class. The professor would have happily shared the excellent material with students.

For many kids, the search for primary sources is the high point of the inquiry process. It takes them out of schools and into the world. It helps satisfy their natural curiosity and thirst for meaning. This is learning at its most fun.

The Personal Interview

• • • • • • • • • The personal interview is one of the most effective primary research tools:

> Get people talking. Learn to ask questions that will elicit answers
> about what is most interesting or vivid in their lives. Nothing so ani-
> mates writing as someone telling what he thinks or what he does in
> his own words. (Zinsser 1990, 81)

We need to teach students how to conduct interviews. Designed questions
assigned by the teacher lack authenticity. Kids can design their own questions based on what they need to know. As they gather information, they
acquire new knowledge that should help them ask better questions.

A Demonstration Interview

Mary and I demonstrate interviewing for her fourth graders. We sit in chairs
facing each other as the kids crowd around on the floor. We explain that our
objective is to learn as much as we can from the interview, since it may be
our only chance to find out what this person thinks and knows.

I decide to interview Mary about running. I am aware that Mary runs,
but know nothing else about it. Before the interview, I jot down some specific questions I want answered: *How many miles does Mary run every week? How
does she train? What runner does she most admire?* Knowing my passion for Tibet,
Mary decides to interview me about my favorite place on earth, and she also
records some questions in her notebook.

Interviews must be flexible. Although interviewers have questions they
need answered, the interview itself directs the line of questioning. In Hector's
interview with Dr. Arnold, his designed questions were useless. Just sitting
and listening provided the best means for getting information. Mary and I
demonstrate how to listen carefully and ask *a follow-up question,* one that follows from the answer to the previous question. Strong interviews engage
subjects and follow the subject's train of thought.

Specific interview questions often fall into two categories: personal questions and universal questions. A personal question might be, *Have you ever
run a marathon?* A universal question might be, *Who is the world's fastest woman
runner?* Mary and I ask each other questions of each type and encourage students to distinguish between them during the demonstration interview.

Some people are difficult to interview. Although specific questions stem
from the interviewer's desire to know more, there are generic "safety net"
questions for the interviewer who struggles with a noncommunicative subject. We list some of them below, but we don't recommend using them verbatim. We've all seen young interviewers ignore responses as they wait anx-
iously to ask their next prepared question.

• How did you develop your interest or expertise in this field?
• How did you find out more about your interest?

- Who helped teach you what you know?
- What knowledge do you have about this field from personal experience?
- What knowledge do you have that goes beyond your personal experience?
- Whom do you admire in your field?

At the conclusion of an interview, the following questions are useful:

- Who else should I talk to about this?
- What publications should I take a look at?
- Is there anything I haven't asked you that I should have?
- May I please call you later, if I have any further questions?

Mary and I begin our interview:

STEPHANIE: Mary, for years I've wanted to know more about your running. Let's start with how often you run.

MARY: It varies. It depends on my level of motivation or whether I'm in training. Right now I'm recovering from an injury, so I'm running about five times a week for thirty minutes, which translates to about twenty miles a week. That's not as much as I'm used to.

STEPHANIE: Is that how runners keep track, by miles?

MARY: Yes, I try to run a certain number of miles a week, but the injury interferes with my routine.

STEPHANIE: Talk about your injury.

MARY: I'm a distance runner, which means I'm generally more interested in how far I go than how fast. Distance running really taxes the hamstring muscle, which is the muscle that I've injured. It's unfortunate, because I was going to run the Chicago Marathon this fall, but now I won't be able to do it.

STEPHANIE: That's too bad. How do you train for a marathon?

MARY: I make sure I'm running at least twenty miles a week, which is my base. Then I begin a training program written by Jeff Galloway, a world-class runner. I start six months out and increase my mileage by ten percent each week. He recommends running a full twenty-six-mile day three weeks before the marathon.

STEPHANIE: How did you develop your interest in running?

MARY: I grew up with older brothers. They were terrific athletes, particularly with ball sports. I really respected them, but I wasn't any good at throwing and catching. My dad suggested I join him on his daily run down at the lake near our house. He ran at six a.m. every morning. At first I hated getting up so early, but I grew to love it, and soon found myself running track in high school, although I didn't like the competition. I didn't do well in races.

STEPHANIE: Why not?

MARY: I loved to run for the sake of running, not to win or lose.

STEPHANIE: Are there formal organizations that help you with your running?

MARY: There is a culture of runners. There are long-distance-running groups. I wanted to get faster, so I joined a group called Pheidippides. They work on improving your time. Pheidippides was the Greek god of running. He ran the first Greek Marathon. In ancient Greece, they ran marathons to carry messages to distant villages. Legend has it that poor Pheidippides collapsed and died when he reached his final destination.

STEPHANIE: That's strange. Who in the running field today do you most admire?

MARY: Women weren't allowed to run the marathon in the Summer Olympics until the 1970s. The Olympic governors didn't believe women were strong enough to compete. Many women since then have blazed the trail. I particularly admire Uta Pippig, who is currently ranked the number one woman runner in the world. She fled East Germany, because they restricted her freedom. She lives in the U.S. now, but she still speaks longingly about her country. She cares a great deal about the German people, but she needed the freedom to run. She had to break out of constraints to run free. People who face adversity and yet break out to pursue their passion are my true heroes.

Next we switch roles, and Mary interviews me about Tibet. The kids see the patterns of both sets of questions. When we finish, we discuss our demonstration with the class, noting what we learned and what we still need to know. We check our questions against the generic questions listed above. We point out examples of follow-up questions, like my asking Mary to tell me about her injury. Mary asks the kids to differentiate between personal and universal questions, and several share examples. We share unexpected findings. I mention Mary's surprising revelation that she dislikes competition. I record in my wonder book the new information about who Pheidippides and Uta Pippig are. Finally, we evaluate the information we have found and jot down questions that remain.

Practice Interviews

Practice interviews prepare students for the authentic interviews they will conduct later. Much interviewing instruction consists of teacher modeling and guided practice. Kids need opportunities to see interview techniques in action and practice these techniques themselves.

After our demonstration interview, the students interview each other. Mary and I wander around eavesdropping and assisting when needed. I listen in as Gregory interviews Martin about the Holocaust:

GREGORY: When did you first hear about the Holocaust?

MARTIN: It was a couple of years ago. My mom sat down and told me about it. I had so many questions. I was so interested in it. I just wanted to get more in depth. I couldn't stop asking questions. Why would anyone ever do something like this?

GREGORY: Who taught you about the Holocaust?

MARTIN: My mom and the rabbis mostly.

GREGORY: How long did it take you to figure out why the Holocaust happened?

MARTIN: After my mom and I talked, it took me about a month to stop thinking about it all the time. You see, I am Jewish so I hear a lot of stories from the rabbis. I still haven't figured out why it happened exactly, but I understand more than I did before hearing the rabbis and reading.

GREGORY: What have you read about the Holocaust?

MARTIN: My parents are charter members of the Holocaust Museum in Washington DC. We have a book from there. I read it all the time. The photographs tell a shocking story. I also read a really powerful fiction book called *Number the Stars*. It tells the story of a Danish Jewish family who are smuggled out of Denmark by Danish fisherman to avoid the Nazis. And then the rabbis gave me stories.

GREGORY: Are your other family members as interested as you are in the Holocaust?

MARTIN: I don't think so. Sometimes my sister asks questions about the Holocaust, but in my family I am the one who's the most interested so I keep on learning.

GREGORY: Do people ask you stuff about the Holocaust?

MARTIN: Yea, mostly questions about how people got killed. I know that most were killed by gas or being shot.

GREGORY: How do you feel when you hear that Jews were killed, and you are Jewish?

MARTIN: It's sad. It's so sad. It's almost like Mrs. Urtz said in her running interview about the runner that wasn't free. It's the same with the Jews. All they wanted was to be free. Why couldn't they be free? I don't understand.

GREGORY: Is there anything you can understand about the Holocaust?

MARTIN: I can definitely understand why the Allies wanted to stop it. I don't think I'll ever understand why Hitler wanted to kill people. And there is another thing I can't understand. Why would Americans ever put the Japanese in internment camps after fighting against the Nazis for putting Jews in concentration camps? That just doesn't make any sense at all.

When Gregory and Martin finish, I distribute copies of their interview to the class. We review it together. Mary and I encourage kids to highlight and code examples of follow-up questions, personal and universal questions, generic questions, etc. Emily points out Gregory's follow-up question about the reading Martin did about the Holocaust. Brandon highlights the part where Gregory asked Martin who taught him about the Holocaust, a generic question. When we've finished discussing the interview, Mary suggests that kids record in their notebooks any new information they've learned about interviewing techniques.

In Allison's wonder book entry on her sample interview with Colin (see Figure 9.1), she says that follow-up questions were tough. She recognizes that she needs more time to watch and practice.

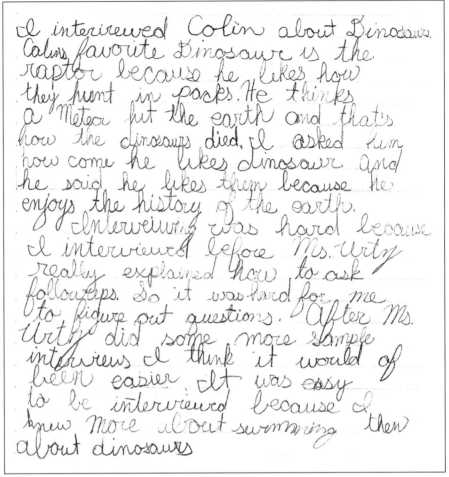

I interviewed Colin about Dinosaurs.
Colins favorite Dinosaur is the
raptor because he likes how
they hunt in packs. He thinks
a Meteor hit the earth and thats
how the dinosaurs died. I asked him
how come he likes dinosaur and
he said he likes them because he
enjoys the history of the earth.
Interviewing was hard because
I interviewed before Ms. Urty
really explained how to ask
followups. So it was hard for me
to figure out questions. After Ms.
Urty did some more sample
interviews I think it would of
been easier. It was easy
to be interviewed because I
knew more about swimming then
about dinosaurs

Figure 9.1 *Allison writes about follow-up questions in her wonder book.*

Marisa notes that a good interview demands strong listening skills (see Figure 9.2). She mentions that her questions came mostly from listening to Brandon's answers, and she includes an example of a follow-up question she asked.

After a week of studying interviewing, Ashley interviewed Amie about dogs, a subject Amie knew well. Figure 9.3 is Ashley's first attempt at recording an interview in writing, a difficult task even for adults. Ashley's interview contains examples of follow-up questions, personal questions, and universal questions. She designed them herself, mostly while the interview was in process. Quite an accomplishment!

From this point on, Mary kept her ears and eyes out for authentic interview possibilities in and around the school. She sought out visitors to the school as possible interview subjects for interested students. She twisted the arms of teaching colleagues. Kids need as much practice as they can get to build the requisite skills to become proficient interviewers.

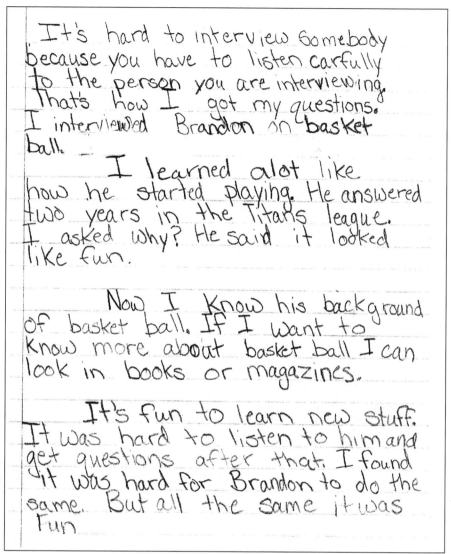

It's hard to interview somebody because you have to listen carfully to the person you are interviewing. That's how I got my questions. I interviewed Brandon on basket ball.

I learned alot like how he started playing. He answered two years in the Titans league. I asked why? He said it looked like fun.

Now I know his background of basket ball. If I want to know more about basket ball I can look in books or magazines.

It's fun to learn new stuff. It was hard to listen to him and get questions after that. I found it was hard for Brandon to do the same. But all the same it was fun

Figure 9.2 *Marisa reflects on her interview with Brandon.*

Interview Guidelines

After a great deal of practice, kids in Mary's class came up with the following interview guidelines:

- Listen carefully to the subject—you may find surprising information.
- Ask follow-up questions—they take the interview deeper.
- Ask mostly open-ended questions—yes and no questions can kill an interview before it gets off the ground.
- Ask specific personal and global questions—both types can provide rich information.

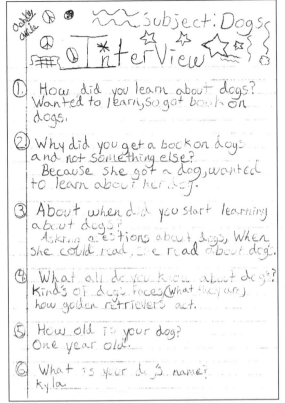

Figure 9.3 *Ashley records an interview in writing.*

- Let the interviewee do the talking—live with the silence in order to find out more.
- Take charge when interviews go astray—if the interviewee rambles, redirect the focus by asking a generic question.
- Jot down key words and short notes during interviews—these should jog your memory later.
- Record important information in notebooks as soon as the interview is completed.

You might design additional lessons focusing on some of these techniques. Also, check out a copy John Brady's *The Craft of Interviewing* (1976). It's written for adults, but it's jam-packed with the nitty-gritty of conducting personal interviews. It's a terrific resource that you can adapt for your classroom.

Learning from Professionals

You can bring real-world practicality to interviewing instruction by bringing in professionals who conduct interviews for a living—a reporter, a newscaster, a researcher, a consultant. Let the kids grill the griller.

Bill Husted, a veteran reporter for the *Denver Post* offers this tip: "Never mistake an interview for a conversation. The interview is not about revealing yourself. The interview is about having the interviewee reveal himself. Don't talk, listen. Live with the silence. Sit and wait. The interviewee may reach deeper because of the silence. Natural talkers are drawn to this profession. They need to keep quiet and listen."

Television is loaded with interview programs—*60 Minutes, The Today Show, Oprah Winfrey*, you name it. *Biography*, a popular nightly program on the Arts and Entertainment channel, includes interviews—usually one with the subject if the person is still living. A&E recently added *Biography for Kids,* a weekly program about people of particular interest to young adults and children; there is a related monthly magazine loaded with profiles and who-am-I type quizzes. An all-biography cable channel is in the works for 1998. Teachers and kids can prepare and post a list of interview programs and their weekly time slots, so kids can watch and compare.

Many magazines, among them *Parade,* which is included in many Sunday newspapers, offer regular interview columns. Establish a list and encourage kids to bring in examples of strong print interviews when they find them.

National Public Radio journalist Susan Stamberg has written an annotated collection of some of her interviews entitled *Talk: NPR's Susan Stamberg Considers All Things* (1993). The book describes her thoughtful interviews for the network and the annotations add a fascinating perspective. Susan Stamberg knows how to "ask the unexpected question and more important listen and respond to the answers" according to the blurb on the jacket flap. A recent book from *New York Times* interviewer Claudia Dreifus, titled simply *Interview* (1997), covers her interviews with subjects she categorizes as saints, philosophers, citizens, media "phreaks," and poets. The opening section, on saints, begins, much to my delight, with two interviews of Tenzin Gyatso, the fourteenth Dalai Lama.

Brian Lamb, host of C-Span's weekly hour *Booknotes,* a program dedicated to interviewing authors about their work, has written a compilation of the show's most memorable interviews in *Booknotes: America's Finest Authors on Reading, Writing and the Power of Ideas* (1997). Children's book writer Pat Cummings interviews fourteen favorite children's book illustrators in *Talking with Artists* (1992). In *The Place My Words Are Looking For* (1990), a book of poetry particularly suited to intermediate and middle school students, anthologist Paul Janeczko interviews each poet about the nature of poetry and places the response adjacent to the poem. All of these books offer wonderful models of interview techniques. Read them with kids and discuss what they reveal about the interview process.

An editor I know suggested that teachers record any or all of NPR's top-notch interviewers and share the tapes with students. A collection like that would provide exceptional models of interview strategies and techniques. Students, of course, can listen to radio and television interviews at home and perhaps occasionally tape one to share with classmates.

Phones, Snail Mail, Surveys, E-mail, and Bulletin Boards

• • • • • • • • • The telephone, letters, and e-mail narrow the distance between kids engaged in inquiry and professionals with valuable information. To get needed information, kids must know how to use the phone (and the phone book), write a good letter, design a survey, compose comprehensible e-mail, or post an on-line bulletin. Primary research offers kids an opportunity to hone their skills in these areas.

Shelley Harwayne notes that one way of determining who's important in school is by noticing who's receiving faxes, phone calls, letters, and e-mail. At schools that value inquiry, everyone receives mail and phone calls, kids included.

Using the Phone Book and the Phone

Having a phone and several current phone books in the classroom is invaluable when doing research. The amount of information in the phone book is staggering. Some phone books contain an information guide that highlights zip codes, maps, street addresses, public transportation routes, and important phone numbers. The phone service pages are helpful when researchers need area codes and service information.

Besides being an important instrument in the search for information, the phone book is also an effective teaching tool. Encourage kids and other members of the school community to bring in old phone books when new ones arrive on their doorstep each fall. You can use them to teach your students about:

- *The purpose and organization of each section.* The yellow pages are arranged alphabetically by category of business or service; the entries in the white pages are presented alphabetically by last name (private residences) or first important word (businesses). The white pages often list residential and business numbers separately. Many phone books include blue pages for government listings.

- *Alphabetizing.* Phone books demand an understanding of alphabetizing. Kids can practice by looking up people who have the same last name as they do. They can search for names of friends and celebrities. And they can look up phone numbers of people or organizations that may provide information on a topic they are researching.

- *Guide words.* Dictionaries, encyclopedias, and phone books depend on the concept of guide words. Teachers can use the phone book to teach guide words, and kids can practice using the guide words at the top of a page to assist them as they look up telephone numbers.

- *Categorizing.* There's no better place to teach categorizing than the yellow pages. Suppose someone is studying asthma. Where might she or he find information on this condition? You can demonstrate a yellow page search. You might first try doctors, which would likely refer you to physicians, where you might then find asthma and allergy specialists, and finally determine a number to call.

Knowing how to use the phone is indispensable in the quest for information. Good phone manners are also critical to the researcher's success. It's not hard to hang up on someone when you feel like it. Teachers can demonstrate polite, authentic information-seeking phone calls and make time for kids to practice with each other before they make real calls in search of information. Appropriate use of the telephone will serve kids well both in and out of school.

Letter-Writing Tips

Research often requires sending away for information. Kids need to know how to write letters requesting information. Teachers can demonstrate this by writing one for their own inquiry study and by sharing examples of business letters they've written or received. Here are some tips (many of them apply to electronic mail as well):

- If students know the name of the person to whom they are directing their inquiry, they should begin the letter with that person's name. A phone call first to determine the best contact is a good idea, but not always practical. If the recipient is unknown, non-gender-specific greetings are essential. Women may take offense at receiving a letter addressed *Gentlemen* or *Dear Sirs*. Writers may choose from several salutations: *To Whom It May Concern, Dear Madam or Sir*, or my favorite, the simple *Greetings*. And remind kids that salutations in business letters are followed by a colon rather than a comma.

- Teach students to state the purpose for writing. Mentioning a school project increases the chance of a quick response.

- Encourage students to be polite. They need to understand that the recipient is doing a favor if he or she responds. Remind them to say thank-you before closing.

- Encourage students to be specific. Tell them to ask for exact information. This reduces the possibility that the recipient will misunderstand and saves everyone's time.

- Encourage students to get to the point quickly and close. Business letters should rarely be more than one page.

- Encourage students to ask to be placed on an organization's mailing list.

- Teach students to use the full block format when writing a business letter. In full block, everything is left justified, including the sender's name, address, and date. The paragraphs are not indented and there is a space between them. Most people use full block because it's simpler than other formats. If the school has stationary with letterhead, kids should use it. If not, they might develop their own on an available school computer.

- Encourage students to use warm words for the closing—*Sincerely* or *Yours truly*. (*Love*, the closing with which they are most familiar, is too personal in this context.)

- Encourage students to start with a rough draft and go back to check both content and mechanics before preparing the final copy.

A sample letter of inquiry follows:

Stephanie Harvey
13 Rangeview Drive
Cataract, CO 80008
August 25, 1997

Colorado Friends of Tibet
3095 Lafayette Drive
Boulder, CO 80303

Greetings:

I teach a fourth-grade class in Denver. We are presently engaged in independent research projects in which each student chooses to investigate a topic of interest. Because I'm interested in Tibet and I believe in learning along with the students, I have chosen to research the plight of Tibet. Having once visited that country, I feel a deep affinity with the Tibetan people. The local chamber of commerce suggested I contact your organization for information.

For my project, I plan to research the historic relationship between China and Tibet. I am particularly interested in any information you have regarding the Chinese incursion. I would also appreciate being placed on your mailing list so that I will be notified of any upcoming events, workshops, or lectures focused on Tibet. Please send this information at your earliest convenience.

Thank you so much.

Sincerely yours,

Stephanie Harvey

Remind students that it may take a while for a written response and suggest that they go on to another step in the process while waiting to hear from the recipient.

Surveys

Distributing surveys can prove useful in acquiring information on a specific topic. Designing, writing, implementing, and interpreting surveys is a terrific way to weave math into the inquiry process and get needed information at the same time. Surveys also provide a window into the thinking of others. Kids can do phone or written surveys from home or school.

Katie, a fourth grader studying UFOs, was primarily interested in whether aliens have visited earth. Although she had read that many hoaxes had been perpetrated on people throughout history, she still found numerous examples of unexplained phenomena related to UFOs. She decided to conduct a survey to ascertain the opinions of people in the school. She surveyed second graders, fourth graders, and adults, asking simply, *Do you think aliens have visited earth?* She graphed results by age and converted the responses into percentages. The trends indicated that most second graders believed that aliens have visited this planet, most fourth graders did not, and the adults had decidedly mixed responses. Katie attempted to make sense of these trends, grappling with the information in relation to her research questions.

Surveys are a useful tool for gathering information. Here are some tips to help kids with surveys:

- Explain what a sample is and how to select a sample. When choosing the sample population, ask, *From whom do I need to solicit information to help answer this question?*

- Teach students how to design survey questions. Most survey questions are either objective or subjective. Teach students the difference. Objective questions can be answered quantitatively, or with a yes or a no. Subjective questions require explanations. Surveys typically include more objective questions, because they are easier to tabulate and interpret.

- Emphasize the importance of clear, unambiguous questions. One of the dangers inherent in poorly written surveys is that respondents don't understand the questions. This skews the survey results. Help kids evaluate their questions for clarity.

- Show kids examples of surveys from newspapers, magazines, or other print material. Discuss how to read the results.

- Weave math into the inquiry study by figuring percentages and graphing or charting the survey results.

It is important to talk to students about both the usefulness and the limitations of surveys. Surveys give us a general idea of what a group of people think about a specific issue or topic. Surveys are limited by their sample. They don't give a universal response. Remind students that personal or focus-group interviews dig deeper and elicit more in-depth information than surveys do.

Quality E-Mail

The first thing Nancy Burton's intermediate kids do every morning is check their e-mail. Some of their e-mail is of the one-time-only variety. They write e-mail to request information and then check responses. Other students are involved in ongoing telementoring relationships. Still others are hooked up with a public-private partnership called GLOBE (Global Learning and Observation to Benefit the Environment). In GLOBE classrooms around the world, kids collect and enter atmospheric data about the ecosystem in which they live and send it to scientists for interpretation. GLOBEMail links classrooms worldwide for the purpose of exchanging environmental information and bringing those issues to the fore.

Nancy sees e-mail as an important way for students to gather primary information and develop global relationships that will expand their horizon. After several years of experience with GLOBE and other electronically linked networks, Nancy observed, "Not all kids want to maintain an e-mail relationship. I see some kids who enjoy connecting, and others who don't seem to care about it. For our generation, it's magic to send a letter to Kenya and hear back in an hour. It's not magic for these kids. They've seen it throughout their lives. A boring book or a boring e-mail, what's the difference? It's still boring. Kids need a trigger. Technology is not exempt. There has to be something that sparks them and sustains their interest."

One morning, fifth graders Kai and Jessie opened their GLOBEMail to find a message seeking environmental information about their hometown of Boulder, Colorado, from a student at Tabor Academy in Marion, Massachusetts. They promptly did some research and e-mailed him back. The following morning, another message arrived asking for additional information.

After several days of recording data and e-mailing information, Kai and Jessie grew weary of their on-line correspondence. Although they enjoyed getting mail, they were tired of data collection and drafting e-mail messages. Just when they were thinking of calling it quits, they received a message requesting information on indigenous Colorado plant life and describing Tabor's maritime environment. It included an address for the Tabor Web page.

Jessie immediately navigated to the Web page. Kai's jaw dropped when he saw the graphics and read the text. Tabor Academy sported a marine lab equipped with state-of-the-art microscopes and computers for aquatic analysis and, unbelievably, a two-story saltwater aquarium. Here was the trigger! For two landlocked kids from Boulder, Colorado, the marine setup at Tabor reignited their interest and kick-started their inquiry into indigenous Colorado plant life.

With visions of the Tabor aquarium dancing in their heads, Kai and Jessie researched plants to share with their e-mail partner. With accessible resources in short supply, they slogged through a high school botany text and headed outside to search for examples. They wanted to provide their Tabor e-mail partner with the best possible information and hoped to learn more about Tabor aquatics in the process.

On a walk to nearby Chautauqua Park, they found a ponderosa pine forest, plucked a needle, and sniffed the scent of butterscotch. "If your research comes only from books, you just get the author's point of view. We looked for characteristics in the book and then went outside to find the plant so we could add personal discoveries to our e-mail messages. Going outside turned our information into knowledge," Kai explained. When Kai and Jessie headed into the field, their e-mail messages came to life.

> We are now sending information on ponderosa pines. If we look out our window, we can see seven of these trees. Ponderosa pines are the biggest evergreens in Colorado and they have the biggest needles ranging from four to seven inches long. Older ponderosa pines have rough bark that smells like vanilla or butterscotch. The bark gets

thicker as the tree gets older. Trees which are further apart will have thicker bark.

Forests of ponderosa pine can be found on sunny mountain sides or at lower elevations, such as Boulder. In fact, ponderosas don't grow above 9,000 feet. Unlike other pine forests where the trees are close together, ponderosas are very far apart. In mountain parks, the ponderosas live in stands in the middle of large open areas. These trees can be seen from a distance, because of their flat tops. What we mean by flat tops is that the top of the tree is more flat than pointed.

We have a city park called Chautauqua that has many ponderosa pines. Just like old fashioned chautauquas in the east, there are old wooden buildings and an old auditorium for performances. Sometimes during a summer concert, there is a sudden thunderstorm and the rain is so loud on the roof, you can't hear the music. When you walk the Foothills Trail from Chautauqua to the National Center for Atmospheric Research (NCAR), you are in a ponderosa pine forest.

This is striking e-mail. The emergence of e-mail marks the return of the art of letter writing, rising from the ashes like some cyberflight of the phoenix. Nancy expects high-quality e-mail from her students. She shares examples of her own e-mail as models and reviews each message, demanding the same level of revision and editing given any published piece of writing.

Jessie reported that they sometimes revised four or five drafts before sending the final one. "We do e-mails in detail, because that's the way we've been taught. Occasionally, we have written short one- or two-sentence e-mails just to answer a quick question. But we like to get informative e-mail most, so we try to make most of our messages worth reading."

Well-crafted, informative e-mail has a better chance of pulling that interest trigger than one- or two-sentence messages. Meaningful primary information comes from e-mailers who are invested in the process. Nancy sets high standards for e-mail; the compelling messages speak for themselves. And her students go deeper to provide information and learn from their new on-line buddies.

Public Bulletin Boards

Kids as Global Scientists (KGS), a project similar to GLOBE, sponsors a bulletin board where kids post messages that ask and answer questions or report on an issue. The kids in Nancy's room studied the KGS message board to determine what makes a good posting. They found that most of the interesting postings were written by scientists, not students; this indicated that most students were not paying attention to the craft of their messages.

Studying the postings, they discovered that unlike strong e-mail messages, the best postings were short and to the point. Titles were crucial. If the message had an uninteresting title, kids chose not to open it. Margaret and Jessie opened a KGS message board on temperature and pressure and scrolled to a posting titled Wild Weather. "Now that's intriguing," Margaret commented as she opened it. And sure enough, an interesting paragraph on inconsistent Colorado weather came into view. Next, Margaret saw a posting titled The Coriolis Effect. "Oh I was hoping to find something on this," Margaret said as she opened it.

Jessie noticed the title Hi to Everybody! "Now why would I take the time to open that?" she asked quizzically. "Or the one that says Unusually Mild Temperature in Winter. How about Weird Winter Weather instead? Wouldn't that grab you more? After all, if you are going to take time to post messages, you might as well have someone take a look at them." Jessie recognized that creating catchy titles for message boards encourages respondents to read them.

School Web Pages

Increasing numbers of schools are creating their own Web pages. School Web pages inform Web surfers about a wide range of school-related information. Web pages offer one of the best opportunities for students to publicize their research projects and findings. Project-based classrooms engaged in nonfiction inquiry can also publish information about project design. Designing a classroom Web site develops technical proficiency and offers classroom research and insight to the public.

Creating classroom Web pages requires teachers and students to think carefully about what they want to say and how to say it. Choosing worthwhile graphics and messages can be challenging for young Web architects. Nancy Burton encourages her students to study Web pages and identify appealing characteristics. Kids in Nancy's class list their favorite Web addresses for other kids to check out and evaluate. The more kids are exposed to quality Web pages, the more likely they will construct an excellent one themselves.

Designing a class Web site offers kids a creative, effective way to work as a team, manipulate technology, and publish classroom inquiry projects. The best example I've seen of student and class research projects on the Internet are the virtual museums constructed by students in the Bellingham, Washington, public schools. They have created a series of museums to highlight the curriculum they have researched, from Ellis Island to the history of their hometown. Check them out at http://www.bham.wednet.edu/bpsmuse.htm#Bellingham (McKenzie 1996).

Primary research via e-mail, message boards, and Web pages appeals to kids because it is interesting, authentic, and purposeful. The real power of our expanding worldwide Internet technology lies in the possibility of bringing people from distant points together to exchange ideas and learn from one another. On-line encounters with peers and professionals from around the globe may be the next best thing to the face-to-face interview.

Exploring in the Field: Off They Go

Trips to the zoo to study animals, visits to shelters to gather data on the homeless, interviews with professors, museum tours: field research can produce important information one might not find in a secondary source. Heading into the field as Kai and Jessie did to better understand the ponderosa pine yields a deeper, richer experience and adds texture to the final product.

After practicing interview techniques and contacting sources, kids can venture out to gather primary information. Asking questions and simultaneously writing down answers is challenging. Working in pairs or small groups makes this easier. One student can ask questions while the others take notes (and these roles can be switched in midstream). Tape recorders, video recorders, or cameras often come in handy. And remind young researchers to take along plenty of paper and newly sharpened pencils.

Many fourth graders in Leslie Blauman's class head into the field to contact sources. Some topics rely more on primary research than others do. Nick, who chose to research communicable diseases, realized early on that most available secondary material was too advanced. He headed straight home to talk to his pathologist dad, who suggested other primary resources in the local medical community. Todd headed to the butterfly sanctuary and answered all but one of his burning questions by talking with the staff and reading signs and labels. Ali toured the Molly Brown house and read original primary documents, including the *Denver Post* published the day after the Titanic sank. Georgi interviewed her family vet about dogs. Eric visited a buffalo ranch referred to him by a Denver restaurant that serves buffalo meat.

Not all inquiry topics require field research, and field experiences are not always possible. Phone interviews, e-mail, and letters often suffice. Inquiry is not a lockstep process. But if it is practical for kids to get out of the classroom, the authenticity of real-world research will stay with them long after their project is completed.

My husband, Edward, and I once visited England's Blenheim Palace, the birthplace and boyhood home of Sir Winston Churchill. Our guided tour ended in a room full of school letters from Churchill to his parents. We'd had a long day and were eager to get back to our hotel for a nap. But other people's mail is irresistible. Churchill's letters woke us up. Reading them brought him to life. Witty descriptions of his daily social, academic, and athletic life at school were followed by the thinly veiled pleas for money of a regular teenager.

We remember primary information. It sticks with us. Tracking down primary sources spurs kids on and enriches their nonfiction inquiry. Talking to experts authenticates the research process. Going out into the field invigorates that search. E-mailing brings new perspective. Primary information enhances the researcher's understanding. It breathes life into the inquiry project. Give kids the opportunity to pursue it.

10

Organizing Thinking: There's No One Way

Much of life's routine revolves around organization, that five-syllable incantation responsible for punctual arrivals, completed homework, and returned calls. When organization succumbs to the fast-paced nineties life, chaos reigns, even at school. Getting organized is the key to productive nonfiction inquiry. Organizing and recording thinking is the glue that holds the research process together. The degree to which kids succeed at organizing their thinking directly affects the quality of the final product. Organization makes the work easier for everyone.

But organizational styles, preferences, capabilities, and deficiencies are highly variable; no single method, no single tool, no single technique, can be taught or relied on. Visualize for a moment a row of seventh graders' lockers, open to view. Some notebooks hide beneath backpacks, jackets, and empty Cheetos bags; others are stacked neatly on the top shelf. Teachers need to keep in mind the varying organizational needs of kids and their matching strategies. Teaching skills for organizing one's thinking, from major structural systems that focus scattered thinkers to little reminders that support natural organizers, is a pedagogical challenge.

Organizing Reading, Writing, and Research

After uncovering and identifying the information that is important (see Chapter 7), students need to sort, sift, and synthesize this information. Traditionally, reports have been organized around a formal outline. The recent trend toward more informal outlining and note-taking strategies allows students to choose from techniques such as indenting, listing, webbing, and mapping in order to organize information. These varied organizational strategies lend themselves to varied organizational styles.

124

Teachers who require a specific number of note cards or a rigid formal outline from every student do a disservice to all students. We need to expose kids to a wide range of organizational strategies, build in time for exploration and practice, and ultimately let them choose those strategies that most aptly fit their styles.

Informal Outlining

Every research report needs a skeleton—a structural framework—around which to organize content. Outlines, both formal and informal, give writers a plan for content and sequence. Formal outlines are arranged around a fixed system of numbers and letters. Informal outlines provide a less rigid structure for organizing content.

I recall wrestling with formal outlining in junior high. I could never remember whether to use a number here or a letter there. I contemplated the employment of *a* versus *A* for hours on end. I worried about the size of the indentations. I treated the outline as an end in itself, rather than as a way to structure my report. Rigid formal outlines tend to stress structure to the detriment of content.

No one showed me informal outlining techniques. Outlining involves chunking information around individual subtopics. Informal outlines accomplish this without a complicated system of letters and numbers. Informal outlines use simpler content groupings that can be supplemented with a finer substructure when necessary. Creating an informal outline using one of the strategies below can be a very helpful initial organizational step.

Listing. I'm convinced the population is divided into two categories, those who make lists and those who don't. I am a list maker. My purse bulges with lists: grocery lists, errand lists, work-related lists. Sometimes I think I need a list of my lists. If I don't write things down, I forget them. If I lose my daily planner, my life dissolves.

Listing serves me well as a writer, too. Ideas for this book hit me while I'm driving, teaching, standing in the checkout line, or tossing and turning at 3:00 A.M. I carry a notebook and jot my thoughts down wherever I am, adding them to my chapter outlines later. Listing is a natural way for writers to organize thinking, young ones included.

Students can start by listing topics, as several in Mary's room do in Chapter 2. As they read and do research, they acquire more and more topic information. Mary encourages kids to list the ideas they feel should be included in their written piece. After deciding on the most important concepts, students can arrange these concepts sequentially to give the writing structure.

Joyce uses lists to frame her research on Helen Keller. First, she lists the important facts she wants to include (see Figure 10.1). Then she attempts to organize the sequence in which she will present them (see Figure 10.2).

Indenting. Indenting subservient information, with or without the bullets and dashes that have come to replace the maze of numbers and letters in

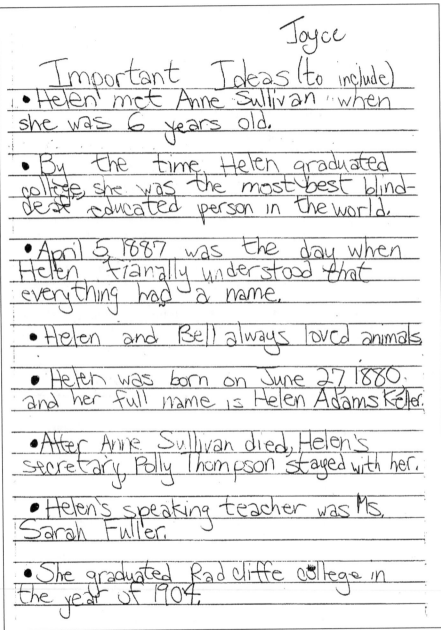

Joyce

Important Ideas (to include)

• Helen met Anne Sullivan when she was 6 years old.

• By the time Helen graduated college, she was the most best blind-deaf educated person in the world.

• April 5, 1887 was the day when Helen fianally understood that everything had a name.

• Helen and Bell always loved animals.

• Helen was born on June 27 1880. and her full name is Helen Adams Keller.

• After Anne Sullivan died, Helen's secretary, Polly Thompson stayed with her.

• Helen's speaking teacher was Ms. Sarah Fuller.

• She graduated Radcliffe college in the year of 1904.

Figure 10.1 *Joyce's list of ideas to frame an inquiry report on Helen Keller.*

formal outlines, offers many writers a useful framework for their nonfiction writing. I share my own informal outlines with students to model the use of indentation and bullets. Jessa, a sixth grader, constructed the outline in Figure 10.3 after her teacher demonstrated indentation and bullets on the overhead.

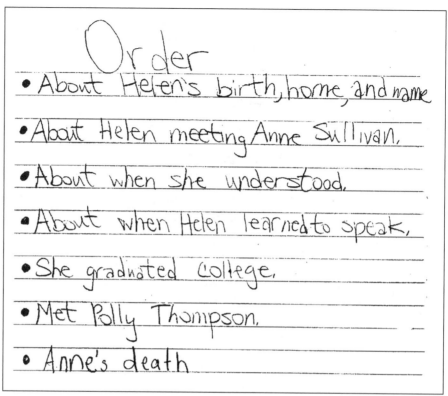

Figure 10.2 *Joyce's sequence for organizing her Helen Keller inquiry.*

Webbing. Webbing is a form of graphic outlining that helps kids develop subtopics and details around their main topic. In a web, the information is clustered visually. Some students, particularly those who operate in a more visual realm, are more comfortable with webbed groupings than with linear lists. Caroline, an eighth grader, webbed the battle of Chickamauga for a Civil War research project (see Figure 10.4). She chose battle preparation, setting, and the two critical battle dates as her pivotal areas of organization and grouped the details around them.

Concept Mapping. Concept maps link related ideas graphically as a way of developing a fuller definition of a person, a term, or an idea. Unlike looking up a static dictionary definition, the process of concept mapping encourages students to integrate their existing knowledge and thus form a deeper, richer understanding (Schwartz and Raphael 1985).

Nonfiction concept mapping sorts main ideas and supporting details according to the following questions: What is it? What is it like? What are some examples? (or, alternatively, Who is it? What is he or she like? What are his or her contributions?). Concept maps guide students through research and track their inquiry. Jessica framed an eighth-grade science study around a concept map of famed primatologist Dian Fossey (see Figure 10.5).

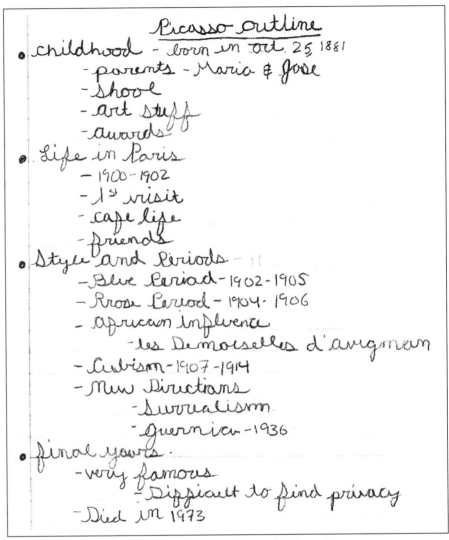

Figure 10.3 *An informal outline using bullets and indentations.*

Outlines must be flexible. Even with a detailed outline, unexpected ideas may pop up and need to be worked in. Writing is an act of discovery. Fresh thinking often adds depth and breadth to inquiry projects. A mark of developing expertise is the confidence to incorporate new information and ideas. Teachers can stress how important it is for students to stay flexible yet organized as they sift through their material.

A final word on formal outlines. Although few writers use them to frame their writing, students will nevertheless encounter them in textbooks, encyclopedias, reference materials, and standardized tests. We need to expose kids to formal outlines so that they will know what they are and understand the concept.

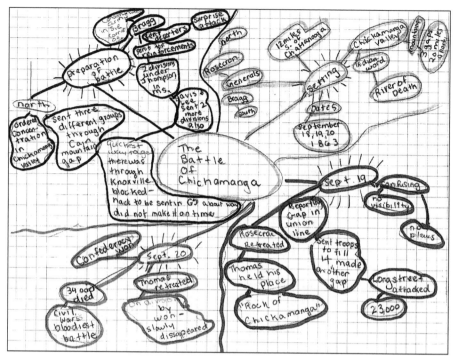

Figure 10.4 *Caroline's web of the battle of Chickamauga.*

Figure 10.5 *Jessica's concept map of Dian Fossey.*

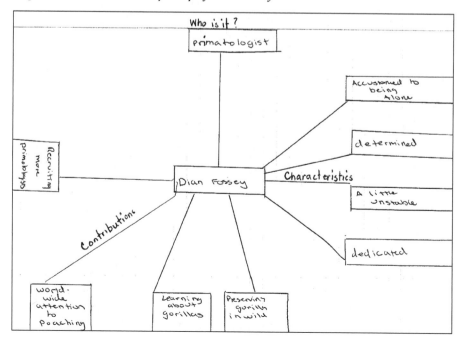

Why Take Notes?

• • • • • • • • • • We take notes to remember ideas and details we might otherwise forget. Period. End of story. Note taking is not an end in itself, but rather a means to an end. In this case the end is a thoughtful, accurate, well-written research report. Note taking is purposeful. Note taking should support students in their inquiry, not torture them.

I once found my daughter hunched over her desk, madly scrawling notes on index cards. The final deadline for her eighth-grade research project on Dian Fossey was fast approaching, so why was she still taking notes? She'd completed her research, and had begun writing her report several days earlier. As I looked more closely, I realized she was copying over notes she'd taken previously! When I asked why, she said her notes were going to be graded, and she wasn't sure her teacher could read them. I asked her if she could read them.

"Of course, I can read them," she answered incredulously.

"That's all that matters," I told her. But she remained unconvinced and continued to waste time on a worthless copying exercise.

Looking at notes as a way to monitor progress is an important diagnostic tool for teachers. But notes are for writers to organize information and clarify their thinking. Grading them for neatness defeats the purpose. When taking notes, handwriting, spelling, and punctuation are secondary concerns. Students take notes to support their learning, not to impress their teachers.

Note-Taking Strategies

Note-taking techniques are as varied as the people who take notes. Marking or coding text is the simplest form of note taking; some kids take their notes on cards; still others use legal pads, sometimes dividing the page into columns. Whatever format is used, time is of the essence. Teachers can encourage kids to:

- Use short phrases, not complete sentences.
- Use their own words.
- Jot down only the most important ideas.
- Not be concerned about handwriting, spelling, and punctuation.
- Devise codes of their own to speed things up: initials, abbreviations, asterisks.

After you've demonstrated note-taking techniques on the overhead projector, send the kids off to practice. It pays off.

Responding to Reading in Writing

Third-grade teacher Norton Moore encourages students to jot down in their nonfiction notebooks the thoughts they have, the questions that come to mind, and the key things they learn while reading. Norton demonstrates by reading out loud and then sharing his musings out loud as he writes them in his notebook. Young readers are remarkably adept at writing about reading if the text is compelling. Before Norton teaches specific note-taking strategies, he gives students plenty of time to become comfortable with writing down their thoughts and responses in their notebook. That way, techniques for recording thinking emerge naturally.

Class Secretary

Carol Newman, the collaborative librarian at Boulder's Heatherwood Elementary, introduces note taking by defining and demonstrating the role of a secretary who takes the minutes of a meeting. After taking notes on a class discussion, she copies them and shares them with the class, showing them her personal codes and idiosyncrasies. Next, she writes a short summary based on these notes, fixing mistakes and writing in complete sentences. She wants kids to see how notes support writing.

Listening and Recording Important Ideas

Most kids are better prepared to take notes if they've had practice with a scaffolding exercise. After the role of secretary has been explained and demonstrated, have the kids form small groups and sit together while you read aloud. After reading a page or two stop and ask the groups to discuss the important ideas they heard while a member of the group who has been chosen to act as secretary records these ideas in a notebook. Continue reading for another page or two and repeat this. Try this several times a week in different content areas and rotate the secretary. It works well with movies and videos too. (The secretary does not take notes during the reading, only during the small-group discussion of important ideas.)

Note Taker of the Day

Judy Davis, Manhattan New School fifth-grade teacher, has come up with a similar concept she calls Note Taker of the Day. After giving a number of note-taking demonstrations, Judy selects a class member to take notes as she reads content-area material aloud to the class. This frees the other students to listen and soak up new ideas. The daily notes are later copied and distributed, so kids are able to jot their own thoughts on them. After each student has had an opportunity to be note taker of the day, everyone has a go at independent note taking.

Note Cards

Carol Newman introduces note cards very gradually. Believing that true research comes from a question, Carol first lists her big questions on the left side of a large two-column chart and includes some smaller related questions on the right.

Big Questions	Small Questions
Why did Egyptians make mummies?	Was it for religious reasons?
Who became mummies?	Was it only for the rich?
How did Egyptians make mummies?	What was the process?
	What materials were used?

Then she divides another large piece of chart paper into a number of smaller segments, holds up a three-by-five note card, and explains that each segment represents a standard note card.

Next, Carol reads aloud from Aliki's *Mummies Made in Egypt* (1979). Discovering that religion was the primary reason for mummification, she writes the word *Religion* at the top of several chart segments and records one religious fact about mummification on each segment. When she finishes writing down the religious information, she turns to the question, Who became mummies? She heads several chart-paper segments with the word *Who* and continues reading. As she encounters text that responds to that question, she again puts one detail on each segment.

Later, instead of using chart paper, Carol substitutes regular eight-and-a-half-by-eleven-inch sheets on which she has photocopied five blank note cards (see Appendix 5). The kids use these sheets to take notes on a main topic, a separate detail on each note-card facsimile. A sheet like this is particularly useful for kids who struggle with organization, since real note cards often make like Houdini and vanish into thin air.

Jeremy's note cards on UFOs are reproduced in Figure 10.6. He has written one detail on each Sightings card. As his note-taking skills evolve, however, he includes many details on the card headed Mistaken Identity.

Figure 10.6 *Jeremy's note cards on UFO sightings.*

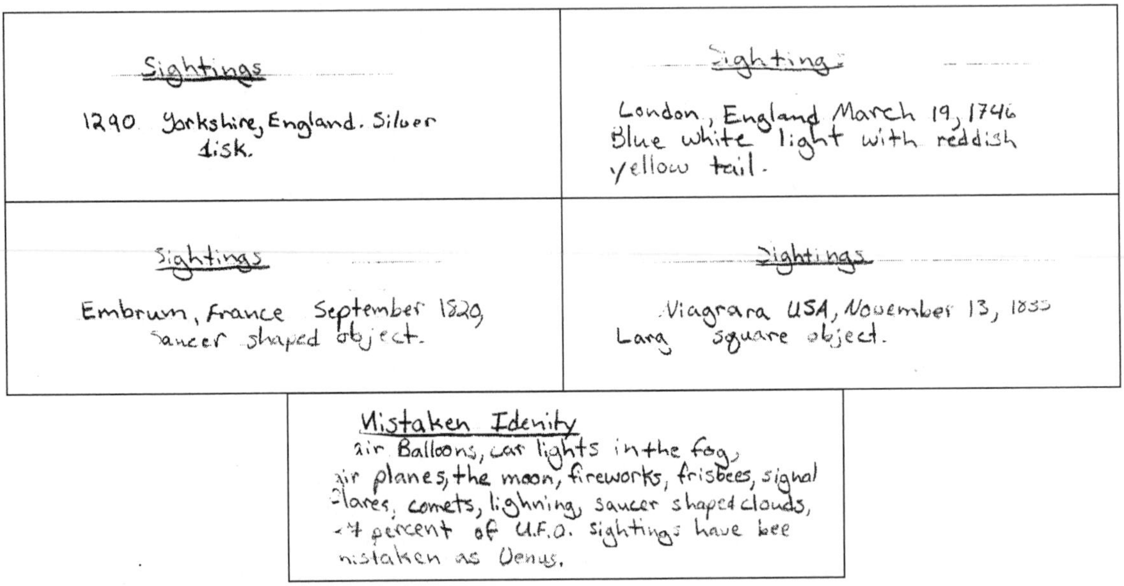

Two-Column Notes

The two-column note is a T chart with two headings. Two-column notes are especially useful, because they are so adaptable. Headings are only limited by the imagination. Teachers can experiment with a variety of forms, each with a specific purpose. Two-column notes described elsewhere in this book are:

- What I Know/What I Wonder (Chapter 3).
- What I Know/What I Learned (Chapter 3).
- Questions/Answers (Chapter 8).
- What's Interesting/What's Important (Chapter 7).
- Big Questions/Small Questions (this chapter).
- What the Text Is About/What It Makes Me Think About (this chapter).
- What the Text Is About/What It Makes Me Wonder About (this chapter).

Here are some others you can try:

- *Opinion/Proof* (Santa et al. 1985). Here the students form an opinion, then look to the text for proof. This strategy increases accuracy and is particularly useful for middle school students. It encourages readers to stay wedded to the text rather than speculating wildly. (The reader, of course, might disagree with the text. A third column explaining the reasons for disagreement can be added.)
- *Facts/Questions.* As students read, they can record factual information from the text and jot down any questions they have about that information. This is a great way to monitor comprehension.
- *Convention/Purpose.* These columns are used to identify and record conventions having to do with the appearance and punctuation of text. When readers encounter boldface print, for example, they note that in the first column and state the purpose in the second. When they encounter a colon, they do the same. (This is often used by students in pairs or small groups, since several heads are often better then one at determining purpose.)
- *Familiar Concept/New Concept.* This form is particularly useful for middle schoolers, because they encounter so many new concepts. As they read, they can jot down familiar concepts and use those as a bridge to new concepts.
- *Direct Quote/Personal Response.* Nonfiction readers encounter text that strikes them, reminds them of their own experience, or speaks to them in some other way. Copying a quotation from the text on a two-column chart and responding to it promotes active reading and thinking.
- *Note Taking/Note Making.* Fifth-grade teacher Judy Davis uses this two-column note form. The kids record information on the note-taking side and add their personal response on the note-making side.

Topic/Details

This is also a two-column note-taking technique, but it is so useful for students as they sift and sort information for inquiry projects that I've given it its own section.

Leslie Blauman introduces this organizational note-taking strategy early in the year, using it in connection with her "featured student" activity. On Monday, the student of the week tells the class her or his life story. The other students take notes and, during the rest of the week, each one writes a narrative about the featured student. The subject of these narratives takes them all home on Friday as permanent keepsakes. What a great memento of fourth-grade life, thirty stories written by your classmates, each one with you as the protagonist!

To model the process, Leslie begins the year by recounting a family camping story featuring her curious husky, Bandit; a wily mountain porcupine; ten porcupine quills lodged in Bandit's mouth; an ineffective pair of pliers; and a midnight return to Denver to ease Bandit's misery. (Leslie knows that a lively, entertaining story provides a much stronger model than a dull description of where she lives and what she does.) As the kids ask her questions after she finishes the tale, Leslie categorizes them.

For example, Bruce asks how many kids Leslie has. "That sounds like a family question," Leslie responds. She draws a chart on the overhead with the headings Topic and Details, noting *family* as the topic. "This topic could become a paragraph in my piece in which I tell about the details of my family life."

After answering further family questions and adding family details on the form, Leslie takes Chris's question about her outside activities. She enters *interests* under the Topic column, making sure to leave some white space in case she needs to add other details pertaining to the family. Her chart now looks like this:

Topic	Details
Family	Two kids—Carolynn, 8, John, 4
	Eric—husband—a consultant who travels regularly
	Bandit—husky
	Cassidy—golden retriever
	Live in suburbs of Denver
Interests	Camping
	Boating
	The outdoors

Additional questions from the students are about family, interests, favorite things, Leslie's school life, the future, and interesting anecdotes. Leslie adds each topic and the related details to the chart. These topics come from the kids' sincere questions. Leslie knows that rich writing comes from genuinely interesting ideas and authentic questions, not from a preordained subset of ideas.

Throughout the week, she demonstrates how her notes support the personal narrative she writes. The following week, Leslie takes notes while the featured child tells his story. Gradually, Leslie encourages students to try their own hand at two-column note taking using the overhead; she is by their side to help them. After much practice, Leslie turns note taking over to the kids completely.

Leslie told me that before she introduced this Topic/Details two-column format, her fourth graders were all over the organizational map. This strategy gave their thinking focus. Now most of Leslie's students routinely use this two-column note technique whenever they read in the content area or do nonfiction research. Leslie also mentioned that this form is useful for quiz preparation. Kids can fold the details side over and practice remembering important details while looking only at the topic.

When kids begin two-column note taking, Leslie invites them to work in pairs if they choose. Jade and Taylor's notes on astronaut training (see Figure 10.7) show their joint foray into the format.

Figure 10.7 *Jade and Taylor collaborate on two-column note taking.*

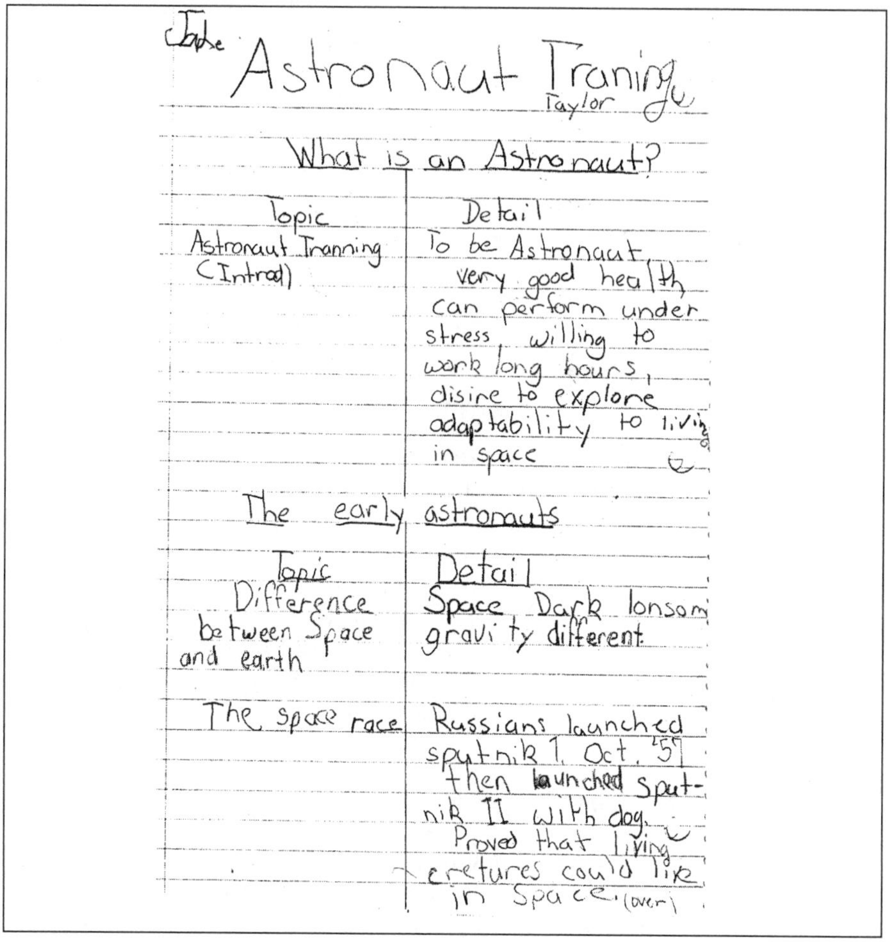

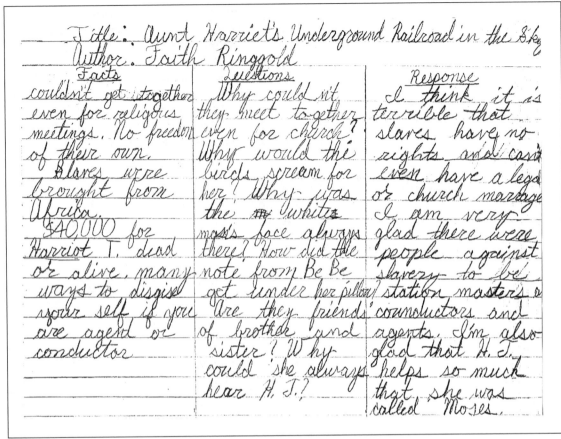

Figure 10.8 *Clare adds a third column for response to a two-column form.*

A Third Column for Response

After teaching two-column note taking, teachers can encourage kids to add a third column for personal response. When readers connect what they read to their background knowledge, they comprehend more deeply. The response column gives ownership to note taking.

Facts/Questions/Response or Topic/Details/Response are particularly useful three-column forms that support readers as they try to make sense of text and organize thinking. Adding a personal response helps students integrate information and begin to synthesize it. Figure 10.8 shows a three-column form from Clare's notebook.

Synthesizing Information

Note taking requires readers and researchers to synthesize what they read. Synthesizing, an important step in the research cycle, is a process akin to working a jigsaw puzzle. In the same way that we manipulate hundreds of puzzle pieces to form a new picture, students must arrange fragments of information until they see a new pattern take shape (McKenzie 1996). The ability to synthesize information takes on increasing importance at the dawn of the twenty-first century. Our information-rich society requires us to sift through ever-increasing amounts of data to make sense of them and act on what we learn (Harvey et al. 1996).

I recently read a *New York Times* review of Savion Glover's award-winning Broadway musical, *Bring in 'da Noise Bring in 'da Funk,* which explores African American history through tap dancing. The reviewer, Ben Brantley, describes Glover's new style of dance as a synthesis:

> Almost all the numbers trace an arc from tentativeness to full-blown assured performances. This is most evident in Glover's splendid second-act solo in which he demonstrates the techniques of legendary tap artists of the past, and then synthesizes them into an exultant style of his own. (1996, C-1)

As Brantley suggests, synthesizing involves combining new information with existing knowledge to form an original idea, a new line of thinking, or a new creation. Through his inventive dance form, Savion Glover puts his personal stamp on the art of tap dancing. In the same way, students distill nonfiction text into a few important ideas or larger concepts that may lead to a new insight or help them form a particular viewpoint. A nonfiction article on famine, for example, might point a finger at governmental food distribution policies. A reader's synthesis of this article could involve forming an opinion about the shortsightedness of the government in question. When students synthesize, they personalize the outcome by integrating their thinking with new information to achieve a new perspective.

The Importance of Summary

Summary is part of synthesis. You can't synthesize information if you don't know how to summarize. Summarizing is the act of briefly presenting the main points. When teaching summary, teachers should encourage young readers to retell information by including important ideas but not telling too much.

Getting the Gist

Cris Tovani talks to her ninth graders about reading for the gist. She begins by asking her students to summarize movies. (We've all heard a kid's retelling of a movie that lasts longer than the film did!) Cris reminds students to recount important ideas and be brief. She models this by writing a summary of a familiar movie.

Cris then explains to students that synthesizing takes summarizing a step further, that synthesizing involves the reader's personal response to the material, whereas summarizing is primarily a straightforward, brief retelling of events, perhaps calling attention to the author's message. She models writing theater, book, and movie reviews that include a statement of the message and a personal critique as well as a summary of the content.

Who? What? When? Where? Why? and How?

Kathy Marquet teaches summarizing and more when she prepares her students for a third-grade tradition at Ponderosa Elementary called *News Spot*. Once a week each third grader at Ponderosa joins a news team to report the news. Assignments include international news reporter, national news reporter, book reviewer, sportscaster, business reporter, entertainment and lifestyles reporter, and environmental reporter. The kids study the newspaper, read relevant articles, write their news summary, practice delivering it orally, and then report the news. Following the newscast, the student reporters take questions from the audience. Individual news reports last from two to three minutes, the entire News Spot segment about fifteen minutes. Each child is videotaped at least once doing a news report.

This process rings with authenticity, deadlines and all. Before turning News Spot over to the kids, Kathy demonstrates the steps at the overhead, including skimming for the gist, rereading more carefully for detail, highlighting for further understanding, writing final news copy, and practicing the oral presentation. (I know some newscasters who could benefit from these focus lessons.)

During her stint as the network environmental reporter, Crystle used the classic questions asked by the investigative reporter to sift through a piece detailing the effects of Hurricane Fran on baby sea turtles (see Figure 10.9). From these notes, she synthesized the information and drafted the empathetic news copy in Figure 10.10.

Personal Response

A number of teachers I work with use a two-column form headed What the Text Is About/What It Makes Me Think (or Wonder) About. Students summarize the content of a piece in the first column and reflect on the piece in the second column. As students get the hang of this, they typically begin to write more in the second column, synthesizing their own thoughts and questions with the material.

From Oranges to Orange Juice: A Focus Lesson

Synthesizing is an abstract concept. Teachers I work with have tried a number of ways to make the process concrete for students. Explicit demonstrations of synthesizing can become anchor experiences.

Sue Kempton, the beekeeping kindergarten teacher, demonstrates synthesis by making orange juice. She shows her energetic kindergartners the can of juice concentrate, the water, the pitcher, and the stirring spoon. Kids follow directions and make the juice. Sue points out that they started with the con-

Crystle

Who: Baby sea turtles (endangered)
What: Hurricane Fran- caused big waves that
washed turtle nests and babies out to sea and
back up on shore. - they were mixed up and
didn't know where they were or how to get
back into water.
Where: Wilmington, North Carolina
When: Last fall
why, Because of hurricane fran
How: Endangered animals - Hurricane
was bad but polluted water even worse!

Figure 10.9 Crystle uses the six questions of the investigative reporter to get information.

centrated juice and the water, which they mixed to form a new and different thing, orange juice. (Sue has also used baking to illustrate synthesizing.)

Poof! It's Water: Another Focus Lesson

Todd Cargill, an eighth-grade science teacher, writes the chemical symbol H_2O on the board and asks kids what it means. Two parts hydrogen and one part oxygen, they answer confidently. He points out that when these elements come together, a synthesis occurs. That synthesis produces water, a new and different substance. Todd also keeps M. C. Escher jigsaw puzzles around as another concrete synthesizing activity kids can engage in when they have a few free moments.

Crystle

Poor little baby sea Turtles got queit a scare when Hurricane Fran smashed into their island off North Carolina. 70% died and 30% lived. Hurricane Fran washed away turtle nests, turtle eggs, and baby turtles. After Hurricane Fran was over, turtle eggs were scatterd all over the island. Some sea turtles were even walking in the streets. People felt sorry for turtles. But Scientests say water pollution is even worse for sea turtles, then hurricanes.

Figure 10.10 *Crystle's news copy on Hurricane Fran's effect on baby sea turtles.*

Synthesis is the opposite of analysis in the classical sense of those terms. Analysis is the breaking down of something whole into its parts, while synthesis is the putting together of separate parts into a new whole. (The H_2O demonstration can be reversed to explain analysis.)

Deriving the Essence of a Paragraph

After demonstrating a few concrete examples of synthesis, Mary Urtz shows her fifth graders how to synthesize information when reading. She begins by reading a rich piece of text from the overhead, one paragraph at a time, circling key words and underlining phrases that may help her extract the important information. To illustrate synthesizing graphically, she then brackets each paragraph and makes a very brief margin note that captures the paragraph's essence.

After Mary's lesson, Nate attempts to synthesize a piece called "Gray Wolf" (Turbak 1996) (see Figure 10.11). Nate grasps the idea of distilling paragraphs into salient points and categorizing the paragraph content. And you can't miss his mini-editorial regarding the article's first line.

Figure 10.11 *Determining important ideas and deriving the essence of a paragraph.*

GRAY WOLF

Canis lupus
STATUS: ENDANGERED

great lead!

It is perhaps the most primeval sound in all of nature: the howl of a wild wolf. Lonely, eerie, haunting, surreal. A cry from the distant past. The sound begins deep within the belly of the beast, rises to falsetto clarity, then trails off into silence. But soon there is another. And another. The wolf's howl is at the same time a call, a query, an announcement and a challenge. It supercedes all other sounds and seems still to own the air even after its maker has quit. No living thing can ignore it.

how they are alike

People and wolves are much alike—social, predatory, competitive, aggressive, the leaders of their respective branches of evolution. Perhaps that is why the howl has for millennia summoned uncounted humans to the front lines of a war against wolves. Maybe that explains why the very word *wolf* inspires images of evil, death, destruction, and searing green eyes glowing in the night. Since long before anyone bothered to record such things, people and wolves have been locked in conflict, a battle that cannot be explained solely by the facts.

once lived

The gray wolf—also called the timber wolf in some places—once ranged from Alaska to Mexico and from Maine to California (and across portions of Europe and Asia). It thrived in any habitat that supported populations of ungulates such as deer, moose, bison, and elk. In this country, only the most arid deserts of the Southwest were devoid of wolves.

characteristics & feachers

Physical characteristics can vary with geography, but generally the gray wolf stands about thirty inches tall at the shoulders, with adult males weighing about ninety-five pounds and females perhaps fifteen pounds less. Their color can range from pure white to jet black, but most animals, true to their name, are shades of gray. Wolves can trot tirelessly for hours and hit thirty-five miles an hour when they need to. When hunting is poor, they can go many days without food.

alphas

Wolves are among the most social—and most hierarchical—mammals on earth. The literal top dog is called (by humans, anyway) the alpha male, and all others in the pack are subservient to him. There is also an alpha female to which all other females are subordinate. From this pair down, a defined pecking order lets each wolf know who ranks above and who lies below. Social standing is frequently reinforced via a complex system of body language and mock fighting—but rarely with real aggression.

hunting

On the hunt, the alpha male makes most of the decisions, takes the lead in the attack, and has first crack at eating the prey. The rest of the pack members dine in the order of their social standing, and if the food runs out before all the bellies are full, the lowest in rank go hungry. Pack size varies considerably, but eight or ten might be about average. Usually only the alpha pair are allowed to reproduce.

mating & babies

They mate in late winter, and nine weeks later from four to seven pups are born, usually in a burrow. Rearing the youngsters can be a truly communal affair. For two weeks or so, the female may forgo hunting entirely to stay with her offspring, during which time the pack carries food to her—either in their mouths or in their bellies for regurgitation at the nursery burrow. When the pups are a couple of months old, the adults often move them to a rendezvous site (usually a meadow with timber and water nearby) where they

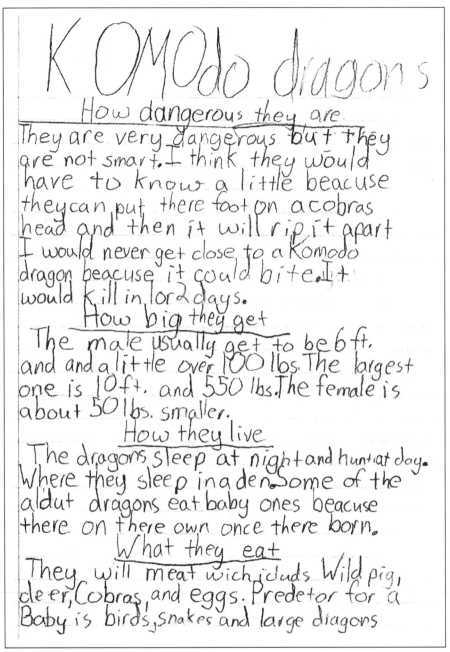

Figure 10.12 *Andrew creates subtopics to organize information on Komodo Dragons.*

Andrew's notes on the Komodo Dragon (see Figure 10.12) demonstrate his independent use of synthesizing. He divided his notes into subtopics he synthesized from his reading.

Anthony struggled with identifying subtopics for his study on frogs. He conferred with Marsha, his teacher, and several other kids in the class before deciding to include the following: habitat, food source, defense, physical characteristics, and enemies. Once Anthony determined these categories, he was better able to read for specific information (see Figure 10.13). Whereas Andrew determined his subtopics *while* reading, Anthony structured his *before* reading.

Figure 10.13 *Anthony uses predetermined subtopics to organize information on frogs.*

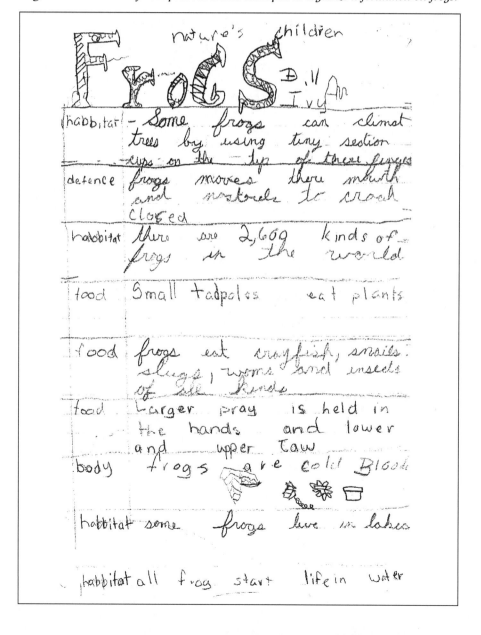

Renaming the Book

The title an author chooses for a book or an article is frequently the briefest synthesis of its content. Young writers can practice the idea of synthesizing by choosing appropriate titles for their writing pieces. Staff developer Colleen Buddy has kids rename the book they're reading. Michelle, a third grader reading Kathryn Lasky's *Monarchs*, renamed it *Flight to Michoacan*. She was intrigued by the impressive monarch migration and its impact on Mexico, and believed this was the most important idea in the book.

Synthesizing to Keep Current

Jay Mahoney, a seventh-grade earth science teacher, engages his class in a weekly synthesizing activity. Each Monday kids are asked to find a current article on earth science that they find interesting. They read the article, tape it to a science notebook page, and write a brief synthesis that includes their own take on the article. At the end of the year, they have an earth science notebook packed with articles on recent scientific events and theories, along with their personal assessment of the information. They appreciate the timeliness of these articles, which supplement their less current textbooks. Geography, world cultures, politics, and science all lend themselves to this technique, which supports knowledge acquisition in the content areas.

Methodical organization is essential to accurate nonfiction writing. But there are as many organizational structures as there are people doing the organizing. It is our job as teachers to help young researchers find the structure that works best for them. We honor students' individual learning styles by modeling the entire spectrum of organizational strategies, encouraging them to practice each a few times, and finally allowing them to select the ones that best fit their needs.

The purpose of the framing strategies discussed in this chapter is to make writing easier. Now that we've glued our thoughts together, we're finally ready to write!

Part 3

Putting It
All Together

11

Getting It Down on Paper

My earliest memories of writing are of scribbling in my childhood books. I still have a copy of Maurice Sendak's *A Hole Is to Dig* that is almost unreadable because of my purple scrawls. As my books succumbed to Crayolas, my mom replaced them with notebooks and sketchpads. I curled up in my bedroom and filled these notebooks with tales of horses, coonskin-capped explorers, World War II battles, and distant ports of call. Little if any writing was done at school—I don't recall any, other than handwriting, until sixth grade. No wonder so many adults are poor writers. We didn't get much practice.

Enter sixth grade. It loomed large in the mind of one frightened fifth grader. And enter Miss Scott, a bigger-than-life sixth-grade teacher. Every Friday at two o'clock, Miss Scott offered creative writing. After assigning some off-the-wall topic like imagining ourselves as a dull pencil, she turned us loose to write, expecting a completed piece when school was dismissed at three.

Miss Scott slumped at her desk correcting papers, while we hunched over ours. I was usually paralyzed by writer's block. As my eyes scanned the room in desperation, I would notice Danny Iwanski, the class clown. Miss Scott loved Danny. Danny's head would be down, his #2 pencil flying over his Big Chief tablet. Forty-five minutes later, Miss Scott would collect the papers. When she returned them, covered with red marks, the following week, she invariably asked Danny to read his. *Danny got it!* He understood what it meant to be an empty glass or a dull pencil, but to my knowledge, he was the only kid in sixth grade who did.

I wondered why we couldn't write about things we knew, understood, and cared about. "This is *creative* writing," Miss Scott told me. "You need to create something. Be clever, don't just write the same old thing." I was struck by the irony of every sixth grader writing on identical, assigned topics in a class called creative writing. I began to believe that I lacked the creativity to write, so I quit—even those stories that filled my spiral notebooks at home. It would be years before I wrote again.

You don't have to imagine yourself as a dull pencil to qualify as being creative. All writing is creative, nonfiction included. The writer coins ideas, chooses topics, struggles with word choice, crafts the piece, and creates new thinking. We celebrate creativity for what it is—an act of discovery, not an exercise in topic cloning.

We can begin to eliminate these breakdowns of confidence by calling writing writing rather than creative writing. I write frequently now about my work, my family, my interests, and my childhood. I know about these things, and I write about them because they intrigue me. William Zinsser speaks to this:

> Ultimately, every writer must follow the path that feels most comfortable. For most people who are learning to write, that path is non-fiction. It enables them to write about what they know or can observe or can find out. This is especially true of young people. They will write more willingly about situations that have reality—experiences that touch their lives—or subjects that they have an aptitude for. (1990, 57)

Self-selected nonfiction inquiry encourages writers to write about their experiences, interests, and aptitudes—real topics that lend themselves to good writing.

The Teacher's Role

• • • • • • • • • • Fortunately, times have changed since Miss Scott's weekly creative writing exercise. Thanks to pioneers like Donald Graves, Nancie Atwell, and Shelley Harwayne, elementary and middle schools across the country feature classrooms in which writing is taught and students and teachers write. Many teachers I know devote an hour to writing workshop at least four days a week. In these lively workshops, young writers have large blocks of time in which to choose topics, write, share what they've written, and confer with teachers and peers.

Like fiction, nonfiction benefits from strong voice, compelling word choice, and clarity. Unlike fiction, nonfiction must convey accurate information coherently. It is the challenge of nonfiction writers to write accurately in a compelling way. We meet this challenge by teaching specific strategies for writing nonfiction. Don Murray reminds us to view writing as a teachable craft:

> Writing is a craft before it is an art. Writing may appear magic, but it is our responsibility to take our students backstage to watch the pigeons being tucked up the magician's sleeve. The process of writing can be studied and understood. Quality nonfiction writing can be

taught if we provide appropriate instruction and give young writers
time to practice. (1985, 4)

The teachers portrayed in this chapter believe that writing can be taught,
practice writing themselves, surround students with examples of high-
quality nonfiction, build in time each day for students to write, and provide
explicit instruction in nonfiction writing.

We learn how to teach writing by doing it. My writing instruction has
come from reading and writing—reading about writing, talking and listening
to writers, attending writing workshops, and sharing my writing. Here are
some resources and activities that help me better understand nonfiction writing and plan my instruction:

- *Books on writing.* A number of books have given me direction, both in
  teaching writing and writing myself. Sharing the lessons of these books
  gives young writers the best possible writing advice. When Leslie
  Blauman has a writing question, she opens her well-worn copy of
  William Zinsser's *On Writing Well* (1990) and shares its secrets with her
  fourth graders. Fifth graders in Judy Davis's Manhattan New School classroom study the qualities of good writing by reading Ralph Fletcher's *What
  a Writer Needs* (1993), a book most often marketed to teachers. Middle
  school teachers who are serious about nonfiction writing often put Strunk
  and White's *The Elements of Style* (1979) on their annual supply list. To
  teach writing well, we must understand what makes good writing.

- *Daily quick-writes.* Writing quickly for about ten minutes each day gets
  writers into the habit of writing. Many teachers and kids in Denver
  enter their classroom each morning, open their nonfiction notebooks,
  and write for a few minutes to maintain their stride as writers. (This is
  in addition to their writing workshop.)

- *Nonfiction study groups.* Choosing a book on writing nonfiction and reading it with a group of interested colleagues encourages cross-grade
  communication and gives common thinking and terminology to nonfiction writing instruction. Student study groups offer similar opportunities.

- *Nonfiction book clubs.* Reading nonfiction in common gives teachers and
  kids insight into the genre and improves nonfiction writing. Nonfiction
  writers must read nonfiction to write it.

- *Writing groups.* For those who are brave enough, sharing writing with
  peers in writing groups provides valuable support and spurs teachers to
  write when they might otherwise think up a million reasons for not
  putting pen to paper. Student writing groups accomplish the same thing.

Several years ago, a writer friend of mine and I summarized Strunk and
White's *The Elements of Style* for young authors. I hand out a copy of this summary to my students so that they can refer to it as needed, and I use these
guidelines to plan my instruction (see Appendix 6).

Of Beginnings, Middles, and Ends

• • • • • • • • • • Writing is best when it is simple, clear, concise, accurate, and compelling. Third grader Allen and his classmates in Norton Moore's room knew this. The first time I visited their classroom, a pudgy nine-year-old with a buzz haircut and a broad smile greeted me by thrusting this letter into my hand.

> Welcome Steph Harvey!
> Here is some stuff we know about writing. Carry a small notebook. Write nonfiction stories because you know about them. Don't forget to show not tell. Writers read books. Read books you can read. First write a rough draft not a final draft. When you are writing your first draft, it is all right to write sloppy. You can practically find paper wherever you go. Pencils too. After you finish writing all you can write, you can have someone help you edit.
> Sincerely,
> Allen

In the rest of this chapter, I explore some of Allen's nonfiction writing strategies, along with others that you and your students may find helpful. And I debunk some myths about writing nonfiction that often hold teachers and kids back.

Leads that Hook

"Born at sea in the teeth of a gale, the sailor was a dog" (Brown [1953] 1992, 1). These words churned in my mind throughout childhood. I return to Margaret Wise Brown's *The Sailor Dog* time and again because of that first line. Nora Ephron says, "I don't write a word of the article until I have the lead. It just sets the whole tone—the whole point of view. I know exactly where I'm going as soon as I have the lead" (Murray 1990, 122). Kids can spend time reading leads, identifying strong leads, categorizing leads, and writing and revising leads. A strong lead sets the stage for a strong piece. William Zinsser says simply, "The most important sentence in any article is the first one. If it doesn't induce the reader to proceed to the second sentence, the article is dead" (1990, 65).

When I introduce leads to young writers, I ask them to think about fishing, to imagine the writer as an angler and the reader as a fish. Writers cast out their first line of words in hopes of hooking the reader and reeling him into the text. Often when readers pull a book from the shelf, they flip to the first page, read it, and reshelve it if it doesn't hook them. There are many fish in the sea. A good lead depends on the best tackle and bait. Good writers care about leads and choose them judiciously.

In Search of Strong Leads. Teachers can begin their focus on leads by immersing kids in great beginnings and calling attention to them. Nonfiction magazines, nonfiction picture books, and newspapers all brim with catchy leads. I model "grabber" leads first, ones that grab readers and make them wonder what comes next. A first line such as the one Barbara Cooney chose for her biography of Eleanor Roosevelt—"From the beginning the baby was a disappointment to her mother" (1996, 1)—reels us into the book by making us wonder why. After sharing a trove of leads, Leslie Blauman and Mary Urtz encourage kids to check out nonfiction text based on the strength of the lead. Kids search for strong leads and mark and share them. Writers think about lead choice after hearing powerful examples.

The Wide Range of Leads. We do young writers a disservice if we teach only one or two types of leads. Good leads do not follow a specific form. Magazines are a great vehicle for comparing a variety of approaches to the same strategy. One morning in Gloria Mundel's sixth-grade classroom in Denver's Horace Mann Middle School, I shared the September 1996 issue of *Faces*, a social studies magazine aimed at middle schoolers. I read the leads to ten articles. The variety was astonishing. For example:

- "In Nicaragua, deaf kids did what no adult could do and what no one had ever seen happen."
- "The Shaman puts on her royal blue vest, ties it with a red sash and dons a wide-brimmed black hat decorated with a tassel of colored yarn and a sprinkling of sequins."
- "Have you ever sent a coded message to a friend across the room, using perhaps a barely visible hand gesture or a subtle facial expression?"

The sixth graders discussed how the ten leads differed and attempted to categorize them on chart paper. Some fell into obvious categories. Others fit under several columns or a column headed Other. The following categories emerged (but remember that some leads will never fit a specific category):

- Leads in the form of a question.
- Leads in the form of dialogue.
- Leads that show, not tell.
- Leads that raise questions.
- Leads that set a tone.
- Leads that inform.
- Leads that surprise.

These categories are helpful for young writers when they begin crafting leads. However, leads in authentic nonfiction are as varied as the articles themselves. Their only requirement is that they hook those fickle fish!

Crafting Catchy Leads. So once we immerse kids in strong leads, how do they actually start writing their own? If kids are stuck, I suggest they begin with the information or event that most struck them during their research. What intrigued them may also capture their audience.

One morning, I pulled a chair next to Cassie, a fourth grader, who had already gone to the pencil sharpener twice, the drinking fountain three times, and the bathroom once during writing workshop. She sat staring at the ceiling with her Mozart research planted in front of her.

"How's it goin'?"

"Okay, but I don't know where to begin. I thought I might start with when and where Mozart was born, but it seemed a little boring," she mused.

"Let's take a look at the leads in some of the material you've gathered," I suggested. As we pored over her resources, Cassie noticed that one book began late in Mozart's life and looked back and that another was told though the eyes of his sister. None began with the standard encyclopedic beginning, "Wolfgang Amadeus Mozart was born in Salzburg, Austria, on January 27, 1756." I asked Cassie what information about Mozart she found most fascinating.

"How young he was when he started playing concerts. He could barely reach the keys and his feet couldn't touch the floor," she noted, turning to a picture in *Mozart: Scenes from the Childhood of the Great Composer* (Brighton 1990), which showed him at the piano. "Look at those tiny hands on the keys. He's only five. I can't believe it!" she said incredulously.

As Cassie talked, I wrote down what she'd said and handed it to her. "I think you might have found a lead here. These are your words in your voice. Think about how you might use some of these words to begin writing." I left Cassie, head down, writing. She was no longer thirsty or preoccupied with shaving her pencil to a needle-sharp point. Her final piece a few weeks later began, "The beautiful velvet curtain rose slowly and the tiny hands began to play. Young Wolfgang Amadeus Mozart sat at the clavier in the Grand Palace Hall playing his first concerto and he was only five years old."

I encourage teachers to share quality leads their students have written. Young writers can benefit by hearing the writing of other young writers as well as published writers. Here are a few striking leads written by students:

It's raining, it's pouring and the whole world is excited. A new baby chimp was born at the London Zoo. Its eyes glow like the midnight moon, and its nose is like the two little eyes of Winkin' and Blinkin'.

Jessica, grade 3

Why did John Hancock sign the Declaration of Independence so big and bold? Because (1) that is the way he writes? or (2) to intimidate the British? The answer is Number 2, to intimidate the British. John Hancock was captured in the first battle of the Revolutionary War. He escaped and King George said if you capture him, you can shoot him. *That* is why he signed so big.

Dan, grade 5

Autumn in Colorado. The golden aspens shimmer across the hillside like a giant fire in the sky. The green spruce trees look almost black next to the changing aspens. Many flowers are gone, but still an occasional burst of purple, red and yellow petals, here and there. The birds still sing, but in trios now instead of choruses. The weather is in practice for the long frosty winter ahead.

Jess, grade 6

It was a windy October evening. The dry leaves whispered in the air as they fell to the ground. The year was 1801. A loud knock echoed through the corridors of the old, colonial family home of Mr. Meriwether Lewis. His devoted servant answered the door. A young man in uniform carried a message with the presidential seal. As Meriwether Lewis read the note, a big smile appeared on his face. President Thomas Jefferson had appointed the twenty-seven-year-old Lewis to be his personal secretary.

Allison, grade 7

A flash of light shines off the alto saxophone, creating a speck of reflection in the listener's fixed eyes. The listener is somewhere far away. He has been kidnapped by the sound. The saxophone is joined by an upright Yamaha, now in the spotlight. The music blends with the rising smoke. Somewhere from the shadows behind the intoxicating duet, flows the sound of a stand-up bass and drum cymbal, synthesized into one sound carrying the piece along. . . . Where did this come from, this form of music commonly known as jazz?

Jerry, grade 8

Don't Forget the Middle

Strong leads are all well and good, but pointless if the middle falls short. The middle of an inquiry piece is a bit like the middle child, more easily overlooked and sometimes left to bump along on its own. A strong middle section develops and supports the central thesis. It requires careful attention.

Earlier in the chapter, I left Cassie crafting a lead for her piece on Mozart. Our next conference found her struggling to go on.

"I have this pretty good beginning now, but I don't know what to do next. I keep looking at the topic/details notes in my notebook. I have notes on his birthplace, his childhood, his family, his music, his adult life, all kinds of stuff. Whew! Where do I go from here? If I organized it like an encyclopedia, I would have started with his birth and continued in order through his life. I know teachers say that's boring, but it would be a lot easier."

I couldn't disagree with Cassie's evaluation, but I knew she could craft a strong piece if I nudged her in the right direction.

"Cassie, when I'm stuck, I usually read what other authors have done in similar circumstances. Let's take a look at how some other writers chose to write the middle section," I suggested.

Cassie and I headed over to the biography book basket and pulled out a few picture books to get a feel for the structure and direction of the writing.

"Look at *Good Queen Bess*." I handed Cassie the book. "Her birth isn't mentioned until the third page after a lengthy description of her father, King Henry VIII, and her mother, Anne Boleyn. Then the author goes back to her birth and follows her life."

The chronological nature of most of the biographies gave Cassie a renewed sense of confidence about her own piece.

"I think my second paragraph can start with Mozart's birth, and then I can use my notes to write about his childhood and go in order from there."

"Great," I said, while perusing her two-column notes, "I do notice though that some of the notes in your column on music refer to his unusual musical talent in childhood. Where will you put that information?"

"I don't know, maybe in the childhood part, because for Mozart music was the most important thing. So I guess I can include music stuff in the childhood section, if it's about music he wrote and performed in childhood."

Here's Cassie's revised second paragraph:

Mozart, the amazing composer, was born in Salzburg, Austria in 1756. When Mozart was only a toddler, he was already showing his musical talent. He would stand in his crib and sing songs he made up that day. When he was three, he started to play the piano all on his own and when he was just four, he drew some notes and wrote his first piece of music. At the age of nine, he wrote his first symphony. No one so young had ever written one and when he was twelve, he wrote his first opera.

As Cassie demonstrates, young writers don't have to use their topic/details notes paragraph by paragraph. They may. Or they may inject information where it fits best. Cassie employs a chronological structure for the most part. As writers practice, they become increasingly effective at weaving a theme through a piece and choosing among a variety of text structures, as described in Chapter 7. Serious revision requires young writers to think and make choices. Teachers can nudge kids to do just that.

Cassie's final piece went on to discuss Mozart's family life, his performance tours around Europe, his relationship with royalty, his sickliness, his adult family, and his later life. Her amazement at Mozart's prodigious musical talent in youth pervaded the entire piece.

Ending When It's Time

Endings are tough but crucial. In fact, many consider the final sentence second in importance only to the initial one. Young writers generally have more trouble winding their pieces down than revving them up. Some just stop when they've had enough, regardless of content. Others ramble on, unsure whether or not they've reached the end. (Half the movies I see these days seem to suffer from this disease.)

Good endings capture the essence of the piece, wrap things up, and conclude with a final sentence that fits. To appreciate an ending fully, you have to have read the entire text, which makes it difficult to model examples. Teachers can mitigate this by concentrating on short pieces—articles, essays, sketches, and picture books.

Eudora Welty has said, "I think the ending is implicit in the beginning. It must be. If that isn't there in the beginning, you don't know what you're working toward. You should have a sense of a story's shape and form and its destination, all of which is like a flower inside a seed" (Murray 1990, 168). One useful technique for helping young writers conclude is to return to the lead and reflect it in the ending. This type of closure brings the piece full circle. Numerous nonfiction books and articles incorporate the lead in the ending.

Leslie Blauman shared a number of circular endings with her fourth graders. One of them was an article on Abraham Lincoln in *Kids Discover* (1995), which began, "Abraham Lincoln grew up in a fast-changing America," and ended, "The face of America certainly was changing—quickly."

Georgi took this example to heart. Her lead in her report on the history of dogs read, "A cry, then a whimper, then nothing. A dog is born. He nuzzles his mother softly as she licks him clean of the blood that drizzles down his tiny forehead." She ended her report this way: "Now it is time for the small puppy to leave its mother. It is a sad moment. They nuzzle and he leaves."

Gerard, a sixth grader investigating Great Britain, sets a tone in the lead that he returns to in the ending. His report begins:

> Royalty, Shakespeare, chivalry, Sherlock and Dickens; what do these things have in common? Great Britain of course. Sometimes beautiful trees, sun and flowers, sometimes dense fog hanging over craggy moors, but it's all part of the tradition of Great Britain.

He concludes it this way:

> So it comes to a day's end. People take one last look at the Tower Clock. A child puts a biscuit in his mouth and washes it down with a glass of milk. A guard at Buckingham Palace puts down his rifle and rests it against his knee. A Bobbie glances down the street to say good night to the banker. And the Queen turns off her light.

When Are You Really Finished?

When writers have said all they want and have to say, they should stop. Teachers can suggest that kids ask several questions to help them determine whether they've reached this point:

- Did I include all needed information?
- Did I tie up loose ends?
- Do I have anything I still burn to say?
- Did I answer my original questions?
- Will the reader feel satisfied or at least challenged?
- Does the ending fit?

Zinsser notes, "The perfect ending should take your readers slightly by surprise, but seem exactly right" (1990, 76). Alexander, an eighth grader in

Meg Philpot's physical science class, ends his first-person biography of the brilliant, physically challenged astronomer Stephen Hawking this way—the last two sentences fit like a glove:

> By this time, I was confined to a wheelchair. Losing my ability to walk was difficult for me. My speech continued to deteriorate. But I continue to study cosmology and ponder the origin and future of the universe. Despite my disability, I've had a good life. Our third child, a son, was born in 1979. My book, *A Brief History of Time*, is a best seller. I've achieved a great deal in my work. But I still ask myself why indulge in these intellectual pursuits in my condition. The answer: although my body is my prison, my mind grants me amnesty. I thrive on it.

A well-crafted piece gives readers something to think about long after the reading is over. Not all questions will necessarily be answered by the end. Nate, a fifth grader in Mary's class, astutely notes that after his deep inquiry into the circumstances of the Vietnam War, new questions bubbled to the surface:

> Why did we lose Vietnam? Was it the enemy's will to fight? If the American people didn't want involvement, why did George McGovern, a largely pacifistic presidential candidate only win one state? Why did Le Duan invade Laos and Cambodia? Still many questions over one of the most puzzling wars in history remain unanswered. Vietnam remains a mystery in many ways.

Myths in Nonfiction Writing

Sadly, the writing instruction I received in school was frequently inaccurate, because writing was taught by people who didn't write or knew little about writing. They propagated the common myths about writing nonfiction:

- Nonfiction is dry. Although it is true that textbooks, manuals, and reference books may be dry, our charge is to teach students to write nonfiction that is informative, lively, and richly voiced. We must choose interesting nonfiction models. Nonfiction is the most widely read genre. If it sounded dull, dry, and encyclopedic, no one would read it.

- Nonfiction is impersonal, so keep it in the third person. "Stay out of the first person. Don't give your opinions. Just write," my high school English teacher admonished. Actually, good nonfiction writing has personality and voice. Kids can fill their pieces with feeling and opinion by writing in the first or second person if they care to.

- Longer is better. "Ten double-spaced pages, minimum," my college professor boomed. Sound familiar? Most of my papers were wordy, long, and laborious, kitchen-sink writing, if you will. Now we know better— brevity is a virtue in writing. George Bernard Shaw once wrote to a good friend, "I'm sorry this letter is so long, but I didn't have time to make it short." Teachers who assign length are dumbing down the craft of writing. Zinsser says, "Writing improves in direct ratio to the number of things we can keep out of it that shouldn't be there" (1990, 14). Writing should be as short as it can be while still saying what the writer needs to say.

- Organized writing must follow a formula in order for it to be clear. Nonfiction writing formulas such as five-paragraph essays have recently been touted as the answer to organizing writing. How often do we see published essays with exactly five paragraphs or paragraphs with a pre-ordained number of sentences? Essays and paragraphs need to be however long the writer needs them to be to say what she or he needs to say. (More on this in Chapter 12.)

- Don't begin sentences with the word *but*. I don't know the goofball who came up with this, but it was routinely taught throughout my education. In truth, *but* kick-starts a sentence. Zinsser notes, "There is no stronger word [than *but*] at the start. It announces total contrast with what has gone before, and primes the reader for a change" (1990, 114). If you think you're using *but* too often, *however* is an alternative. And it can be inserted into the middle of a sentence: "It is, however, an important event." But remember, *but* is stronger than *however*.

We need to debunk these myths. We need to keep nonfiction from dropping off into the realm of the dull, dry, wordy, and formulaic. Showing, not telling; writing with voice; writing with nouns and verbs; staying in the active voice; and a host of other strategies lead to compelling nonfiction writing.

Showing Not Telling: How Not to Sound Like an Encyclopedia

Mary Urtz and Leslie Blauman conduct explicit focus lessons to demonstrate the difference between encyclopedic writing and authentic nonfiction writing. They begin at the overhead by comparing a piece of published nonfiction with an encyclopedia article on the same topic. The following comparison between a piece on sea turtles in *National Geographic* and an article in the *World Book Encyclopedia* highlights the difference between interesting nonfiction and reference nonfiction.

National Geographic
Turtles poured out of the surf in wave after wave through the darkness. Heaving, huffing, gasping, turtles plowed the coarse black sand with their noses, laboring onto shore. On this rain-soaked October night, possibly 30,000 olive ridley sea turtles were converging on a half mile of Pacific beach at Ostional, Costa Rica, in a biological extravaganza called *la arribada*, the arrival.

Following instincts that scientists have not begun to understand, the turtles had gathered offshore for mating and now hordes of females were swimming to this particular beach to lay eggs. By 2 A.M.

the beach looked like a cobblestone street where the cobblestones had come to life. And still more turtles were coming. All night, they advanced and retreated. They collided and piled up in jams. They filled the air with the soft sound of flippers hollowing nests in the sand and a rhythmic thump thump thump as turtles that had finished laying rocked their 80-pound bodies to pack sand over their eggs. (Rudloe and Rudloe 1994, 97)

World Book Encyclopedia (1996)
There are at least seven species of sea turtles. Six of them—the green turtle, the flatback, the hawksbill, the loggerhead, the Atlantic ridley and the Pacific ridley—have bony scut-covered shells. . . .

Female sea turtles do not normally leave the water, except to lay their eggs. The females often migrate thousands of miles or kilometers to reach their breeding beaches. They drag themselves onto a sandy beach, bury their eggs, and then return to the sea.

Writers strive to "show, not tell" in quality nonfiction. Encyclopedias tell information in a dry, straightforward way. Authentic nonfiction paints pictures with words and prints a visual image of the text in the mind's eye. Since we are not in the business of turning out young encyclopedia writers, we need to encourage kids to search the room and the world for nonfiction text that shows rather than tells and to mark those words, phrases, and sentences with sticky notes.

Many kids simply don't notice the language of quality nonfiction. But with instruction and encouragement they can strive to write visually about their topics and paint pictures with words. They can learn to read as writers, noting beautiful language, precise word choice, and interesting ideas. This sentiment from Diane Ackerman's *A Natural History of the Senses* would brighten the walls of any writing classroom:

Words are small shapes in the gorgeous chaos of the world.
But they are shapes. They bring the world into focus.
They corral ideas. They hone thoughts.
They paint watercolors of perception.
(1990, 7)

I Didn't Know Nonfiction Had Voice

The writer Kurt Vonnegut says, "Sound like yourself" (1988). When young writers write in their own voice, the result reads like easy conversation. Writing nonfiction with voice raises it above the encyclopedia. Many teachers ask me, So what is voice, anyway? Ralph Fletcher explains:

When I talk about voice, I mean written words that carry with them the sense that someone has actually written them. Not a committee, not a computer, but a single human being. Writing with voice has the same quirky cadence that makes human speech so impossible to resist listening to. (1993, 68)

Very young kids are particularly adept at writing in their own voice, which is why we find their writing so charming. Typically, the older we get, the more we hide our voice. Self-conscious adolescents are prone to ignore voice altogether. Voice is as important in nonfiction as it is in fiction or memoir. Voice gives life to writing.

Teachers I know demonstrate voice by reading aloud. To instruct her students in how to write with voice, Mary Urtz reads Kathy Wollard's *How Come?* (1993), a humorous informational book on the solar system. It gives her listeners an anchor by which to remember the concept of voice. As Mary reads other pieces of nonfiction aloud, she encourages kids to listen and identify the type of voice being used: humorous, poignant, impassioned, angry.

As students research their inquiry topics and respond in their wonder books to what they read, Mary borrows a phrase from Shelley Harwayne and encourages kids to "underline their gems," those parts that strike them, sound like themselves, and might hook readers. Emily underlined her "gems" in an early draft of her report on coyotes (see Figure 11.1). There's perhaps too much voice here, but Emily can tone it down later. Her natural

Figure 11.1 *Emily's voice comes shining through.*

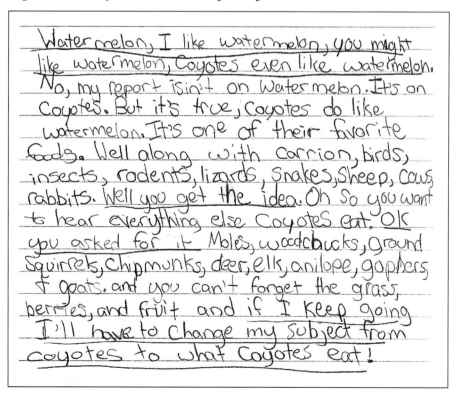

Watermelon, I like watermelon, you might like watermelon, Coyotes even like watermelon. No, my report isin't on Watermelon. It's on Coyotes. But it's true, Coyotes do like watermelon. It's one of their favorite foods. Well along with carrion, birds, insects, rodents, lizards, Snakes, Sheep, Cows, rabbits. Well you get the idea. Oh So you want to hear everything else Coyotes eat. OK you asked for it Moles, woodchucks, ground Squirrels, Chipmunks, deer, elk, antlope, gophers, + goats. and you can't forget the grass, berries, and fruit and if I keep going I'll have to Change my subject from coyotes to what Coyotes eat!

voice lends authenticity, charm, and simplicity to the piece; she sounds like she's talking. Writing with voice eliminates any potential for plagiarizing. When kids are expected to sound like themselves, they are unlikely to copy someone else's words.

The great essayist and short-story writer Raymond Carver once said:

> I think a writer's signature should be on his work. If you hear a few bars of Mozart, you don't need to hear too much to know who wrote that music, and I'd like to think that you could pick up a story by me and read a few sentences without seeing the name and know it was my story. (Murray 1990, 130)

Nouns and Verbs Breathe Life into Writing

"Add more adjectives, make your work descriptive." My eighth-grade teacher's words still resonate. I grew up thinking that stringing a list of adjectives together made the writing stronger. I recall an English teacher who had us write an essay containing at least a dozen adverbs, needed or not. Nouns and verbs give sentences power. The secret to showing, not telling, lies in writing with nouns and verbs. Young writers should look to the nouns and verbs when their sentences need strengthening. They should use adjectives and adverbs sparingly; often these words are just cluttering up a sentence.

We all remember being told to use the active voice, but perhaps we didn't understand what that meant. Active verbs show action. "Javier hit the ball" is active. "The ball was hit by Javier" is passive. "There were twenty-three students in the room" is weak. "Twenty-three students crowded into the room" is stronger. Bringing the object of a preposition out front as the subject and employing an active verb strengthens a sentence and usually shortens it. And precise verbs create a more vivid visual image: "The owl pumped its wings" is clearer than "The owl moved its wings."

Specific nouns add life. "Jawbreaker" is stronger than "piece of candy," because it's concrete. When a noun is specific, adjectives are often unnecessary. A red strawberry is redundant, because strawberries are by nature red. However, young writers can practice using adjectives when nouns alone don't convey the intended meaning. In the Colorado high country, for instance, snow varies greatly. Skiers conjure different images as they anticipate a day spent in champagne powder, deep powder, or corn snow. In cases like this, adjectives are useful.

A Focus Lesson on Specific Nouns and Precise Verbs

At Horace Mann Middle School, a hardball's throw from Coors Field, the home of the Colorado Rockies baseball team, Gloria Mundel's sixth graders joined me at the overhead for a focus lesson on writing with nouns and verbs. When I asked who wanted to select a topic, Pete hopped up and wrote *The Colorado Rockies* on the transparency. I drew a line down the center and headed the resulting columns Stuff/Nouns and What Stuff Does/Verbs.

First we brainstormed nouns, or "stuff," related to the team and then chose precise, active verbs to show what the "stuff" did:

The Colorado Rockies

Stuff/Nouns	*What Stuff Does/Verbs*
crowd	roars
Coors Field	sparkles
balls	fly
bats	crack
pitchers	hurl
catchers	signal
batters	crunch
runners	slide
home plate	waits
Blake St. Bombers	slam
Big Cat	smashes
hot dogs	drip
home runs	soar
scoreboard	flashes

After choosing these specific nouns and precise verbs, we wrote the following group paragraph:

On this warm summer evening, Coors Field sparkles in the distance. The crowd roars as the top of the lineup leads off. Our biggest hitters, the Blake Street Bombers, slammed two homers the night before. They are hot and crunch the ball night after night. Gallaraga steps up to the plate. The pitcher hurls the ball and Big Cat smashes it to right center. Home plate waits for Dante Bichette. His bat cracks the ball. It flies into the left stands. Cat rounds the corner and slides home.

Some Additional Strategies

Creating leads, middles, and endings that show, not tell, and writing clearly and visually in your own voice require constant attention. One lesson on each does not a writer make. These are big ideas that teachers must nurture to help kids grow as writers. Instruction is ongoing. Here are some additional things we can emphasize when we teach the craft of writing nonfiction:

- *Accuracy.* The audience reads nonfiction to learn. Readers rely on accurate reporting. Because nonfiction writers convey information and shape thinking with their words, they owe it to readers to strive for accuracy. The note-taking strategies discussed in Chapter 10 help to ensure accuracy. Identifying source page numbers in notebooks and rechecking copyright information (see Chapter 8) is useful. Conferring with teachers and peers promotes accuracy. Young writers need to transfer information from their notes to their writing very carefully.

- *Transitions.* Writers learn best how to make appropriate transitions from one idea to another by reading nonfiction. Teachers can point out natural transitions as they occur in authentic nonfiction, thus helping their students read like writers. After her lead about a dog's being born, Georgi made the following transition to the rest of her report: "This scene has played over and over many times. Dogs and wolves date back fifty million years." The Topic/Details chart discussed in Chapter 10 supports transition writing by isolating topics; when students write essays, they can treat each topic in its own paragraph, and use transitions to move from one paragraph to the next.

- *Sequence.* In reference books and textbooks, information is presented chronologically. This predictable structure lacks life and bores readers. Georgi's dog piece is an example of an alternative way in which time can be handled in authentic nonfiction. Georgi leads with the generic present, goes back to the past, and moves forward from there. Teachers need to point out examples of alternative ways of sequencing time.

- *The sound of the language.* James Kilpatrick says, "Back when I was growing up, the finest wine glasses were made of lead crystal. At the tap of a fingernail, they gave off a magical chime. If the crystal was flawed, all you got was a clunk. So it is with writing" (1997, 65A). Some words produce that magical chime. Other words clunk. We can train kids to listen to the sound of words and sentences. Does the sentence flow easily or is there a clunky word or syntax that kills it?

- *Dialogue.* Dialogue enhances writing, as long as it's clear who's talking. Teaching kids to identify the speaker is essential. Recently, I've seen classroom charts listing other words to use in place of *said*. These are useful to expand vocabulary, but *said* says quite well what it means to say. Unless the speaker truly *mumbled* or *screamed, said* is the straightforward and unfussy choice.

- *The power of quotations.* After his teacher read aloud from *On Writing Well,* Jeffrey took to heart Zinsser's advice that "whatever form of nonfiction you write, it will come alive in proportion to the number of quotes you can weave into it naturally as you move along" (1990, 81). Jeffrey's piece on the Iroquois tribe came to life when he quoted a harvest prayer:

  > The Iroquois called maple sugar sweet water and often smoked a pipe and spoke this prayer for an abundant harvest. "Partake of this tobacco, O Forest! We beg you to continue making sweet water. And may no accidents befall our children who roam the woods. This day is yours. May you enjoy it."

- *Cutting words.* While writing this book, I learned a valuable lesson: whenever I used a word or phrase that didn't quite work, I cut it. In almost every case, the result was clearer and more concise.

- *Copyediting.* Copyediting is the final step. Revision is an overall editing process that concentrates on the big picture. When a piece has been revised to a writer's satisfaction, it still needs a complete, detailed copyedit. Young writers can view their peers as copy editors and their teacher as the editor-in-chief. Referring to style guides and editing checklists is helpful at this stage. A hint for editing spelling: suggest that kids read their piece backward. Eliminating context gives a better chance of catching misspellings.

Helping Kids Revise

• • • • • • • • • • "But I'm done." Breathes there a teacher anywhere who has not heard this refrain from a student who is being nudged to revise? How do we combat it?

"But don't you want to add that great part about the boa constrictor devouring the kinkajou? That was so interesting, and you said it so well."

"Nope, I'm done." The young writer crosses his arms.

How *do* we get young writers to revise their work? It helps if they're committed to the project. When kids have put a lot of thought and time into something, they want their work to shine. Nonfiction inquiry engages them and pushes them to revise. Commitment is central to revision. Kids will not revise pieces about which they are ambivalent.

The poet Lorna Dee Cervantes tells her writing students at the University of Colorado to insert a hyphen into the word *re-vision* to remind them what it means. To revise is to resee. At a speech before the Colorado Language Arts Society in March of 1997, Ms. Cervantes recounted her antipathy toward revision during adolescence. She refused to revise anything until, at eighteen, she began to garner attention for her writing, which focused on the lives of poor Hispanic and Native American women on welfare. She gave voice to these women in her poetry, and their response so moved Cervantes that she began to revise her work. She wanted to be the best she could be for her audience. Revision became important when the audience became important.

Modeling Revision Techniques

Revision differs from copyediting. Revision refers to changes in words, sentences, and ideas. Copyediting involves grammar, spelling, and mechanics. While these two activities sometimes occur simultaneously, adding punctuation and copying the work over in neat handwriting is not revising.

Teachers can demonstrate revision in front of their students. While researching box jellyfish in Kathy Marquet's third grade, I wrote a page on the overhead and solicited questions. Hands waved wildly. As we discussed what I had written, I crossed out and rewrote certain phrases or sentences. Sometimes kids volunteered word changes and I changed them. Sometimes I declined to change my writing, reminding them that the writer has the final say. When I finished, the page looked as you see it in Figure 11.2. An example of sixth grader Jessa's revision follows in Figure 11.3.

Revising Leads

Third-grade teacher Carol Mooney, who was researching Albert Einstein, conducted a focus lesson on lead revision. (Before this lesson, her students

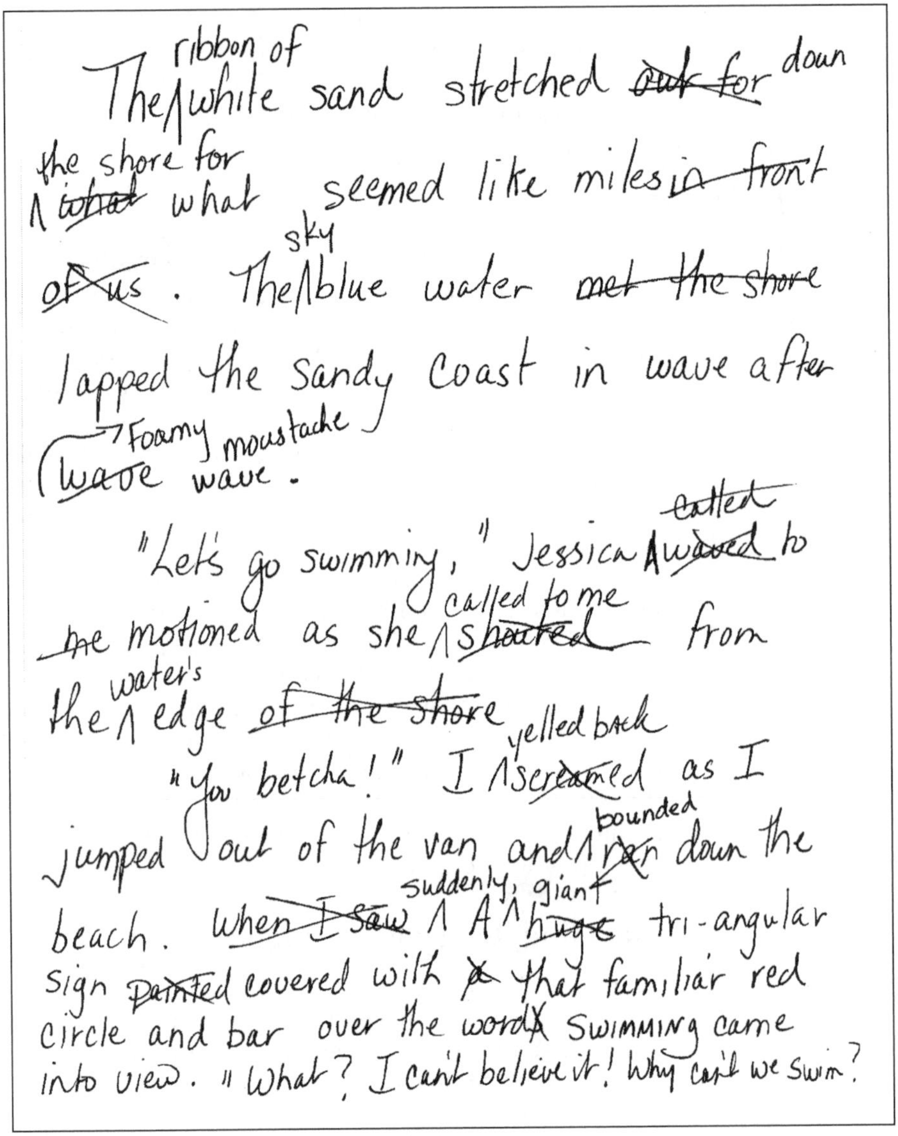

The ribbon of white sand stretched ~~out for~~ down
the shore for
what seemed like miles ~~in front~~
of ~~us~~. The sky blue water ~~met the shore~~
lapped the sandy coast in wave after
~~foamy moustache~~
~~wave~~ wave.

"Let's go swimming," Jessica ~~waved~~ called to
~~he motioned~~ as she called to me ~~shouted~~ from
the water's edge ~~of the shore~~
yelled back
"You betcha!" I ~~screamed~~ as I
jumped out of the van and bounded ~~ran~~ down the
beach. When ~~I saw~~ suddenly, giant ~~huge~~ tri-angular
sign ~~painted~~ covered with ~~a~~ that familiar red
circle and bar over the ~~word~~ swimming came
into view. "What? I can't believe it! Why can't we swim?

Figure 11.2 *I model revision on the overhead projector.*

had spent some time searching for and evaluating leads.) Carol began by
sharing her first attempt at a lead: "Albert Einstein was one of the greatest
scientists of all time." However, when she remembered that leads must hook
readers, Carol felt that this one didn't do the trick. So she wrote three new
possibilities on the overhead:

1. Albert Einstein's mind traveled where no mind had gone before.
2. Although no one would have guessed it during his youth, Albert
   Einstein grew up to be one of the most brilliant mathematicians of all

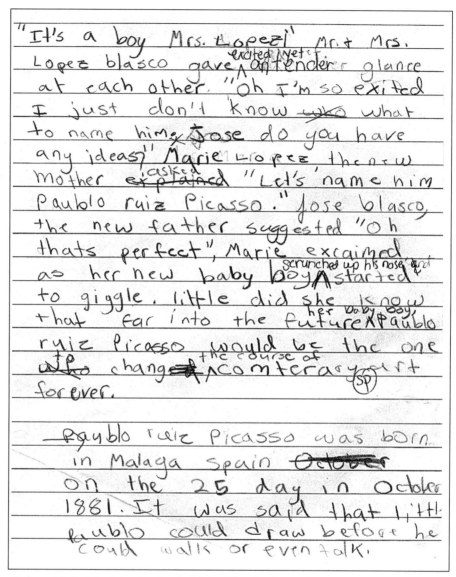

Figure 11.3 *Jessa's beginning revision of her draft on Picasso.*

time. What is it that allows one mind to think of things that most other people don't even know exist?

3. What were you doing in grade school? Were you a dreamer? Did the teacher scold you for not paying attention? That is exactly what happened to one of the world's greatest geniuses, Albert Einstein.

Then she suggested that her students take a stab at revising their own leads.

Mouths turned down and groans filled the room. "But I like mine the way it is," came the joint refrain. Carol held fast, explaining that everyone had to give it a shot, although no one would be forced to use a revised lead if they chose not to. Somewhat placated, the kids revised their leads and, in many cases, improved them.

The Struggle for Clarity

Taylor, a seventh grader struggling with revision, blurted out, "I know why they call it writers *work*shop. It's hard work! And I'm tired of it." Taylor and I had just completed a conference in which I tried to help her write more clearly, and I understood what she meant. I too struggle with clarity. Yet writing clearly is central to strong nonfiction writing.

Some teachers don't teach clarity, because doing so is difficult. Instead, they substitute formulaic, five-paragraph essays that may appear clear on the surface but that prevent writers from writing what they need to say. There is no quick fix for writing a clear sentence. Some need extensive rewriting, the "hard work" that frustrated Taylor. Clear writing comes from rereading and revising, not from following strict form.

To write clearly, writers must think clearly and understand their topic. "Know your subject and say it. Say it your way and say it quickly." This solid advice from Don Murray (in Graves 1994, 35), along with regular practice in the craft of writing, promotes brevity, simplicity and understanding.

Mary Urtz shows how she searches her wonder book for accurate information and crafts a paragraph out of sentences that relate to one another and have the same focus. Leslie Blauman suggests her fourth graders use the two-column note format (see Chapter 10) to support their writing. Organized notes reduce fuzzy thinking, increase understanding, and support clear writing.

Revision and response are central to clarity. Kids can ask themselves the following questions: What am I trying to say? Am I saying it? Does it make sense?

As teachers review blurry paragraphs, they need to ask students what they intended to say. There is no better place for clearing up confusions than the writing conference or the author's chair. Response from an audience will quickly let the writer know whether the writing is clear.

Clear writing grows with practice and discipline. Stick with it! Our schools are falling victim to formulaic, inauthentic writing, which is easier to teach but produces stilted results. The strategies explored in this chapter—matching reading to writing; writing with voice; showing, not telling; writing with nouns and verbs; and revising and editing—promote clarity. As writers think more clearly, they will write more clearly. But, as Taylor knows, writing is still hard work.

12

Inquiry Genres: The Wide Range of Possibilities

When I was a child, books filled every nook and cranny of our house. I couldn't resist turning the pages. By age four, I learned what it meant to be a boss, turning our basement into a zoo and running it with the same iron fist deployed by Gerald McGrew, Dr. Seuss's effervescent zookeeper (Seuss 1950). At five, I discovered Virginia Lee Burton's *Katy and the Big Snow* (1943), a rare example of a rough-and-tumble female who saved the day. At six, Margaret Wise Brown's *The Sailor Dog* ([1953] 1992) carried me off to exotic seaports where dogs draped in striped robes and amber beads balanced water jugs on their heads. Later in my life, romantic faraway places called to me, and I give Miss Brown, Miss Burton, and Dr. Seuss some of the credit for my independent streak and wanderlust. You are what you read.

In first grade, I learned to read with Dick and Jane. At first, they made me feel at home. Like them, I lived in a small town and had a working dad, a stay-at-home mom, a younger brother, and a playful dog. But I soon tired of Dick and Jane's leaf raking, cookie baking, and car washing. As mundane as these activities were at home, they were drop-dead dull in books. Reading had the power to take you anywhere. Books about a family just like mine with a house just like mine in a town just like mine didn't cut it. What was the purpose of reading about that? I knew my life. I wanted to know other people, other places, other things.

The following year, Miss Nelson answered my prayers. Each Friday, Miss Nelson, my second-grade teacher, passed out a miniature newspaper published just for kids, the *Winkly Reader*! I didn't know who Winkly was. But I imagined a twinkle-eyed, rosy-cheeked grandfather for whom I was forever grateful for writing about the world outside my neighborhood. Mr. Winkly introduced me to the Empire State Building, the Boeing 707, Dr. Jonas Salk, the grand opening of Disneyland, the Cold War, and Elvis Presley. To this day,

I remain a current-events nut who can't leave the house in the morning without first reading the paper.

I was nearly twelve when I discovered the truth about this Winkly fellow and sixteen before I could admit my confusion without embarrassment. But I remain in debt to the *Weekly Reader* for my introduction to nonfiction. There are many avenues by which to explore nonfiction; the newspaper is one. Magazines, picture books, textbooks, trade books, reference books, and Web pages are others.

Teachers I work with expose students to a wide range of reading and writing genres from the real world: biography, autobiography, historical fiction, essay, memoir, and poetry can convey factual information in an interesting way—can tell us real things about real people and real events—and are suitable sources for and products of in-depth inquiry. Picture books, magazine articles, newspaper stories, diaries, journals, correspondence, and speeches are popular forms for reporting research findings. Kids need to read the genres they choose to write. Nothing is more critical to quality writing than reading.

Genre and form are closely related to purpose. If a seventh grader is fed up with school lunches better suited to the postsurgery ICU, she might write a persuasive schoolwide petition and deliver it to the powers that be. A class investigation into rain forest ecology could culminate in an environmental newspaper distributed schoolwide on Earth Day. Let's look at some of these forms and genres more closely.

A Place to Start

• • • • • • • • • The kids profiled in this book have been allowed to exercise choice in the inquiry process. Lucy Calkins notes, "If our students' goal is to share their fascination with a topic and their ideas about it, then instead of writing like encyclopedias, they'll be writing in the literary nonfiction tradition of John McPhee and E. B. White" (1995, 439).

For first attempts at this style of writing, picture books and magazines are the most promising models. The rich voice, colorful illustrations, and vivid photographs of informational picture books and nonfiction feature articles are natural forms for young writers. These accessible formats require little instruction beyond the strategies presented in Chapter 11.

If some writers want to explore other genres and forms independently, no problem: teachers can give them the guidance they need in individual conferences.

Informational Picture Books

The nonfiction picture book is well suited to reporting the fruits of an inquiry. Picture book writing and illustrating can realistically be managed by young writers. They can design their own layout and write their text after studying various kinds of nonfiction picture books: pattern books, alphabet books, books that pose questions, narrative biography, etc.

Teacher Mary Lawlor used the picture-book format for her report on sidewinders. Ben, an art lover, offered to illustrate it for her. Mary was delighted since Picasso she wasn't. It was a happy collaboration! (See Figure 12.1.)

Todd, a fourth grader in Leslie Blauman's room, studied nonfiction picture-book conventions before he prepared the page of text in Figure 12.2. His voice, which comes through loud and clear, and his scientifically accurate stickers authenticate his work.

Students in Mary Urtz's fourth grade and Leslie Blauman's fifth grade tried a number of different nonfiction picture-book formats. Nathan's picture book on Charles Lindbergh contained Internet photographs and illustrations

Figure 12.1 *Ben's illustration of his teacher's picture book.*

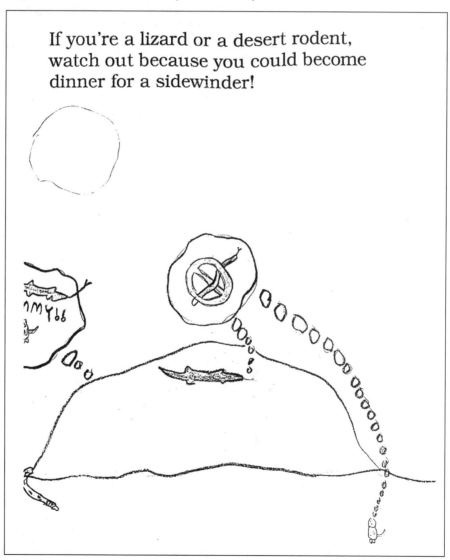

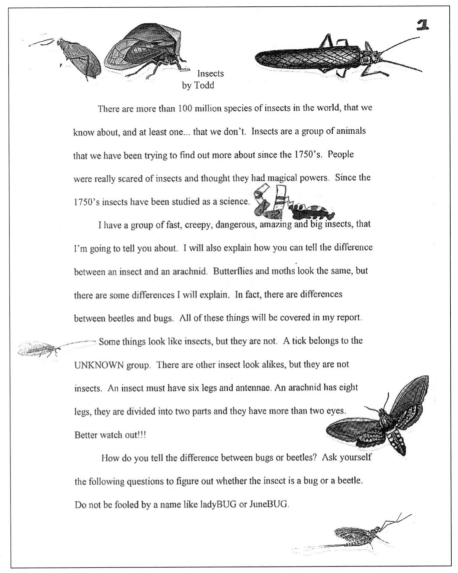

Figure 12.2 *The first page of Todd's picture book.*

of the aviator and his prized Spirit of St. Louis; Brandon photocopied the classic positions in mime and combined them with text to explain the nature of this movement form. Ben used a "fact or fable" format in his book comparing whales and dolphins. His first page asks, *Fact or Fable: Whales and dolphins are fish*. The next page answers, *Fable. Whales and dolphins are mammals*, and includes a definition of mammal. Elissa pasted her Edgar Allan Poe report on sepia-colored paper and included old photographs and illustrations, adding an antique flair.

Magazines: Feature Writing

National Geographics, Smithsonians, and *World Magazines* jam the shelves of the classrooms portrayed in this book. These magazines are more than photography showcases; they are filled with beautifully crafted text and never fail both as resources for great information and strong models for writing.

Feature articles in magazines like these drop us into the setting and bring the scene to life. Young writers can achieve this same style by doing research, writing in their own voice, painting pictures with words, and drawing, photocopying, or downloading illustrations, photographs, and diagrams, all strategies that bring authenticity to text. Some research topics from kids in Mary's and Leslie's room that lend themselves to literary nonfiction include:

- Vietnam: Forever at War.
- Reading the Night Sky in Ancient Greece.
- The Holocaust—Before and After.
- The Lost City of Atlantis: An Unsolved Mystery.
- Sally Ride, An American First.
- The Mysterious Life of the Bengal Tiger.
- Richard Nixon: Hero or Criminal.
- The Tasmanian Devil.
- Dreams: The Language of the Night.
- Shirley Temple: A Life in the Spotlight.
- Mahatma Gandhi, Man of Peace.
- The Puzzle of Hypnosis.

These topics resonate with action and life and are perfect subjects for compelling nonfiction. Erica, a fifth grader, speaks directly to her audience in this piece on the lost city of Atlantis:

> Pretend you are a scientist searching for a lost land that was supposed to have sunk thousands of years ago. You don't know if this land exists or where to look for it. You don't know if it's as large as a city or as large as a continent. You're clueless! Welcome to the tour of the Lost City of Atlantis. *You,* today, are the scientists and *you* will search for this lost city or continent. *You* will decide where Atlantis is located. *You* will decide if Atlantis ever existed. So get ready to make your decision.

Here comes my favorite part:

> To begin this tour, you must know who Plato is. Not the mushy, salty stuff in a container, but the Greek philosopher who described Atlantis thousands of years ago.

Anne, a fifth grader in Leslie's room, uses a conversation between a boy and his grandfather to tell the story of her research into the horrors of the Holocaust. It begins like this:

"Hey Papa what's that number on your arm mean?" a young seven year old boy asked his grandfather one winter evening.

"Well, Jeremy, that's my tattoo, my grim reminder of the horrors done to me and other Jews during those twelve years from 1933 to 1945, the point in time called the Holocaust. Did you know that during the Holocaust six million Jews were killed?"

"But you survived?" the wide eyed young boy asked.

"I lived through liberation in 1945. I was among the two million people who survived."

Jon's assimilation of the *National Geographic* style is apparent in this passage on the Tasmanian Devil:

The Tasmanian Devil, the most interesting night prowler of them all, goes in for the kill. In the distant light, the Devil spots something, a weak wallaby. As the small bear-like Devil darts at full speed towards the prey, the chase is on. The chase continues for about six seconds until the wallaby is violently brought down by the bone crushing jaws of the Tasmanian Devil.

I can't help thinking of the more traditional encyclopedic rendition of this event: "Tasmanians Devils eat wallabies as well as other small mammals." The difference is startling!

Other Genres, Other Forms

When deciding on a specific genre or format, young writers do well to ask: What is the purpose for my writing? What format best suits my piece? How do I communicate this information in an interesting way? Teachers can provide explicit instruction in genres like biography, poetry, essay, historical fiction, and personal narrative, and they can share a variety of formats as well. Matching reading to writing remains paramount. The genres and formats that follow have all met with considerable success in my colleagues' classrooms.

Writing About People, AKA Biography

People make the world go round. You can't flip through a magazine without glimpsing a photograph of Tiger Woods, Hillary Clinton, Tom Cruise. People—kids included—are fascinated by other people. But people don't exist in a vacuum. They are a reflection of where they are and what takes place around them. Young writers often lack the necessary historical background knowledge to write compelling biographies. This is the main reason traditional teacher-assigned biographies do not lend themselves to rich nonfiction writing.

Jean Fritz, award-winning children's biographer, reels us into her narratives by setting the scene and sharing details of events and personalities of the time. In her biography of George III, *Can't You Make Them Behave, King George?*, she explains taxation without representation and describes the Boston Tea Party. Her extensive research moves beyond the life of King George and supplies insight into issues, customs, personalities, and events of the day. Not all kids would have the time or inclination to research adequately the historical events surrounding one person's life.

But once again, choice is the key. When writers *choose* to investigate the life and times of a certain personality, engagement and sustained learning follow. In classrooms where I work, a handful of kids routinely choose to research people in whom they have a special interest. Hector Vilas, the sixth grader who switched from the broad topic of the French Revolution to the narrower topic of Robespierre (see Chapter 9), has a good shot at high-quality reporting because of his passion for Robespierre and his knowledge of the French Revolution. Teachers should encourage young writers who want to delve deep into the historic surroundings of a biographical subject to go for it.

Fourth grader Megan, a tap dancer, chose to write about Shirley Temple. For as long as she could remember, she and her mom had been curling up in bed watching Shirley Temple movies. An excerpt from Megan's final piece shows that interest and prior knowledge are fertile soil in which rich biographical writing can sprout and grow:

> She tap danced and lit up the whole screen. Born in Santa Monica in 1928, she was the smallest and cutest member of her family. When her mother played music, she would get up in her crib and do a little dance. She started singing and acting at age 3 1/2. Known for her curly hair and dimples, she starred in over thirty movies. She is Shirley Temple and she was a big hit! There were Shirley milk mugs, Shirley dolls, Shirley hats, Shirley dresses, Shirley soap, Shirley perms and even Shirley underpants. Have you ever had a drink called a "Shirley Temple"? Well that was named after her, of course.

Biography in the Content Areas

If writing a biography is a curriculum requirement, integrating a biography project with a content area makes sense. A social studies unit focused on a specific concept or time period or a science unit framed around a scientific principle or discovery builds background knowledge for would-be biographers. In a unit on sixteenth-century world exploration, kids can choose from among explorers, royalty, noblemen, peasants, sea captains, and the like as their subject. A middle school physical science unit might lend itself to investigating physicists, their lives, times, and contributions. Young biographers will write more convincingly after having studied a specific content area.

The Biographical Character Sketch

The nonfiction writing strategies discussed in Chapter 11 also apply to biographies. A wealth of narrative picture books provide rich models for biographical writing (see the "Well-Crafted Biography Picture Books" bibliography). Some of these narratives are presented in autobiographical form. Kids might enjoy assuming the personality of their subject, as Alexander did in his portrayal of Stephen Hawking (see Chapter 11). Quality biographical writing may require some additional instruction in technique. For instance, the main character in a biography has to capture the reader's attention. Teaching kids to explore the character in depth enhances the narrative.

As a conclusion to a unit on modern world history, an eighth-grade class wrote biographies of twentieth-century public figures who have made or are making a positive difference. After students researched the person they had chosen, I suggested they write a character sketch. I reminded them that people operate in the context of the times. When I asked what they noticed about their character, Ashley, who had researched Mother Teresa, mentioned her distinct clothing.

"Her clothing is part of her physical description. Should that be included in Ashley's character sketch?" I asked.

"If it's important, it should," Josh said. "I mean if she just wore jeans and a T-shirt like everyone else, it wouldn't matter." Several heads nodded in agreement.

"But she wears these clothes because she is a nun who forgoes material things and devotes herself to the plight of the poor," Ashley chimed in. We all agreed that Mother Teresa's apparel was central to her essence and should be included.

Chad added that we needed to look at our characters across the course of their lives. "If you know what kind of person someone is in a regular circumstance, it helps you understand why they did what they did in extraordinary circumstances." After further discussion, we generated a short list of elements we thought were instrumental in character development:

- Physical appearance.
- Personality and interests.
- Education and/or intellectual pursuits.
- Childhood and family life.
- Experiences that made an impact.
- The impact of surrounding events and times.

To demonstrate the craft of creating a character sketch, I read aloud *Teammates* (Gollenbock 1990), a powerful picture book that describes Jackie Robinson's breakthrough into the segregated major leagues. We listed Jackie's characteristics on the overhead as they came to light while reading. *Courageous, determined, dedicated, restrained, athletically superior, sad,* and *lonely* emerged as paramount. Over the next several days, class members read more about Jackie Robinson and we then wrote a brief character sketch as a group:

Little did his friends and relatives know that the name Jackie Robinson would one day be synonymous with one of the most gallant individual efforts ever mounted against injustice in U.S. history. Jackie Robinson, the first man to break the major league color barrier, needed to be an extraordinary athlete who was brave enough not to fight back when players shunned him, called him names, or attempted to hit him with pitches. A truly awesome responsibility for one man, this burden may have contributed to his premature death from diabetes and high blood pressure at age 53. So what was life like for one of the twentieth century's most courageous individuals? How did Jackie feel on the inside? Lonely; sad and lonely.

Poetry Anthologies: Exploring the Effects of War

Poems and poetry anthologies related to a curriculum unit or an individual inquiry appeal to aspiring poets. Carol Quinby finds that poetry is often the genre of choice for kids in her class who are learning English. Poetry is convention free and at its best when short, crisp, and expressive. Many kids in her fifth-grade class, English and Spanish speakers alike, write striking poetry. While investigating the Civil War, Daniel chose to write a series of poems about the brutality of war. This is one of them:

The Civil War
Guns are shooting
bullets piercing
people dying
churches burning
men fighting
And the war has
just begun

I asked Daniel what gave him the idea for his gripping poem. "Civil War books and my grandma," he answered. "My grandma's house was sprayed in a drive-by shooting. The bullet went through the front window and out the kitchen. She was sleeping in the living room and it just missed her. I thought how the Civil War was like the 'hood. As a matter of fact, if I changed the title from *The Civil War* to *The 'Hood,* my poem would still make sense."

For Daniel, the poetry he used to explore Civil War violence was connected to a disturbingly real aspect of his own life and led to insight.

Diaries, Journals, Correspondence, Scrapbooks, and Speeches

Primary sources such as diaries, journals, letters, scrapbooks, and speeches capture the imagination of young writers. They are a user-friendly way to chronicle a person's life and times and mark important events, challenges, or achievements. These formats serve a variety of genres, including biography. Most young writers have personal experience with at least one of them. If the teacher is a journal keeper, a letter writer, or a public speaker, her own artifacts may have the most impact on young writers. Teachers can also keep their antennae poised for interesting examples of primary documents, clipping published letters, journal entries, and speeches to share.

A class visit to the library is an excellent way to expose the students to primary sources. The Denver Public Library recently exhibited thirty-five handwritten diaries of both famous and obscure Coloradans, fascinating relics of the state's western heritage. The Internet and CD-ROM encyclopedias are rife with historically important documents. Many books are written in primary forms (see the "Models for Diary, Journal, Notebook, Letter, Speech, and Newspaper Writing" bibliography). The Library of Congress is an excellent source of historic documents, including the letter from Clara Barton below. Teachers can demonstrate these forms when reporting their own inquiry findings. Students can use one primary form or include examples of several.

Many primary documents are difficult to understand. Kids may need help when negotiating primary text. Encourage them to stick with it. Primary sources reveal the writer's inner thoughts and feelings. During a Civil War study, teacher Carol Quinby tracked down a copy of an original letter from Clara Barton penned to her cousin Vira from an army post in Virginia on the eve of a major battle. Letters like this provide models for young writers who want to take a crack at writing in period style:

> December 12, 1862
>
> The camp fire blazes with unwanted brightness, the sentry's tread is still but quick. The acres of little shelter tents are dark and still as death, no wonder, for as I gazed sorrowfully upon them, I thought I could almost hear the slow flap of the grim messenger's wings as one by one he sought and selected his victims for the morning sacrifice.

Diaries

The diary form captivated fifth grader Anna, who keeps a diary herself. When her class did research on Ancient Rome, Anna chose to explore Roman life through the diary of Juno, a rich noblewoman. She covered her diary in gold lamé and tied it closed with a fancy golden ribbon.

> 321 B.C.
>
> Dear Diary,
> I'm back. Boy do I have a lot to tell you today. Guess what? The Appian Way was just completed. It's about time! I can tell it will probably last a long time. Oh, that must be my husband. Gotta' go.
> Juno

Journals

Young writers can use the journal format to document a person's response to both daily life and historic events. The journal of a young pioneer girl heading west by covered wagon might include illustrations of unfamiliar plants and animals, details of wagon-train life, or a map of the westward route. A scientist's journal might chronicle the steps leading to an important discovery. Photo journals allow writers to comment on scientific, cultural, or historic events through the use of photographs and parallel text.

During the fifth-grade study of Ancient Rome, Ashley chose the journal format to record historic events from the point of view of several memorable Romans. The personalities of both Julius Caesar and Marc Antony are evident in these entries:

An entry from Julius Caesar's journal

51 B.C.

I am the greatest of the Romans. Many people have told me that I am, but I was never sure until now. I have beaten Vercingetorix in battle and forced him to leave. Today, I was walking along the Appian Way towards Compua when I realized that I really was wonderful!

An entry from Marc Antony's journal

41 B.C.

I now realize why Caesar loved Cleopatra. I love her too. Everything around me reminds me of her. Concrete most of all. I know it sounds funny, but she makes me feel lighter than a feather, instead of being made with sand, lime and water, she is made with love, joy and kindness. I love Cleopatra and I love Cesarion. I would love to be his father.

After choosing autobiography as the form in which she wanted to present her research on noted primatologist Jane Goodall, Sarah, a Ponderosa third grader, incorporated a journal entry as well (see Figure 12.3). Sarah had uncovered entries from Goodall's journal and found that keeping a journal was central to Goodall's life and work. (In addition, Sarah illustrated her piece with African woodcut designs representative of those present in Goodall's surroundings.)

Letters and Speeches

Writing authentic letters to newspapers, magazines, or public figures is an excellent way for students to experience nonfiction writing. People listen to well-written, persuasive letters, and writers write powerfully when they have a purpose. Students can get to know the power of the pen early on.

In addition, young writers often choose the letter format when reporting findings. Letters lend themselves to conveying information from afar: a young Civil War soldier writing his family from the war-ravaged front lines, early American settlers contacting friends who stayed behind in Europe, a logger in the Pacific Northwest writing the newspaper to give his perspective on the spotted owl. The letter provides a lens into the writer's character.

In a Russian history project in Tom Rice's class, Harvey, an eighth grader, revealed Stalin through a variety of primary documents, including a personal journal; correspondence from family, friends, and foes; and a speech

Figure 12.3 *Sarah's interpretation of Jane Goodall's journal.*

written by his successor, Nikita Khrushchev. The following excerpts show how Harvey captured the flavor of this tumultuous period in Russian history:

Josef

I know you will not read this letter and even if you do, you would not understand, for I love another man long forgotten. Koba, the man who I believed in, the man I married, not the present leader of Mother Russia who I no longer recognize. You disavowed your son for marrying a Jew. That is no crime! How could you turn from your own son resulting in a self inflicted attempt on his life? And the stories I hear of mass murder. What has happened?. . . Some day, Stalin when you are dead and gone, history teachers will teach the history and life of our gallant revolution, but when they come upon Stalin, they will teach of a dictator and a villainous mass murderer. Russia's grandchildren will be taught to hate your very name: Josef Stalin. I remember Koba, but know you not. Good-bye.

Nadezhda

Speech by Nikita Khrushchev to the Politburo

Friends and Comrades! The leadership of Stalin was a reign of terror. Three nights ago, the terror ended. It is time for me to expose it so

that we might know our hearts before we move on. Stalin was para-
noid and distrustful. He created an atmosphere of fear all around
him. He sent our comrades to their deaths for crimes they did not
commit. Gentlemen, don't be ashamed of yourselves for not taking
a stand, for if you had, you would most assuredly not be here today.
The strange legacy of Stalin is that Russia is a stronger international
and economic force than before. Is this gain worth twelve million
lives? Many would speak a resounding no. In truth, it does not matter now, because Stalin and the twelve million are gone. Now, we
must carry on Lenin's torch and leave Stalin to the history books.

A compilation of primary sources along with artifacts such as postcards,
illustrations, photographs, and newspaper articles allows for an in-depth
look into the subject at hand. Scrapbooks can trace the life and times of
famous figures, mark important discoveries, report historic events, chronicle
scientific phenomena, and convey information about other places.

An *afterword* is a useful feature in connection with a primary document
or compilation. At the conclusion of an Egyptian slave's journal explaining
the mathematical calculations necessary to construct the Great Pyramid,
Lida, an eighth grader, used an afterword to address important mathematical
relationships discovered by scientists centuries later, difficult information to
incorporate in a dated journal entry but important to include.

Afterword

It is likely that the Pyramid builders did not understand the exact
relationship of circumference to pi. They did not know that the
equation for a circle is 2D × 3.1416. After the Great Pyramid was
examined, however, scientists discovered that the difference
between the longest and shortest sides is less than eight inches; the
corners are almost perfect right angles, .09% error; the base is per-
fectly flat, .004% error; and the casting stones are so accurately posi-
tioned that it is impossible to fit even a hair between the joints. They
were amazing ancient mathematicians.

Primary documents personalize history in a way that stirs the soul and
spurs action. Reeled into the personal realm by primary information, young
writers gain a deeper understanding of events and times.

From the Personal to the Universal

• • • • • • • • • Narrative can lead to in-depth inquiry. Kids generally write easily about their
own experiences. While memoir is often too personal a reporting format for
nonfiction inquiry, the personal narrative may reveal passions and curiosities
ripe for further research.

Danny, a third grader who adores his police officer dad, revised a piece
on his dad's job into an informative report about the Denver Police

Department. Danny's firsthand account of his dad's life on the force, augmented by information received by making phone calls and writing letters to the Denver Police Department, made for a fascinating report. Teachers can nudge kids beyond the realm of the personal into that of the universal.

Early in the year, Jamie, a fifth grader in Mary Urtz's room, wrote a personal narrative describing her scuba certification class and her first dive. Later, when the time came to explore a passion, Jamie chose to research scuba diving and concluded by writing a narrative about the sport:

> A splash and in you go! You sign to your buddy that you're going down with a downward point of the thumb. As you dive deeper, it gets darker. You flip on your flashlight, ready to explore a whole new world, scuba diving, what a great activity you think as the ocean floor comes to life. You enjoy yourself unconcerned about the dangers of diving. You've learned to follow safety rules like sticking with a buddy and surfacing slowly. Not to worry, you'll be all right. You're far from running out of air. The cylinder on your back holds plenty of compressed air and attaches to a regulator that hooks up to your mouth so you can breathe. . . .

Jamie continued with details of beautiful sea creatures, a wealth of scuba terms, and a harrowing moment requiring quick thinking underwater. These narratives make for informative reports with a personal touch. In pieces like this, writers use personal experience to create a broader, more universal appeal.

Essays: Freedom Versus Formula

A subgenre known as the five-paragraph essay has crept in the back door of upper elementary schools across the country. This highly structured form demands an introductory paragraph, three supporting paragraphs, and a concluding paragraph. It is the result of teachers' attempts to organize student writing, a noble goal, but in this case a misguided one. Phillip Lopate notes, "The essay is a notoriously flexible and adaptable form. It possesses the freedom to move anywhere, in all directions" (1994, 37). Five-paragraph essays restrict this movement and freedom.

Teachers should concern themselves with the true purpose of essay writing and begin instruction from there. Essays make a point. The best ones make it in a powerful, literary way. E. B. White, one of America's greatest essayists, does this time and again in whatever number of paragraphs he needs.

An essay should reflect its writer's needs. As a teacher, you can share great essays with your students. Collect essay anthologies. Check *Time* and *Newsweek* for the contemporary essays that conclude the magazine each week. The stronger the essays young writers hear, the better their own will be.

Sam, a seventh grader, returned from a visit to Mexico so stirred up after witnessing a bullfight that he simply had to write this essay. His passion shines through:

An Uneven Match

Why are there bullfights? I know your answer. Tradition. But how could a bloody, terrible murder with hundreds of excited witnesses be a beloved tradition? After seeing a bullfight from a rooftop in San Miguel, Mexico, I no longer like the children's book *Ferdinand the Bull.* The book does not give small kids a true taste of what a bullfight is really like. Then the small child grows and grows and soon the grown thirteen-year-old doesn't know a real bullfight and actually believes that the bull is deadly and the matador has a good chance of dying.

Near the beginning of the bullfight, the picadors, men in capes on prancing horses, stick the bull in its back with ten long sharp spears. The poor bull suffers a severe blood loss and can't even walk straight. Soon the matador withdraws his three foot sword from its sheath and plunges it into the bull's spine. A slow, painful ten seconds goes by, and finally, the bull collapses to the ground in a puff of dust. Now, if you can believe this, the matador cuts off the bull's ear, and the crowd cheers wildly. The matador bows, bows and bows again waving the ear in the air.

So the next time you open up the childhood favorite *Ferdinand the Bull* to read out loud to little kids, remember this: The proper name for a bullfight is a bull kill.

Sam benefited from the freedom his teacher encouraged. Some students, however, may need more support with form and structure. It is our job as teachers to share the wide range of possibilities for writing. Demonstrating a five-paragraph essay as a scaffold to organization is appropriate. Encouraging writers to practice helps them get in the groove. But then let writers choose whether they need this formula. Those it helps can and should use it. But don't hold the five-paragraph essay up as a standard. Sadly, it limits the possibilities of the birth of a truly great essay.

Extra! Extra! Read All About It!

Reading the daily newspaper breeds an informed citizenry. Reading the newspaper in school promotes literacy. Kids can learn about the newspaper by examining it section by section and feature by feature. Reading the newspaper makes writing one possible. To many students, creating an entire newspaper seems daunting. A class project to produce a newspaper focused on a common topic is a popular alternative.

After eight weeks spent studying the Civil War with their students, eighth-grade history teachers Kevin Plummer and Tom Rice collaborated with middle school technology specialist Dennis Griebel to produce a successful newspaper. Kevin and Tom oversaw the content. Dennis talked about the sections and features of a newspaper and taught the students how to design a layout using QuarkXPress, a desktop publishing program.

The kids decided the paper would include interviews with famous Civil War figures, feature articles on important battles, reports on the progress of the war, editorials on slavery, eyewitness accounts of executions, quotes from soldiers and civilians, recruitment solicitations, advertisements for military uniforms and warm blankets, classified ads selling weapons, obituaries, political cartoons, and advice columns. Then students chose topics about the Civil War that interested them and a format in which they wanted to couch what they learned. After they had researched their topics electronically and in print, they wrote first drafts, usually in history class, and then revised the pieces in the computer lab, where they also did the layout. The content was informative and the design compelling. The newspaper, printed in color, rivaled *USA Today* (see Figure 12.4).

Historical Fiction

Most kids are natural storytellers. Historical fiction gives kids the chance to tell stories. As writers, it allows them to convey accurate information embedded in rich fictional narrative. When factual information about people and events from a specific period in history is woven into the fabric of fiction, readers take note. The best historical fiction produced by students usually emerges from a common topic of study.

Glenda Clearwater's High Plains fifth graders were studying immigration. They began this inquiry by reading Russell Freedman's powerful *Immigrant Kids* (1980), a nonfiction photojournalistic account of immigration in the late eighteenth and early nineteenth centuries. The story unfolds through a series of authentic photographs and primary source accounts enhanced by Freedman's compelling narrative. Historical fiction seemed a logical genre for individual inquiry projects focused on immigration.

Glenda immersed students in a wealth of nonfiction and historical fiction picture books and magazine articles, as well as the social studies text and other reference materials. Since realism is a prime feature of historical fiction, Glenda encouraged students to record important facts and interesting details that would bring authenticity to their writing. Some writers kept two-column notes like the ones below:

Factual Information	Interesting Details
Most immigrants were poor.	Slept on crowded decks.
Left in search of a better life.	Never forgot the Statue of Liberty.
Steerage was crammed and uncomfortable.	Only took what they could carry.
Most landed at Ellis Island.	Tied clothes in bed sheets.
All underwent medical exams.	Dr. chalk marked shoulders for further inspection.
Most settled in New York.	Some had never seen a banana.
Letters from family members in America encouraged others to come.	

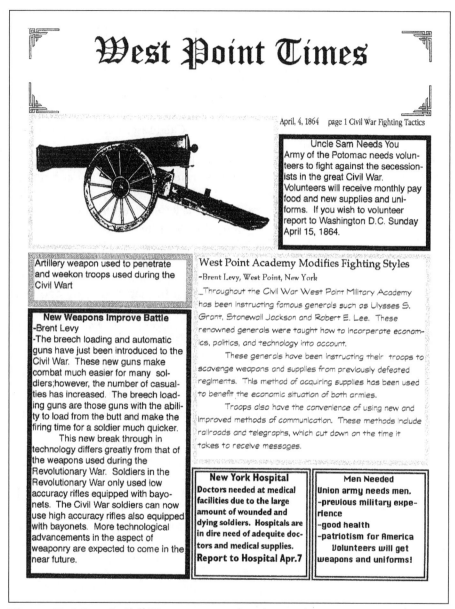

West Point Times

April, 4, 1864   page 1 Civil War Fighting Tactics

Uncle Sam Needs You
Army of the Potomac needs volunteers to fight against the secessionists in the great Civil War. Volunteers will receive monthly pay food and new supplies and uniforms. If you wish to volunteer report to Washington D.C. Sunday April 15, 1864.

Artillery weapon used to penetrate and weekon troops used during the Civil Wart

West Point Academy Modifies Fighting Styles

–Brent Levy, West Point, New York

_Throughout the Civil War West Point Military Academy has been instructing famous generals such as Ulysses S. Grant, Stonewall Jackson and Robert E. Lee. These renowned generals were taught how to incorperate economics, politics, and technology into account.

These generals have been instructing their troops to scavenge weapons and supplies from previously defeated regiments. This method of acquiring supplies has been used to benefit the economic situation of both armies.

Troops also have the convenience of using new and improved methods of communication. These methods include railroads and telegraphs, which cut down on the time it takes to receive messages.

New Weapons Improve Battle
-Brent Levy
-The breech loading and automatic guns have just been introduced to the Civil War. These new guns make combat much easier for many soldiers;however, the number of casualties has increased. The breech loading guns are those guns with the ability to load from the butt and make the firing time for a soldier much quicker.

This new break through in technology differs greatly from that of the weapons used during the Revolutionary War. Soldiers in the Revolutionary War only used low accuracy rifles equipped with bayonets. The Civil War soldiers can now use high accuracy rifles also equipped with bayonets. More technological advancements in the aspect of weaponry are expected to come in the near future.

New York Hospital
Doctors needed at medical facilities due to the large amount of wounded and dying soldiers. Hospitals are in dire need of adequite doctors and medical supplies.
Report to Hospital Apr.7

Men Needed
Union army needs men.
-previous military experience
-good health
-patriotism for America
Volunteers will get weapons and uniforms!

Figure 12.4 *Brent's Civil War newspaper done in QuarkXPress.*

After several weeks of reading and research, kids interviewed parents and other relatives about their ancestors. Phone wires buzzed with calls to great uncles in Miami and grandmothers in New York. Snail mail and e-mail messages to distant relatives stuffed mail boxes and filled cyberspace. Rich stories about family immigration were uncovered. All students wrote partially fictional, historically accurate accounts of the lives of these brave immigrants. Lisa's story of her great-great-grandfather, titled *Finding Home: The Hardships of an American Immigrant,* begins:

Part One: Letter From America

"Mama! Papa! We have a letter from America!" Maria jumped up and down, her hair flying from the scarf that draped around her head. It was 1892 in Calabrese, Italy. Italy was in distress, and people were hungry.

Papa snatched the letter from Maria. Frank's spoon froze in his mouth and Mama stopped with a pot in her hand. The coffee dribbled down the side. Papa tore the letter open. He was still angry with Uncle Ralph, who fled to Hazleton, Pennsylvania in America years ago.

> Dear Brother and Family,
>
> Everything is well in America. The land is rich and good here. I have married and have seven healthy children. Brother, I beg you. Bring your family to America. They will live a good life. They can learn to read and write and will eat well. Do not worry. There is church in America and lots of Italians. Your traditions will not be taken away. America is a free country. Frank, listen if your father won't come, you come and tell him yourself how good it is! Best to all of you,
>
> Uncle Ralph

Frank smiled. He liked Uncle Ralph . . .
(In case you're wondering, Frank took his uncle up on his offer.)

Stephanie included a detail about her great-grandmother's first encounter with an unfamiliar banana: "I tried to take a bite of this strange yellow fruit. It was hard and difficult to eat. A gentleman took it. Then he neatly peeled off the rubbery outside and handed it back to me. My teeth sunk into it easily this time. It was delicious!"

When Adrienne's great-great-grandfather Charles was detained in the Ukraine, he rushed home and "pulled the sheet off his bed, got out three sets of clothes, food that would not spoil, one blanket, shoes, photographs of his family and his favorite book. He placed these carefully in the sheet and took the four corners of his sheet and tied them together at the top. It was time. He would leave for America tomorrow."

Final pieces included illustrations, photocopies of primary documents, old family photographs, and assorted computer images. The dedications were particularly moving: "Dedicated to all those immigrants who suffered to give us the name Americans. Thank you!" Individual author's notes completed each piece, elaborating on the protagonist's relationship to the author and separating truth from fiction. In her author's note, Lisa wrote:

> The story of Frank Saccomanno is indeed true. But there are fictional parts. Frank was a real person. He did leave Calabrese starving at

21, hoping to find a better life. He could not speak English or write in either language. He did have relatives in Hazleton, Pennsylvania who wrote for him to come to America, but I'm not sure who. He came to Ellis Island after fourteen days at sea. He lived in Hazleton until he met and married Josephine who was also an Italian immigrant. They moved to Colorado. In Colorado, Frank had eight children. The oldest being my great-grandfather. I live in Colorado to this day and so do many of his relatives. Everything else is fictional. The conversations are made up. I am not sure about Mama, Papa or Maria. It might not have been Frank's uncle who wrote. I just took a guess. Frank could have come with his family or alone. He probably met friends on the way, or not. A lot of things in my piece could have happened, but probably not. But after all, what would this story be like without a little fiction?!

These fifth graders studied immigration in depth, taking ownership of the project by exploring their family histories through a piece of historical fiction. This was an extraordinary inquiry into the lives and times of another generation, one the students will always remember.

A Hazard of Historical Fiction

Historical fiction challenges young readers to think critically. Confusion may surface when young readers try to separate historical facts from the story. A group of fifth graders studying colonial history struggled with this problem. Meeting in historical fiction book clubs of five or six members, they recorded three-column fact, question, and response notes as they read (see Chapter 10). Staff developers Anne Goudvis and I worked along with librarian Nel Box and teacher Marilyn Berkey, conferring with groups. Comments such as "Her mother died of tuberculosis when she was merely two" or "Oceanis Hopkins was born on the Mayflower" filled the facts column. At one point, Stacey raised her hand: "Was Oceanis Hopkins really born on the Mayflower?"

"Interesting question," Anne responded.

"I'm having trouble figuring out what's true and what's made up just for the story," Michael added sheepishly.

The adults glanced at each other. Leave it to kids to shake things up. In our planning, we neglected to recognize this roadblock to comprehending historical fiction. After a brief huddle, we set to work. Anne drew three columns on a piece of poster paper: Historical Truths/Invented Truths/Further Research Required. As kids hashed out confusions, they recorded them on sticky notes and placed them in the appropriate column. If a sticky note ended up in the research column, interested research teams took it on.

Anne joined a small research team interested in whether Oceanis Hopkins was a real figure from history or not. They conducted an Internet search and located the Mayflower passenger list. Oceanis was on the list! Stacey moved the sticky note to the column headed Historical Truths. As the kids became familiar with this note-taking technique, they employed it in their notebooks. This was not easy. Answers often eluded adults, as well. But awareness of this potential confusion made comprehending historical fiction easier.

Viewing History Through Several Lenses

• • • • • • • • • • Fifth-grade teacher Jody Cohn facilitated a collaborative classwide inquiry into three periods in American history: the American Revolution, the Civil War, and World War II. Students examined these periods through the lenses of economics, culture, government, and history. The primary goals were to identify events and people in history and investigate the link between them, explain the effects of historical relationships on Americans living today, develop an appreciation for human diversity, and compare and contrast the organization of societies.

Jody selected a wide range of historical texts, including picture books, novels, and even songs—"Yankee Doodle," "Dixie," and "When Johnny Comes Marching Home." Kids read books in many genres and joined historical fiction book clubs. Big Band music occasionally wafted through the room.

As the students read, wrote, and talked, questions arose. Research took shape from these inquiries. Students chose to explore one of these historic periods through the eyes of an economist, an anthropologist, a historian, or a government specialist. They met in one of three war groups to define their roles and responsibilities. After much discussion, they chose to report findings in a newspaper format. Jody encouraged each specialist to read newspaper sections that closely matched her or his expertise: the business section for the economist, the lifestyles section for the anthropologist, and so on. As they studied newspaper features, their notes evolved into newspaper writing.

Ultimately, each group published a newspaper containing feature articles, cartoons, poetry, essays, and other standard newspaper features written authentically from the perspective of an expert. Lisa created a brochure to describe the inquiry and list the schedule for visitors on presentation day (see Figure 12.5).

The Sky's the Limit

• • • • • • • • • There are other forms for writing nonfiction than the ones I've mentioned. The following list comprises authentic writing forms used daily in the world outside school. Teachers and kids should think about the wide range of possibilities for reporting and add whatever forms they like.

- *Scripts.* A script is an excellent way to delineate an encounter between two people—John Adams and Thomas Jefferson discussing slavery, for example.
- *Songs.* Songs can mark special occasions. My daughter wrote both the music and lyrics to a song for her school celebrating the twentieth anniversary of Earth Day.
- *Logs.* "Captain's Log: Stardate 2098" certainly captured our imagination!

Figure 12.5 *Lisa's brochure to inform visitors about class schedules and activities.*

- *Cartoon strips.* Kids love to doodle. This gives them a legitimate reason.
- *Advertisements.* "Come all separatists! Tired of taxes. Join us on a nautical adventure to the New World . . . "

- *Postcards.* These provide a visual (a drawing or a photograph) and textual account of a topic and can include a writer's personal thoughts.
- *Brochures.* Travel or sales brochures can explain a variety of things: whales and whale watching, climbing Mt. Everest, etc.
- *Catalogues.* Catalogues can describe artifacts from a specific time period or culture—weapons and armor from the Middle Ages, the dress of various Native American tribes, and so on.
- *Field guides.* Field guides are useful forms for science writing, providing writers with an opportunity to classify and describe animals, plants, and habitats.
- *Dictionaries.* These define common terms from a historic period or from the cultural or scientific realm. Maribel's bilingual Civil War dictionary was a big hit in Carol Quinby's bilingual fifth grade (see Figure 12.6).
- *Alphabet books.* Alphabet books can be designed around a specific theme such as women in World War II.
- *Manuals.* Instruction booklets may be written on many subjects—how to operate a software program, how to care for the class iguana, how to

Figure 12.6 *Maribel's bilingual Civil War dictionary.*

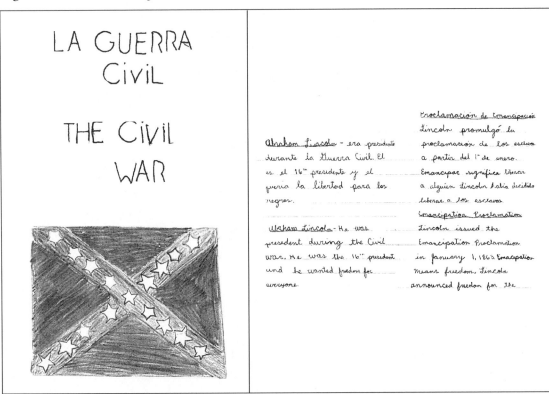

access certain Web sites on the Internet. Classroom opportunities for manual writing are limited only by the imagination.

- *Travel guides.* These are useful for writing about the culture and history of specific places.

- *Course syllabuses and textbooks.* Kids can design courses on a topic and even write a companion textbook.

Schools where wonderful and imaginative research writing bubbles to the surface practice diversity in reading and writing. Nancie Atwell says, "When teachers admit the many possible forms that school reports might take, they also admit the strong possibility that writers will enjoy writing as well as learn from it" (1990, 163). Writing to learn is one of the highest purposes for putting words on paper. The many possible forms and genres in which research writing may be couched breathe life into it, give it authenticity, promote engagement, and foster deep learning. What more could a teacher ask for?

13

Managing Nonfiction Inquiry Projects

I n the town where I grew up, a traveling carnival set up on the high school playing field each Fourth of July. For this small, upper-midwestern lumber town, the carnival was both a welcome guest and a welcome host who helped us celebrate our nation's independence.

A static excitement crackled in the air the week before the rides, tents, and booths appeared. The day the carnival arrived, hordes of Norman Rockwell kids on Schwinn bicycles churned over to watch the trucks roll in, their trailers sky-high with Ferris wheel and roller-coaster scaffolding. There too was I, waiting patiently for the last crate to empty. But the Ferris wheel or Tilt-a-Whirl crates were not the object of my scrutiny. I lurked around the crates holding the games: the shooting gallery, the fishing booth, the pitching contest, and my favorite, Whack-a-Mole.

For those of you who missed Whack-a-Mole in the Coney Islands of your youth, it is a game like no other. The Whack-a-Mole table resembles a large pinball machine minus the glass top. A dozen holes about four inches in diameter and three inches apart cover the tabletop. When play begins, puppetlike creatures remotely resembling moles pop up helter-skelter out of the holes in the table. A single player with a mallet hits the moles on the head as fast as possible to keep them below the table surface. Sound easy? It's not. Just when you strike one mole, two more pop up.

Isn't classroom management a little bit like that? Just when things seem to be rolling along, the carpet is finally installed during testing week, the nurse comes in for a head-lice check, the principal requests a new form of reading instruction, the district mandates a new literacy program. The only gophers you don't want to send back underground are the kids, most of the time anyway! Far too many teachers are engaged in an endless game of Whack-a-Mole.

At this point you may be asking, This inquiry stuff is all well and good, but how can I possibly do a good job of teaching all these nonfiction reading, writing, and research strategies, guide students in their practice, confer, respond, and still teach math, Spanish, and earth science? Good question! The nonfiction inquiry process is huge.

In a vignette in Chapter 4 featuring a research project on Australia, Kathy Marquet had a similar concern. She worried about the logistical nightmare that would result if every student researched a different topic. How could she possibly monitor them all?

The surprising truth is, if you want to be sure to turn a research project into a living nightmare, *ignore* your students' passion and assign each one a rigid animal report. Engagement falters, and kids who find animals boring (believe me, there are some) will quickly find a way to give you night sweats. Cloned final products usually disappoint, and long-term learning suffers. And if you really want misery, while you're at it design a process that ensures that you do more work than the students: assigning topics, developing research questions, designating content, taking full responsibility for evaluation.

Individual inquiry, on the other hand, keeps kids interested and involved and develops student independence. If kids take ownership of the research process, learning will skyrocket and a well-managed classroom will be a given. We mustn't forget to set high expectations for student commitment and hard work. It's our job to monitor their engagement and nurture it when it dwindles. But let kids do the work!

Trust Your Instincts

• • • • • • • • • The moles win in classrooms where teachers try to do the impossible: confer with every student every day, read every nonfiction notebook nightly, and teach every reading, writing, and research strategy in eight weeks. We can't do it all, and we shouldn't be expected to. Inquiry-based teaching and learning is ongoing and systematic, stretching out over time, one strategy building on another in the march toward insight.

This chapter offers a few examples of management strategies that have worked in other classrooms. But remember, no one knows better how to run a classroom than the teacher who works there. No one fights schedule changes more effectively than the class that is disrupted. No one understands better the need for long blocks of time than the teacher who is interrupted every ten minutes. And no one is more effective at luring a distracted twelve-year-old back from outer space than the teacher who knows that child's passion.

Management comes from within. It comes from decisions you make as a teacher living in a crowded room with thirty shorter humans. It comes from understanding your kids and knowing what they need.

Spend Time to Save Time

• • • • • • • • • How can a teacher cram a major undertaking like nonfiction inquiry into an already overambitious schedule? Long-term, in-depth research projects take time, and time is a precious commodity. Long blocks of time built into the daily schedule are a boon to management minus nightmare. Allotting extended periods for nonfiction inquiry minimizes time-wasting transitions and maximizes organization. Setting aside one or two hours a day in which you and your students will read, research, and write is a must. Teaching non-fiction reading and writing strategies over the year, not only during the research unit, will save you time. Completing mini-research projects as a pre-cursor to in-depth inquiry also pays time dividends.

Curriculum Integration

Integrating the curriculum allows you to make better use of the time you have, and nonfiction inquiry is particularly well suited to it. Encouraging the class to choose individual topics from under the shade of a broad umbrella makes sense (see Chapter 4). Since many inquiry topics are derived from sci-ence or social studies, time spent on these inquiries can come from that devoted to science or social studies instruction.

Implications for departmentalized middle schools are clear. Forty-five-minute periods four or five days a week don't allow students time to get into the reading, writing, and research groove. Subject-area teachers, language arts teachers, librarians, and technology specialists can collaborate on inte-grated study units, thus together providing the amount of time needed for these projects. The eighth-grade newspaper project mentioned in Chapter 12 combined a Civil War study with instruction in the operation of the QuarkXPress desktop publishing program. Students worked on the project in both history and technology class.

Testing the Waters

As mentioned in Chapter 3, Norton Moore and others encourage kids to try a few mini-research projects before diving head first into a long-term inquiry project. By first dipping their big toe in the inquiry pond, kids learn valuable research strategies and acquire a taste for nonfiction inquiry. After wading through strategy instruction, Leslie Blauman and Mary Urtz aim for their students to complete two or three long-term research projects over the course of the year. Guiding students through the process more than once allows time for additional instruction and practice. Some teachers find that an umbrella project first, followed by an independent inquiry project later, facilitates a smoother-operating inquiry-based classroom.

The Nitty-Gritty: Time and Pace

• • • • • • • • • How much time does a nonfiction inquiry project take? How do you know the kids are where they need to be? When do you leave one phase of the research cycle and move on?

Well, my colleagues and I find that an inquiry project usually takes from six to ten weeks, start to finish. To get a sense of what happens and how the time gets used, let's peek in on Leslie Blauman's fourth-grade class.

Leslie begins nonfiction inquiry with a letter to students explaining her expectations. (Teachers can adapt these guidelines to fit their expectations.) She attaches several forms, including a general research project overview, a simple contract, a statement of topic, a form for research questions, a week-to-week time line, and the research requirements. Leslie gives each student two copies of the time line and the research requirements, one to use at home, the other to keep in school. Here's her introductory letter:

Date

Inquiry Project

Dear Students,

Today you are going to begin your first independent inquiry project. Because you all have so many interests, this is an opportunity for you to ask questions and find answers to a topic you have always wanted to learn more about. I know you are going to learn much, and I also know that I am going to learn a lot from you.

Because this is the first time you will do a research project like this, I am going to work with you at every stage of learning. I'm also going to give you a time line to help with organization. This will be your first long-term assignment, so you may need some help from your parents with organization. However, this is *your* project, so you need to be responsible for your own work.

Each Wednesday, we will spend an hour in the media center researching our topics. This should let you get most of your research done at school. If you need to visit the library any other time, talk to me and the librarian to arrange it. You may need to go to the public library for additional information. The Internet is available both here and at the public library if you need it. I also encourage you to find experts on your topic and interview them if possible. Resources such as the phone book are in the room. I will help you find and acquire as many additional resources as possible. Try to find a topic with a variety of sources of information (books, magazines, etc.). You may check encyclopedias, but try not to rely on them for the bulk of your research. Please be prepared to do research at school every Wednesday. You may sometimes be asked to take notes at home as well.

Today you are going to begin exploring topic possibilities. Remember to choose something you want to learn more about and can find quite a bit of information on. I am attaching two copies of the requirements for your project and the due dates. I suggest that you post one set somewhere at home where you can check them regularly. I also want you to show this letter to your parents and talk about your topic. By next Wednesday, please choose a topic, fill out the research contract (also attached), sign it, and have a parent sign it to show that they also know the requirements.

I'll be doing a research project too. We are all going to learn so much from each other. I can't wait to see what you choose to study.

Sincerely,

Mrs. Blauman

The contract, signed by Leslie, the student, and a parent, states simply: *I have chosen _____ for my research project. I understand that this is to be my project. I also understand the time lines and requirements.*

Along with their contracts, kids turn in a research-question form (see Figure 13.1) for Leslie to review and respond to. Leslie reminds them that more questions may emerge through research, but these early questions give the researcher a place to start and let Leslie know where she or he is headed.

So that you can get an idea of the pace of instruction, I've adapted the research time line below from the schedule Leslie sends home with her students. This time line assumes a ten-week cycle, including presentations. For the first six weeks, students spend maybe an hour or so a day on their inquiry study during reading/writing workshop. At week seven, they begin to use the entire literacy period and maybe a content-area period to write and finalize the project, about two hours a day total. Students generally finish their reports by week nine and then begin preparing for their final presentations, which are delivered during weeks nine and ten.

Research Time Line for First Inquiry Project

- *Week 1.* Teacher has proper resources in place. The classroom is filled with ample nonfiction text from the school library, the public library, her own collection (see Chapter 5). A wide range of genres is represented: magazines, newspapers, trade books, CD-ROMs. Teacher sows seeds, whets student appetites. Gets them thinking of possible topics. Shares own passions, collections, and possibilities for study.

- *Week 2.* Teacher builds background knowledge by reading out loud and conducting focus lessons on determining text importance, highlighting, and using general reading strategies (see Chapter 7). Students immerse themselves in possible topics, reading anything of interest and narrowing their choice.

- *Week 3.* Students commit to topic. Student, parent, and teacher sign contract. Teacher responds to student research questions and helps students generate further questions as needed. Students continue reading to find more information, coding and marking text with sticky notes. Teacher continues reading-strategy instruction and begins to demonstrate note-taking techniques. Generally, intermediate students have already had some practice in webbing, mapping, and listing. If not, now is the time to give them some.

- *Weeks 4–6.* Research and note taking continue. Students work on note-taking strategies and take notes on their questions. They add new questions as they arise and research those questions. Teacher continues teaching organizational and synthesizing strategies to support research

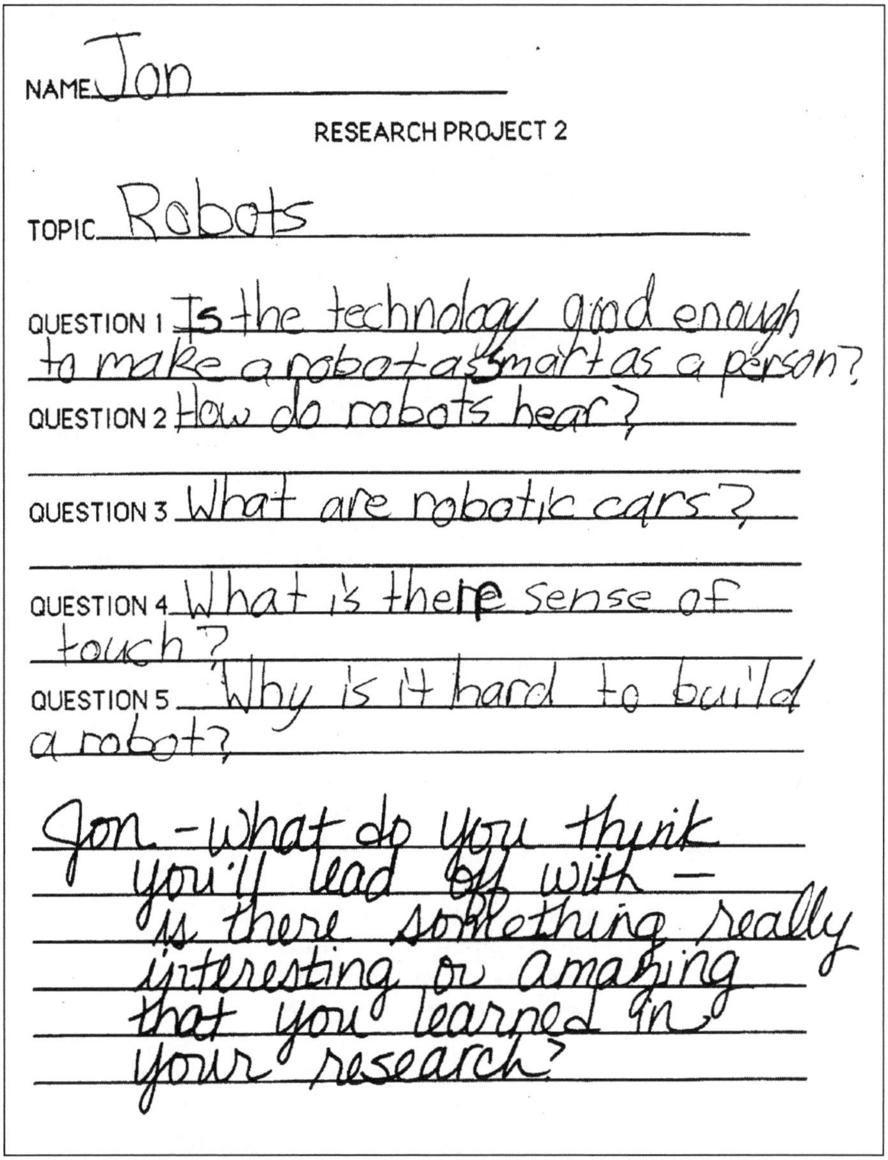

NAME Jon

RESEARCH PROJECT 2

TOPIC Robots

QUESTION 1 Is the technology good enough
to make a robot as smart as a person?

QUESTION 2 How do robots hear?

QUESTION 3 What are robotic cars?

QUESTION 4 What is there sense of
touch?

QUESTION 5 Why is it hard to build
a robot?

Jon - what do you think
you'll lead off with -
is there something really
interesting or amazing
that you learned in
your research?

Figure 13.1 *Leslie Blauman's form to respond to student research questions.*

efforts as elaborated in Chapter 10. Teacher confers with each student every week, a brief check-in if there isn't time for more. Teacher begins teaching writing strategies as described in Chapter 11.

• *Weeks 7–8.* Writing time! Teacher further instructs how to put the report together, what genre(s) to choose, how to organize the writing, and how to craft well-written nonfiction. Focus lessons include a range of those described in Chapters 11 and 12. Time is spent by teacher and students reading well-written nonfiction as models. Writing needs to be done mostly at school to guarantee the student's primary involvement. Students determine presentation dates and send out invitations.

- *Week 9.* Finalize papers. Work on visual aids. Organize props for presentation. Practice oral presentations. Begin final presentations.
- *Week 10.* Complete final presentations.

This time line is based on student needs during a first-time inquiry study early in the year. As a general rule, less time is needed to complete these projects later on, because students have more reading, writing, and organizational strategies under their belts. Some teachers and classes need more time. Some need less. Middle school teacher Sue Collins planned about three weeks for an independent inquiry project in the spring of the year. Mary Urtz generally devotes about six weeks to research projects. Be flexible. Know your kids and respond to their needs.

Unfortunately, in some schools inquiry is not emphasized and nonfiction literacy strategies go untaught. This doesn't make in-depth inquiry impossible, just more difficult. Less experienced kids take longer to wade through a research project and emerge with a strong product. Don't be alarmed! Teach reading, writing, and research strategies all year, not just as a preamble to an inquiry project. You can nudge others in the school to devote more time to reading, writing, and research-strategy instruction. The benefits of an inquiry approach to research are compounding, cumulative.

Sample Research Requirements

1. *Notes.* You may use either note cards or your nonfiction notebook for note taking. You are required to have a minimum of four questions about your topic and to have notes about each of those questions. Or you may have one big question with three subquestions. Don't forget to use a variety of sources and record them for a bibliography.
2. *Written paper.* This paper may be typed (double spaced) or written in ink (single spaced on one side of the paper only). It must be long enough to answer your questions thoughtfully and give the reader substantial information about your topic. Supporting research should be included as needed. The writing needs to be interesting and engaging. Your voice must come through. We will spend time in class learning how to write a research paper that does these things, and you will have time to write and revise it in class. You will need a cover page that includes your name, date, and title.
3. *Presentation.* This is your opportunity to teach the class about your topic. Don't read it verbatim, but feel free to use note cards to support your presentation. Your presentation should be at least five minutes long, but no longer than fifteen.
4. *Props and visual aids.* These help your audience understand your topic more thoroughly. Props need to be big and bright enough for the audience to see easily. Some possibilities include maps, charts, graphs, overhead transparencies, videos, etc. And, remember, quality is better than quantity.

Sample Time Line

Sept. 15–30	Immersion, topic exploration, and topic choice
Oct. 1–21	Read, research, and take notes
Oct. 22–Nov. 12	Start drafts, write, revise, and edit
Nov. 13–21	Present findings

Project Management

Independent inquiry should develop independence. We can support developing independence through the gradual release of responsibility. Early research projects require a great deal of teacher involvement. As the year progresses, teachers can gradually release responsibility for the role of project manager to the student. Calendars and planners, mentioned first in Chapter 5, are a necessity to support young project managers. Teachers can model their use by sharing their own calendar. Here are a few suggestions for helping kids manage their projects.

Contracts and Plans

Contracts and research plans help kids stay on course through occasionally choppy research waters.

To ensure that students take responsibility for their projects, middle school teacher Sue Collins enters into a contractual agreement with each student. Students begin by selecting a topic of interest (see Appendix 7). Together Sue and the students state the purpose, objectives, rationale, resources, and means of evaluation (see Appendix 8). In a contract conference, they discuss the research plan and time schedule. Sue agrees to provide as much help as needed.

On the reverse side of the contract, students fill in their work plan each day in the form of a log beginning with Day 1 and ending with Day 18 (see Appendix 9). Students begin the daily nonfiction workshop by completing their plan for that day and evaluating the previous day's plan. This is a regular reminder to stay the course. Kids and teachers can quickly see if they are on target or lagging behind.

Many teachers I work with use an informal three-column form to monitor the research plan: Date/What I Did Today/What I Plan to Do Tomorrow. Students fill it out in their nonfiction notebooks during the last five minutes of the nonfiction workshop, and teachers check to see that kids are monitoring themselves.

The Nonfiction Workshop

Because kids engaged in self-selected nonfiction inquiry are investigating different topics and answering different questions, they must proceed individually. The reading and writing workshop allows for this. A predictable workshop with time allotted to instruction, individual reading and writing, conferring, and sharing supports student inquiry and contributes to a well-managed classroom.

An in-depth description of the reading and writing workshop is beyond the scope of this book. Don Graves, Nancie Atwell, Jane Hansen, and others have written extensively on the reading and writing process. Their work is the foundation for the inquiry-based teaching and learning described in this book, and readers may want to check out what they have to say. Below I highlight a few workshop techniques that are particularly valuable in managing an inquiry-based classroom.

- *Light-touch conferences.* A normal anxiety for the dedicated nonfiction inquiry teacher is the inability to touch base with every kid every day. In a class of thirty-two kids researching thirty-two different topics, a teacher may be able to have a ten-minute conference with sixteen of them by Thursday. On Fridays, she can then circulate through the classroom, crouch down next to those sixteen students whom she hasn't seen that week, and ask them how it's going and where they are in the research process. On Monday, she begins longer conferences with those students she didn't meet with in depth the week before. This rotation guarantees contact with every student every week.

- *Urgent conferences.* Certain students will need to confer more often than others. Mary Urtz has a conference sign-up sheet that hangs in the room. Kids sign up if they need to see Mary, checking the "urgent" box if they need to see her now.

- *Compass groups.* Some kids talk more than others; sometimes quiet kids rarely get a chance. Compass groups are a formal technique that helps teachers manage classroom talk and gives equal access to everyone for at least a half hour or so. The kids position themselves, either on the floor or at tables, in groups of four, one student at each point of the compass. The teacher announces North's turn. After five minutes, the teacher prompts North to conclude. A minute or so later she announces East's turn, and so on. After about twenty-five minutes, each child will have had a turn to share for about six minutes. Teachers can wander and eavesdrop, comfortable in the knowledge that this process guarantees even the most reticent talkers a chance to be heard.

- *Writing support groups.* Amy Tan dedicates her best-selling *The Joy Luck Club* (1989) to her writing group, without whom she couldn't have written the book. Norton Moore shares this fact with his class and invites kids to join writing support groups. Norton arranges a time for them to meet at least once a week. The respondents comment on those parts that strike them as well as those parts they wonder about. They come to know each other as readers and writers. They rely on their writing pals to help them weather the rugged spots as well as celebrate strong writing.

- *Sitting up close.* I like kids to be close to me when I'm delivering instruction or facilitating a discussion. I can sense the level of student engagement by watching them at close range. And a stronger feeling of community emerges when kids sit close together. Some kids choose the floor, especially younger ones. Others may want to pull up a chair. No problem, as long as they are close enough to participate naturally in the lesson. And what about the kids who always sit in back, or their enthusiastic counterparts who race for a position in front? Every so often when kids bunch around the chair for a discussion or focus lesson, I stand up and move to a chair at the back of the crowd and then ask everyone to turn around on their bottoms, placing front-row regulars in back and the usual back-row suspects in front. It doesn't take long for kids to seek out the most convenient space rather than the previously coveted front or back row.

Research Teams

Research teams provide built-in opportunities for peer response and facilitate smooth classroom management in the process. Last spring, I visited Manhattan New School teacher Karen Ruzzo while her class was researching New York City, a focus of the social studies curriculum. In a meeting to plan their New York study, Karen asked kids what interested them most about New York. "The Empire State Building," one child blurted out. Another waved her hand: "Central Park." Madison Square Garden, the Brooklyn Bridge, and the Statue of Liberty completed the list. Karen then formed five research teams, each focused on a separate New York institution, and guaranteed the students their first or second choice.

Research included reading a wide variety of text, searching the Internet, hearing from New York experts, and lots of conversation. When students had built sufficient background knowledge, research teams made site visits. Karen spent a day in the field with each research team. Each team brought cameras to record the day's events and discoveries.

The site visits narrowed the research focus. Having just read Roald Dahl's *James and the Giant Peach* (1996), the Empire State Building team decided to study books and films that featured the structure. The team investigating Central Park was so struck by the park's beauty that they researched the life, work, and genius of Central Park designer Frederick Olmstead. The Brooklyn Bridge team investigated the Manhattan skyline. The Madison Square Garden group couldn't resist learning more about the New York Knicks. And the Statue of Liberty team decided to research the sheer size of the bronze lady. These inquiries culminated in team presentations and photojournalistic accounts in beautifully bound scrapbooks.

The research team concept replicates the way in which authentic research is conducted. Twentieth-century research efforts are increasingly carried out in teams; medical scientists search for cancer cures, social scientists analyze growth patterns, and environmental scientists study ozone depletion. Research pairs and teams frequently share Nobel prizes.

The research team notion gives kids a chance to practice working together cooperatively. Team members have high expectations and hold one another accountable for organization and deadlines. Haggling over resources is less likely, and job assignments are divided equitably. Peer response is readily available. And management is facilitated, because the number of topics is reduced and their focus narrowed.

14

· ·

Presentations and Assessment

E rin looked nervous. Her fourth-grade classroom had become a small auditorium full of kids, unfamiliar invited guests, and her mom, sitting in front. Erin taped a hand-drawn illustration and some photographs delineating the difference between frogs and toads on the chalkboard. Using a yardstick to direct attention to her visual aids, Erin began, "For the past three months, I have been studying frogs and toads. The biggest frog is approximately two and a half feet long." Her pointer a measuring stick again, Erin demonstrated a length of two and a half feet.

Audible gasps filled the room as the audience took in the size of this giant frog. More relaxed now, Erin passed around a basketball and said that the surface closely replicated toad skin. These props were a stroke of genius. They put this previously unknown information in a context that would help Erin's audience remember it.

Final presentations take a wide range of forms. Some kids report their findings orally with the help of creative props, as Erin did. Some dress in costume and perform. Others use overhead transparencies, charts, graphs, and posters. Some share journals, newspapers, or scrapbooks. Some give speeches. Others create audiotapes, videotapes, and computer simulations. Final presentations are limited only by the imagination.

In presentations in Mary Urtz's class, Megan performed "On the Good Ship Lollipop" dressed as Shirley Temple; Brandon concluded his discussion of the art of mime with a game of Charades; Andrew displayed an intricate hand-rendered diagram of a saltwater fish habitat; Jeffrey spoke about the Iroquois's homeopathic approach to healing while a tape of a medicine man's initiation ceremony played softly in the background; Nick showed a video of the rain forest habitat at the Denver Zoo; and Emily handed out slices of watermelon after telling everyone about coyote nutrition.

Final presentations are cause for great celebration. Most kids are bursting with pride at having worked so diligently over a sustained period on a topic of great interest to them. Bringing a project to life in a final presentation is a way to share knowledge and is an invaluable means for the presenter and the teacher to assess the depth of learning. Proud classrooms invite parents, other classes, school staff, and interested community members to come and be intellectually stimulated.

Nancy Burton's sixth graders at Jarrow Senior Elementary synthesize their projects into a single paragraph and include these summaries in a festive invitation to attend their presentations. This preview allows interested parties to mark their calendars. Here are two examples:

Rodents: The Good, the Bad and the Ugly

Why are rodents so unique? How are hamsters different from other animals? Rodents have a bad reputation just like wolves do. Yet, isn't it strange that almost every kid wants a hamster or a gerbil for a pet? Remember they were the first mammals. They've lived since the end of the dinosaur era. They are fascinating fictional characters from Templeton in *Charlotte's Web* to Mickey Mouse. Rodents run rampant.

Eating Disorders in Young Women

When a person looks in the mirror, who do they see or who do they want to see? Everywhere you turn, there are beautiful, thin, famous women. Girls want to be like these women. This is not a problem, until wanting to be like your thin idol forces you to starve yourself to become thinner. Cultural slenderness in the name of fashion has caused many young women to develop eating disorders. What's being done to combat this societal problem?

Ongoing Assessment

"But how do you grade these?" middle school teacher Gloria Mundel asks me. "I mean the students work so hard, reading, doing research, sifting through, taking notes, and finally writing and presenting. And they learn so much! The final written product can't possibly reflect the time and effort that went into this overall project. It seems a shame to grade the final report and say that's that."

Gloria is right, of course. Nonfiction inquiry is far too big an endeavor for a single grade. The grade on the final report is for the final report only. It doesn't reflect the many strategies learned and experienced during the various inquiry phases. Assessment of long-term projects needs to be ongoing and sustained, to include an evaluation of interim work products and milestones—the process as well as the product.

Designing Rubrics

Students are the educational consumers. It's only natural that they be involved in assessing what goes on in the classroom. While I was visiting Judy Davis's fifth grade last spring, her students were designing a rubric for the upcoming oral presentations that would conclude their Revolutionary War inquiry.

"So what do you think we should assess when you start making your oral presentations next Monday?" Judy asked.

"It shouldn't be too long. It will bore people," Adar said.

"Yea, and you have to speak loudly," Chris added.

Other suggestions tumbled out, and Judy recorded them on the overhead. There was much discussion, but within half an hour, Judy's class had written the following rubric suitable for their American history presentations (and any others, for that matter):

_____ Presentation did not exceed fifteen minutes nor take less than ten.

_____ Voice was loud and steady and pronunciation was clear.

_____ A visual aid was included that helped support information.

_____ Information was well organized and accurate.

_____ Note cards were used unobtrusively.

_____ Presentation was lively and energetic.

_____ Body language helped express content.

_____ Presentation engaged the audience the whole time.

_____ Audience learned something they didn't know before.

Incorporating math into this activity, the students assigned point values from 0 to 3: 3 = very good, 2 = average, 1 = needs more practice, 0 = poor. Multiplying the total number of rubric components by the highest point value gave 27 as the highest possible score. The students decided that a score of 23–27 was excellent, 18–22 allowed room for improvement, and below 18 was disappointing. The kids agreed that people who worked really hard needed to be rewarded and those who slacked off probably deserved a disappointing grade.

Teachers and students can design rubrics throughout the research process. They can collaborate on rubrics to evaluate the quality of the writing, rubrics to evaluate the steps of the research process, rubrics to evaluate comprehension strategies. When students help design rubrics, they learn what's important and they are more likely to remember what they have learned.

Linking Assessment to Instruction

Instruction and assessment need to be linked. Ongoing assessment informs instruction by helping teachers determine what students need and then design an appropriate instructional response. For assessment to be valid, it must measure what was taught.

If a teacher provides instruction in note taking, assessing that strategy is appropriate and should yield information about student progress and teacher effectiveness. For example, a good grade would not stem from neat two-column notes, but rather from evidence that the writer has assimilated the information that effective notes use single words, brief phrases, and codes.

To inform their own instruction, teachers can ask students the following questions:

- What worked for you?
- What was new information?
- What do you need to continue?
- What suggestions do you have for next time?

Ultimately, how students do in long-term research projects is best measured by how effectively they research and report findings in subsequent attempts.

Identifying Possible Rubric Components

Teachers and students can develop rubrics for each phase of the inquiry project: selecting a topic, developing research questions, reading for information, designing research strategies, organizing information, synthesizing information, writing the report, and presenting the report. The rubric components detailed below are some possibilities. You don't have to use them all. But the rubrics you create should include enough detail to explain why the final product came out as it did.

- *Selecting a topic:*
  Choosing a compelling topic.
  Choosing a realistic topic.
  Settling on a topic within an appropriate time frame.
  Narrowing the topic.
  Expanding the topic.

- *Developing research questions:*
  Choosing questions with a clear focus.
  Choosing big questions that require problem solving.
  Choosing sincere, compelling questions.

- *Reading for information:*
  Choosing the best text resources.
  Activating background knowledge to help comprehend information.
  Asking questions before, during, and after reading.
  Determining what's important in text and using the information.
  Using fix-up strategies to understand unfamiliar vocabulary.
  Inferring answers to specific questions.
  Overviewing the text to decide what to read.
  Coding the text to help comprehension.
  Highlighting important parts only.
  Recording bibliographic information for further use.

- *Designing research strategies:*
  Practicing observational skills.
  Deciding on the best research tools for a specific purpose.
  Making appropriate decisions about the use of technology.
  Using both secondary and primary sources.
  Choosing from a variety of primary assessment tools.
  Using the Internet to gather information.

- *Organizing information:*
  Designing an informal outline.
  Taking short, quick notes for easy reference.
  Becoming familiar with a wide range of note-taking strategies.
  Choosing the organizational strategy that fits best.
  Meeting project deadlines.

- *Synthesizing information:*
  Sifting important information from interesting details.
  Summarizing material.
  Using background knowledge to help understand new information.
  Writing short summaries that include the writer's take on the content.

- *Writing the report:*
  Writing in your own voice.
  Matching reading to writing.
  Showing, not telling.
  Using the active voice.
  Writing with nouns and using adjectives sparingly.
  Writing with verbs and using adverbs sparingly.
  Writing strong leads.
  Writing endings that fit.
  Making appropriate transitions.
  Checking for accuracy.
  Changing words, sentences, and thoughts when revising.
  Checking mechanics when editing.
  Choosing the best genre and format.
  Using appropriate resources to help with writing.

- *Presenting the report:*
  Speaking loudly.
  Speaking clearly.
  Using but not reading note cards.
  Making eye contact with the audience.
  Taking cues from the audience about pacing.
  Using gestures when appropriate.
  Using expression.
  Using appropriate props and visual aids.
  Answering appropriate questions afterward.

The literacy behaviors above are just some of those that teachers and students can assess during nonfiction inquiry. Choose those that merit assessment, keeping in mind that we should only assess what we teach.

If you need or want to give a letter grade to the whole project, you can first assign a numeric value (1 to 5, with 5 being an A) to each nonfiction inquiry behavior and then assign a final grade that justly reflects the measured components. But remember that when a project comes to an end, teachers, students, and parents should be able to identify which steps in the process were areas of strength and which ones require more attention.

Rating the Teacher and the Process

Leslie Blauman understands that no one knows her teaching effectiveness better than the kids who live with her every day. They are her best evaluators. Therefore, as her students move through the inquiry process, Leslie asks them to evaluate her instruction in their nonfiction notebooks. For example, when they finish their final draft, they tell Leslie what they learned from her focus lessons on the craft of writing. These comments help Leslie assess her own teaching; she uses the information when planning the next research project. Let's look over Leslie's shoulder and see what some of her students have to say:

Nikki on Topic Exploration

I like doing research, because you are free to research what you want to learn. Sometimes the topic is too big, so you have to narrow it down. That's fun, because you learn just exactly what you want to. Some research topics are really hard to find information on, so you have to write away or interview some one. And you have to find addresses, too.

Chelsea on Presentations

I learned that when you do a presentation, you need to stand up straight, speak loudly and do NOT read from your note cards. I also learned not to write the report by hand. I did my Anasazi report by hand, and I could hardly read it myself. So I needed to stay up really late and type it on the computer the night before my presentation.

Jon on Content

I learned so much about a lot of stuff. First I learned about the Tasmanian Devil, my research report. I also learned about robots, the World Cup, the Sand Dunes and a couple of other topics when kids shared their reports. Doing research was a great learning experience.

Leslie also asks her students to comment on the entire process. Ben sums up nonfiction inquiry this way and gives us some food for thought:

The research projects that we have done taught me a lot. How to do a report, how to take notes, how to make a visual aid, how to present what I've learned and more. I still think that instead of rubrics and grades being emphasized, teachers need to bring more attention to learning. Because when I'm thinking only about how good my project will be, I forget to learn. I loved the research projects and I feel that they got me ready to take on other assignments. Research projects made me feel the responsibility of big projects.

Let's heed Ben's gentle advice and remember that the purpose of research is to find things out and the purpose of education is to enhance understanding. Did Ben attend the same Howard Gardner workshop I did?

A Final Word

I t's no coincidence that this book is chock-full of stories: teaching stories, learning stories, childhood stories, coming-of-age stories. For years, I kept these stories to myself. Although I loved stories, I failed to see their connection to my life as a classroom teacher, even though my best stories came from real things—my childhood, my kids, and the kids I taught. The older I grew, the more stories I collected. And it was only when I began to spill these stories in front of teachers and kids, their eyes wide, their expressions fixed, that I realized the power of narrative in inquiry-based teaching and learning.

Stories are the lifeblood of teaching. Richard Feynman's story taught me about the nature of inquiry. Elizabeth and her baby doll reawakened me to the power of strong models. Albert Einstein reminded me that there are never, ever any stupid questions. We remember stories. The roots of understanding take hold in their telling. Discover your stories and share them with kids. Find them, listen to them, and give them away.

When students work as hard as the young researchers in this book have, fifteen-minute presentations may not leave them with enough sense of fulfillment. You and your students can design a forum for a project beyond the final presentation. When projects live beyond the classroom, kids invest in them. Authenticity is no longer just a big word. Let's take a look at a few projects that teachers and kids refused to let die on the classroom floor.

Our obsession with clean hands, clean counters, and spick-and-span floors became a seed of wonder for a New Jersey high school sophomore. She hypothesized that perhaps our wild antibacterial spraying and wiping were triggering the breeding of a new class of bigger, nastier, more powerful bacteria that would resist these chemical agents. She tackled this for the science fair and found indications to support her hypothesis. A university researcher got wind of this project and with the student's help and permission, received a substantial grant to further her research. Sure enough, her hypothesis was confirmed. These repulsive, giant germs have mutated to resist Lysol and other bacterial cleansing agents. The professor's interest had breathed additional life into this project.

Nanette Newman's third grade combined a study of Helen Keller and blindness with a picture-book writing project. Students wrote biographies, informational books, alphabet books, etc. But after classroom presentations, the project seemed incomplete. Nanette and her students brainstormed some possibilities for project life beyond the classroom and decided to record their own picture books and other treasured published books on tape and donate them to the library of a local school for blind children. They created a budget and raised the money to cover costs. The project expanded, lived on, and changed the lives of others.

These are not isolated examples. After reading Henry David Thoreau, third graders at the Rocky Mountain School of Expeditionary Learning built their own Walden House on their campus, a permanent structure for "solitude and reflection." Fifth graders and sixth graders at Graland, unhappy with shared lockers, stated their case in persuasive essays and received individual lockers when the school underwent renovation. Students in the Barnstable Grade Five School invented their own board game, marketed it, and have netted $30,000 for the school to date. Three hearing-impaired students in Wheatridge, Colorado, wrote a handbook for teachers, students, and friends with suggestions on how to support the hearing impaired. A local school district purchased it for teacher training. Students at Denver's P.S.1 won the right to inscribe poetry on the new entrance to the public library after submitting a detailed proposal to the city.

And let's not overlook one of the easiest ways for projects to live beyond the classroom presentation. Kids can share their findings with other classes in the school. I can't think of a better way to help a second grader gain some background knowledge about a future third-grade unit of study than by hearing a third grader present information she learned in a third-grade umbrella inquiry project.

Inquiry-based learning leads us to think beyond the classroom walls. The need students have to apply their project springs from the project's authenticity. Let kids know that inquiry knows no bounds. And be there to help them think through even the wildest, most unrealistic ideas. Teachers and kids can do just about anything if they put their minds to it. True research not only explores the world, it changes it.

Nonfiction inquiry starts with one condition, and it simply will not lift off without it: wonder. Teachers must find and fuel student curiosity into a state of wonder and a need to know more. The most likely place to unearth such wonder is in the realms where the person already has a passion, interest, or developing knowledge.

Questioning is the sextant that guides the inquiry process. The best and biggest questions come from those things we know and love. Teachers can work to harness student passion and direct it toward further inquiry. If questioning, born of wonder, breeds a passion for an answer or a drive to understand, the student is halfway to his or her destination of enhanced understanding. From that point, the teacher can encourage deep inquiry by acting as tour guide, orchestrating the instruction, response, environment, options, resources, tools, structure, and evaluation to help ensure a successful journey.

Area of Interest and/or Expertise Resource Form

Name _____

Phone # _____

Date _____

I. Please list several areas of interest or expertise that you have.

  1. _____

  2. _____

  3. _____

  4. _____

  5. _____

II. Please list any areas of interest or expertise you would share.

  _____

  _____

  Please indicate a good time to come in and share your interest.

  _____

III. Would you be willing to teach an area of interest or expertise?

  Yes   No

  If so, please list several possible time slots that you might come in and teach your area of interest or expertise.

  1st Choice _____

  2nd Choice _____

  3rd Choice _____

Parent and Special Friend Resource Letter

Greetings,

We love it when the people in our students' lives are involved in our school and classroom. Our students have many adult relatives and special friends, who have varied careers, interests, and talents. The school community can only benefit from this wealth of expertise. If you think you can spare some time to come in and talk about what you do and what you know, we would very much like to hear from you.

If you regularly have extra time, we encourage you to participate in our Mentors for Students program. Adults in this program spend some time each week with a student in a mentoring relationship. Activities range from helping with homework or sharing an interest to inviting the student to your work place to give him or her a new perspective.

We recognize that time is a precious commodity, but hope that you can see your way clear to spend a bit with us. Please return the form below if you can spare some time. We think you'll reap big rewards in the process! Thank you so much,
Warmly,

Name _____

Phone # _____

Please list several areas of interest or expertise that you would be willing to share at school.

_____

_____

Please indicate if you would be willing to teach an area of interest or expertise?   Yes   No

Please indicate if you would be willing to participate in the Mentors for Students program?   Yes   No

When is the best time for us to call you to talk about these opportunities?

_____

Copyright © 1998 *Nonfiction Matters* by Stephanie Harvey, Stenhouse Publishers, York, Maine

Text Cues

Some common signal words and their corresponding text structures.

Cause/Effect
since
because
this led to
on account of
due to
may be due to
for this reason
consequently
then, so
therefore
thus

Comparison/Contrast
in like manner
likewise
similarly
the difference between
as opposed to
after all
however
and yet
but
nevertheless

Problem/Solution
one reason for that
a solution
a problem

Question/Answer
how
when
what
where
why
who
how many
the best estimate
it could be that
one may conclude

Sequence
until
before
after
next
finally
lastly
first/last
then
on (date)
at (time)

(Dole 1997)

Vocabulary
Have a Go

Word	Guess (from context)	Dictionary (if needed)

Note Cards Facsimile

Topic _____

①

②

③

④

⑤

Reminders for Young Authors

(adapted from Strunk and White's The Elements of Style*)*

- **Write naturally.**
  Use words and phrases that come easily to you. Sound like yourself.

- **Write with nouns and verbs.**
  The adjective or adverb doesn't exist that can pull a weak or inaccurate noun or verb out of a tight place. This is not to disparage adjectives and adverbs; they are indispensable parts of speech. In general, however, it is nouns and verbs, not their assistants, that give good writing its toughness and color.

- **Revise and rewrite.**
  Revising is part of writing. Few writers are so expert that they can produce what they are after on the first try. It is not a sign of weakness or defeat that your manuscript needs major surgery. This is common to all writing, even that produced by the best writers.

- **Make sure the reader knows who is speaking.**

- **Use the active voice.**
  Active voice makes for forceful writing. Use active verbs unless there is no possible way to get around it.

- **Be clear, be brief, be bold.**
  Since writing is communication, clarity can only be a virtue. When you become hopelessly mired in a sentence, it is best to start over. Strong writing is concise. A sentence should contain no unnecessary words, a paragraph, no unnecessary sentences, for the same reason a drawing should have no unnecessary lines and a machine no unnecessary parts. Often a word that causes difficulty can just be gotten rid of. Say what's on your mind. Be brave. It's worse to be irresolute than to be wrong. No need to run and hide!

- **Writing is an act of faith, not a trick of grammar.**
  If one is to write, one must believe in the truth and the worth of the scrawl, in the ability of the reader to receive and decode the message.

THE WHOLE DUTY OF A WRITER IS TO PLEASE AND SATISFY HIMSELF, AND THE TRUE WRITER ALWAYS HAS AN AUDIENCE OF ONE.

Independent Study Contract

Part 1 I'm interested in _____

I'm interested in this because _____

_____

Part 2 While I explore this for ____ days, I plan to do these things:

1. _____

2. _____

3. _____

4. _____

5. _____

Part 3 Doing those things will help me develop myself in these ways:

1. _____

2. _____

3. _____

4. _____

5. _____

Part 4 After ____ days, I will share my work. I can change my mind, but right now, I think I will share my work in this way:

_____

_____

_____

Part 5 I understand that fulfilling this contract will take a lot of self-reliance and responsibility. I agree to ask for help, meeting with my teacher 1-on-1 during recess if necessary, if I don't know what to do or if I'm not getting anything done.

(Student signature) _____

Procedures for

_____'s

Independent Study on

_____

Objectives

1. _____

2. _____

3. _____

4. _____

5. _____

Rationale

_____

_____

Resources

_____

_____

_____

Evaluation
Commitment and Guiding Questions

_____

_____

_____

Independent Study Log

Day 1   (Date)   Create a Contract

Day 2   / /   _____

Day 3   / /   _____

Day 4   / /   _____

Day 5   / /   _____

Day 6   / /   _____

Day 7   / /   _____

Day 8   / /   _____

Day 9   / /   _____

Day 10   / /   _____

Day 11   / /   _____

Day 12   / /   _____

Day 13   / /   _____

Day 14   / /   _____

Day 15   / /   _____

Day 16   / /   _____

Day 17   / /   _____

Day 18   / /   _____

Self-Assessment _____

_____

_____

_____

Bibliographies

Well-Crafted Nonfiction Books About Animals

Clyne, Densey. 1995. *Spotlight on Spiders*. St. Leonards, Australia: Little Arc.

Dangerous Animals. 1995. The Nature Company Discoveries Library. New York: Time-Life.

Esbensen, Barbara Juster. 1991. *Tiger With Wings: The Great Horned Owl*. New York: Orchard.

Grace, Eric S. 1993. *Elephants*. San Francisco: Sierra Club.

Guiberson, Brenda. 1991. *Cactus Hotel*. New York: Holt.

Hunt, Joni Phelps. 1995. *A Chorus of Frogs*. Parsippany, NJ: Silver Burdett.

Lasky, Kathryn. 1993. *Monarchs*. Orlando, FL: Harcourt Brace.

Lewellyn, Claire. 1996. *Disguises and Surprises: Camouflaged Animals*. Cambridge, MA: Candlewick.

Lewis, Sharon. 1990. *Tiger*. New York: Harper and Row.

Lovett, Sarah. 1992. *Extremely Weird Endangered Species*. Santa Fe, NM: John Muir.

McGovern, Ann. 1976. *The Underwater World of the Coral Reef*. New York: Scholastic.

Pallotta, Jerry. 1996. *The Freshwater Alphabet Book*. Watertown, MA: Charlesbridge.

Pfeffer, Wendy. 1997. *Arctic Wolves: Creatures in White*. Parsippany, NJ: Silver Burdett.

Ryder, Joanna. 1997. *Shark in the Sea*. New York: Morrow.

Simon, Seymour. 1989. *Whales*. New York: HarperCollins.

———. 1993. *Wolves*. New York: HarperCollins.

———. 1995. *Sharks*. New York: HarperCollins.

Turbak, Gary. 1993. *Survivors in the Shadows*. Flagstaff, AZ: Northland.

Waldrop, Victor, Debbie Anker, and Elizabeth Blizard. 1988. *The Unhuggables*. Washington, DC: National Wildlife Federation.

Wright, Alexandra. 1992. *Will We Miss Them?* Watertown, MA: Charlesbridge.

Well-Crafted Biography Picture Books

Adler, David. 1997. *Lou Gehrig: The Luckiest Man.* San Diego: Harcourt Brace.

Aliki. 1989. *The King's Day.* New York: Crowell.

Bedard, Michael. 1992. *Emily.* New York: Doubleday.

————. 1997. *The Divide.* New York: Doubleday.

Bruchac, Joseph. 1994. *A Boy Called Slow: The True Story of Sitting Bull.* New York: Philomel.

Bruns, Robert. 1986. *Thomas Jefferson.* New York: Chelsea House.

Cooney, Barbara. 1996. *Eleanor.* New York: Viking.

Cooper, Floyd. 1994. *Coming Home: From the Life of Langston Hughes.* New York: Philomel.

Demi. 1991. *Chingis Khan.* New York: Holt.

Fraden, Dennis. 1996. *Louis Braille: The Blind Boy Who Wanted to Read.* Parsippany, NJ: Silver Burdett.

Freedman, Russell. 1987. *Lincoln: A Photobiography.* New York: Clarion.

————. 1991. *The Wright Brothers: How They Invented the Airplane.* New York: Holiday House.

————. 1996. *The Life and Death of Crazy Horse.* New York: Holiday House.

Fritz, Jean. 1976. *Will You Sign Here John Hancock?* New York: Coward McCann.

————. 1977. *Can't You Make Them Behave, King George?* New York: Coward McCann.

Gollenbock, Peter. 1990. *Teammates.* Orlando, FL: Harcourt Brace.

Hayley, Gail. 1973. *Jack Jouette's Ride.* New York: Viking.

Kramer, S. A. 1995. *Baseball's Greatest Hitters.* New York: Random House.

Krass, Peter. 1988. *Sojourner Truth, Anti-Slavery Activist.* New York: Chelsea House.

Krull, Kathleen. 1993. *Lives of the Musicians.* Orlando, FL: Harcourt Brace.

————. 1994. *Lives of the Writers.* Orlando, FL: Harcourt Brace.

————. 1996a. *Lives of the Artists.* Orlando, FL: Harcourt Brace.

————. 1996b. *Wilma Unlimited.* Orlando, FL: Harcourt Brace.

Lasky, Kathryn. 1994. *The Librarian Who Measured the Earth.* Boston: Little, Brown.

Miller, William. 1994. *Zora Hurston and the Chinaberry Tree.* New York: Lee and Low.

Mochizuki, Ken. 1997. *Passage to Freedom: The Sugihara Story.* New York: Lee and Low.

Orgill, Roxanne. 1997. *If I Only Had a Horn: Young Louis Armstrong.* Boston: Houghton Mifflin.

Pinkney, Andrea. 1994. *Dear Benjamin Bannecker.* San Diego: Harcourt Brace.

————. 1996. *Bill Pickett, Rodeo Ridin' Cowboy.* Orlando, FL: Harcourt Brace.

Ross, Stewart. 1997. *Charlotte Bronte and Jane Eyre.* New York: Viking.

Schroeder, Alan. 1996. *Minty: A Story of Young Harriet Tubman.* New York: Dial.

Sis, Peter. 1995. *Starry Messenger.* New York: Farrar Strauss.

Stanley, Diane. 1990. *Good Queen Bess.* New York: Macmillan.

————. 1992. *The Bard of Avon.* New York: Morrow.

————. 1994. *Cleopatra.* New York: Mulberry.

————. 1996. *Leonardo Da Vinci.* New York: Morrow.

Winter, Jeanette. 1991. *Diego.* New York: Knopf.

Well-Crafted Science Picture Books

Anderson, Peter. 1997. *A Grand Canyon Journey: Tracing Time in Stone*. New York: Franklin Watts.

Aronson, Billy. 1996. *Nature's Blackouts: Eclipses*. Danbury, CT: Franklin Watts.

Bash, Barbara. 1989. *Tree of Life: The World of the Baobab*. San Francisco: Sierra Club.

Bosfeld, Jane. 1997. *While a Tree Was Growing*. New York: Workman.

Brandenberg, Jim. 1995. *An American Safari: Adventures on the North American Prairie*. New York: Walker.

Couper, Heather, and Nigel Henbest. 1997. *Big Bang: The Story of the Universe*. New York: DK.

George, Jean Craighead. 1995. *Everglades*. New York: HarperCollins.

de Golia, Jack. 1989. *Fire: The Story Behind a Force of Nature*. Las Vegas, NV: KC.

Grupper, Jonathan. 1997. *Destination Rainforest*. Washington, DC: National Geographic Society.

Kramer, Stephen. 1992a. *Avalanche*. Minneapolis: Carolrhoda.

———. 1992b. *Lightning*. Minneapolis: Carolrhoda.

———. 1992c. *Tornado*. Minneapolis: Carolrhoda.

Lasky, Kathryn. 1997. *The Most Beautiful Roof in the World*. San Diego: Harcourt Brace.

Murphy, Jim. 1995. *The Great Fire*. New York: Scholastic.

Nicholson, Cynthia Pratt. 1994. *Earthdance: How Volcanoes, Earthquakes, Tidal Waves and Geysers Shake Our Restless Planet*. Toronto: Kids Can.

Pratt, Kristin Joy. 1994. *A Swim Through the Sea*. Nevada City, CA: Dawn.

Stelson, Caren. 1988. *Safari*. Minneapolis: Carolrhoda.

Stille, Darlene. 1995. *Extraordinary Women Scientists*. Chicago: Children's Press.

Wick, Walter. 1997. *A Drop of Water*. New York: Scholastic.

Well-Crafted Social Studies Picture Books

Ancona, George. 1995. *Fiesta USA*. New York: Lodestar.

Ballard, Robert. 1988. *Exploring the Titanic*. New York: Scholastic.

———. 1991. *Exploring the Bismarck*. New York: Scholastic.

Belinda, Rochelle. 1997. *Witnesses to Freedom*. New York: Puffin.

Bisel, Sara. 1990. *The Secrets of Vesuvius*. New York: Scholastic.

Brenner, Barbara. 1991. *If You Were There in 1492*. New York: Macmillan.

Buettner, Dan. 1997. *Africa Trek: A Journey by Bicycle Through Africa*. Minneapolis: Lerner.

Chang, Ina. 1991. *A Separate Battle: Women and the Civil War*. New York: Puffin.

Fisher, Leonard E. 1997. *Anasazi*. New York: Atheneum.

Foreman, Michael. 1989. *War Boy*. New York: Little, Brown.

Freedman, Russell. 1980. *Immigrant Kids*. New York: Scholastic.

Fritz, Jean. 1983. *SHH! We're Writing the Constitution*. New York: Putnam.

———. 1994. *Around the World in a Hundred Years*. New York: Scholastic.

Giblin, James Cross. 1995. *When Plague Strikes: The Black Death, Small Pox and AIDS*. New York: HarperCollins.

Gintzler, A. S. 1994. *Rough and Ready Prospectors: True Tales of the Wild West*. Santa Fe, NM: John Muir.

Hakim, Joy. 1995. *A History of US*. New York: Oxford.

Harness, Cheryl. 1997. *Abe Lincoln Goes to Washington, 1838-1865*. Washington, DC: National Geographic Society.

Jakes, John. 1986. *Susannah of the Alamo*. New York. Harcourt Brace.

Krenski, Stephen. 1996. *Breaking into Print Before and After the Invention of the Printing Press*. Boston: Little, Brown.

Kroll, Steven. 1994. *By the Dawn's Early Light: The Story of the Star Spangled Banner*. New York: Scholastic.

————. 1996. *Pony Express*. New York: Scholastic.

Lamb, Nancy. 1996. *One April Morning: Children Remember the Oklahoma City Bombing*. New York: Lothrop.

Levine, Ellen. 1993. *If Your Name Was Changed at Ellis Island*. New York: Scholastic.

Mochizuki, Ken. 1993. *Baseball Saved Us*. New York: Lee and Low.

Murphy, Jim. 1990. *The Boy's War*. New York: Clarion.

————. 1992. *The Long Road to Gettysburg*. New York: Clarion.

————. 1996. *A Young Patriot: The American Revolution as Experienced by One Boy*. New York: Clarion.

Osborne, Mary Pope. 1996. *One World, Many Religions*. New York: Knopf.

Perring, Stefania, and Dominic Perring. 1991. *Then and Now*. New York: Macmillan.

Reynolds, Jan. 1991. *Himalaya: Vanishing Cultures*. San Diego: Harcourt Brace.

Sandler, Martin W. 1996. *The Civil War: A Library of Congress Book*. New York: HarperCollins.

Ward, Geoffrey, Ken Burns, and S. A. Kramer. 1994. *Baseball, the American Epic: 25 Great Moments*. New York: Knopf.

————. 1994. *Baseball, the American Epic: Shadow Ball—The History of the Negro Leagues*. New York: Knopf.

Wright, Courtri. 1994. *Journey to Freedom: A Story of the Underground Railroad*. New York: Holiday House.

Nonfiction Magazines for Kids and Young Adults

Calliope World History for Kids. Cobblestone Publishing, 7 School Road, Peterborough, NH 03458.

Cobblestone: The History Magazine for Young People. Cobblestone Publishing, 7 School Road, Peterborough, NH 03458.

3-2-1-Contact. Children's Television Workshop, 1 Lincoln Plaza, New York, NY 10023.

Dolphin Log. The Cousteau Society, 870 Greenbrier Circle, Chesapeake, VA 23320.

Dramatics. Educational Theater Association, 3368 Central Parkway, Cincinatti, OH 45225.

Faces: People, Places and Culture. Cobblestone Publishing, 7 School Road, Peterborough, NH 03458.

Kids Discover. Kids Discover, 170 Fifth Avenue, New York, NY 10010.

Literary Cavalcade. Scholastic, 555 Broadway, New York, NY 10012.

Muse. Carus Publishing. The Cricket Magazine Group. 332 S. Michigan Avenue, Sutie 2000, Chicago, IL 60604.

National Geographic. National Geographic Society, 1145 17th Street NW, Washington, DC 20036.

Ranger Rick. National Wildlife Federation, 8925 Leesberg Pike, Vienna, VA 22184.

Smithsonian. The Smithsonian Institution, 900 Jefferson Drive S.W., Washington, DC 20560.

Sports Illustrated for Kids. Time Inc., Time Life Building, Rockefeller Center, New York, NY 10020.

Tomorrow's Morning. Tomorrow's Morning Inc., 160 N. Thurston Avenue, Los Angeles, CA 90049.

Time for Kids. Time Inc., Time Life Building, Rockefeller Center, New York, NY 10020.

The Weekly Reader. Scholastic, 555 Broadway, New York, NY 10012.

Wild Outdoor World (formerly *Falcon Magazine*). Rocky Mountain Elk Foundation, P.O. Box 8249, Missoula, MT 59807.

Wildlife Conservation. The International Wildlife Park, Bronx, NY 10460.

World Magazine. National Geographic Society, 1145 17th Street NW, Washington, DC 20036.

Zillions: Consumer Reports for Kids. Consumers Union, 101 Truman Avenue, Yonkers, NY 10703.

Zoobooks San Diego. Wildife Education Ltd., 9820 Willow Creek Road, San Diego, CA 92131.

Models for Diary, Journal, Notebook, Letter, Speech, and Newspaper Writing

Diaries

Dannenberg, Barry. 1996. *When Will This War Be Over? The Civil War Diary of Emma Simpson Gordonville, Virginia 1864.* New York: Scholastic.

Filapovic, Zlata. 1994. *Zlata's Diary.* New York: Penguin.

Frank, Anne. 1952. *The Diary of a Young Girl.* New York: Bantam Books.

Gregory, Christina. 1996. *The Winter of Red Snow: The Revolutionary War Diary of Abigail Jane Stewart, Valley Forge Pennsylvania 1772.* New York: Scholastic.

Johnson, Delores. 1994. *Seminole Diary Remembrances of a Slave.* New York: Macmillan.

Lasky, Kathryn. 1996. *A Journey to the New World: The Diary of Remember Patience Whipple, Mayflower 1620.* New York: Scholastic.

McKissack, Patricia. 1997. *A Picture of Freedom: The Diary of Clotee, a Slave Girl, Belmont Plantation Virginia 1859.* New York: Scholastic.

Ryan, Cary. 1993. *Louisa May Alcott: Her Girlhood Diary.* New York: Troll Medallion.

Talbot, Hudson, and Mark Greenberg. 1997. *Amazon Diary: The Jungle Adventures of Alex Winters.* New York: Putnam.

Journals

Bowen, Gary. 1994. *Stranded on Plimoth Plantation.* New York: HarperCollins.

Fraser, Mary Ann. 1994. *Sanctuary.* New York: Holt.

Kalman, Esther. 1994. *Tschaikovsky Discovers America.* New York: Orchard.

Krull, Kathleen. 1997. *Wish You Were Here: Emily's Guide to the 50 States.* New York: Doubleday.

Leigh, Nila K. 1993. *Learning to Swim in Swaziland: A Child's-Eye View of a Southern African Country*. New York: Scholastic.

Matthaei, Gay, and Jewel Grutman. 1997. *The Ledgerbook of Thomas Blue Eagle*. New York: Lickle.

Mullen, Frank, Jr. 1997. *The Donner Party Chronicles: A Day by Day Account of a Doomed Wagon Train*. Reno, NV: Nevada Humanities Committee.

Schanzer, Rosalyn. 1997. *How We Crossed the West: The Adventures of Lewis and Clark*. Washington, DC: National Geographic Society.

Thomasma, Kenneth. 1997. *The Truth About Sacajawea*. Jackson, WY: Grandview.

Notebooks and Scrapbooks

Baylor, Byrd. 1986. *I'm in Charge of Celebrations*. New York: Scribner.

Brewster, Hugh. 1996. *Anastasia's Album*. New York: Hyperion.

Wright-Frierson, Virginia. 1996. *A Desert Scrapbook: Dawn to Dusk in the Sonoran Desert*. New York: Simon and Schuster.

Letters

Brisson, Pat. 1989. *Your Best Friend Kate*. New York: Bradbury.

———. 1990. *Kate Heads West*. New York: Simon and Schuster.

———. 1992. *Kate on the Coast*. New York: Bradbury.

Dear Laura: Letters from Children to Laura Ingalls Wilder. 1996. New York: HarperCollins.

Nichol, Barbara. 1993. *Beethoven Lives Upstairs*. New York: Orchard.

Parks, Rosa. 1996. *A Dialogue With Today's Youth*. New York: Lee and Low.

Stewart, Sarah. 1997. *The Gardener*. New York: Farrar Strauss.

Yildirim, Eljay. 1997. *Aunty Dot's Incredible Adventure Atlas*. Westport, CT: Joshua Morris.

Postcards

The Discovery Library of [a series of countries around the world]. 1994. Vero Beach, FL: Rourke.

Leedy, Loreen. 1993. *Postcards From Pluto: A Tour of the Solar System*. New York: Holiday House.

Williams, Vera. 1988. *Stringbean's Trip to the Shining Sea*. New York: Scholastic.

Speeches

King, Martin Luther. 1997. *I Have a Dream*. New York: Scholastic.

Lincoln, Abraham. 1995. *The Gettysburg Address*. Boston: Houghton Mifflin.

Philip, Neil. 1997. *In a Sacred Manner I Live: Speeches by Native Americans*. New York: Clarion.

Newspapers

Fleishman, Paul. 1996. *Dateline: Troy*. Cambridge, MA: Candlewick.

Langley, Andrew, and Phillip De Souza. 1996. *The Roman News: The Greatest Newspaper in Civilization*. Cambridge, MA: Candlewick. Additional titles in this series include *The Greek News*, *The Egyptian News*, *The History News: Medicine*, and *The History News: Explorers*.

Quotations

Burleigh, R. 1997. *Who Said That? Famous Americans Speak*. New York: Holt.

References

Ackerman, Diane. 1990. *A Natural History of the Senses.* New York: Random House.

Aliki. 1979. *Mummies Made in Egypt.* New York: Thomas Y. Crowell.

Atwell, Nancie. 1990. *Coming to Know.* Portsmouth, NH: Heinemann.

Ballard, Robert. 1988. *Exploring the Titanic.* New York: Scholastic.

Barry, Dave. 1991. *Dave Barry's Only Travel Guide You'll Ever Need.* New York: Fawcett Columbine.

Baylor, Byrd. 1986. *I'm in Charge of Celebrations.* New York: Scribner.

Bisel, Sara. 1990. *The Secrets of Vesuvius.* New York: Scholastic.

Bowen, Gary. 1994. *Stranded on Plimoth Plantation.* New York: HarperCollins.

Brady, John. 1976. *The Craft of Interviewing.* New York: Vintage Books.

Brantley, Ben. 1996. "Flying Feet Electrify the Sweep of History." Review of *Bring in 'da Noise Bring in 'da Funk. New York Times,* Weekend section, April 26, C-1.

Brennan, John. 1984. *A Is for Australia.* Melbourne: Dent Ply.

Brighton, Catherine. 1990. *Mozart: Scenes From the Childhood of the Great Composer.* New York: Doubleday.

Brown, Margaret Wise. 1942. *The Runaway Bunny.* New York: Harper.

———. 1992. *The Sailor Dog.* Racine, WI: Western, 1953. Reprint, New York: Golden Books.

Burton, Virginia Lee. 1943. *Katy and the Big Snow.* Boston: Houghton Mifflin.

Calkins, Lucy. 1995. *The Art of Teaching Writing.* 2nd ed. Portsmouth, NH: Heinemann.

Chanzit, Gwen. 1996. Curator of Contemporary Art, Denver Art Museum, Nov., personal interview.

Cooney, Barbara. 1996. *Eleanor.* New York: Viking.

Crotchett, Kevin. 1996. *A Teacher's Project Guide to the Internet.* Portsmouth, NH: Heinemann.

Cummings, Pat. 1992. *Talking with Artists.* New York: Bradbury.

Dahl, Roald. 1996. *James and the Giant Peach.* London: Puffin.

De Bruycker, Daniel, and Martine Noblet. 1995. *Tintin's Travel Diaries: Tibet.* New York: Barron's.

Dole, Jan. 1995. Public Education and Business Coalition Reading Comprehension Workshop, Denver, CO (October).

———. 1997. Public Education and Business Coalition Reading Comprehension Workshop, Denver, CO (April).

Dreifus, Claudia. 1997. *Interview.* New York: Seven Stories Press.

Faces: The Magazine About People. 1996. Vol. 13, No.1 (September).

Feldman, David. 1989. *Who Put the Butter in Butterfly?* New York: Harper and Row.

Feynman, Richard. 1985. *Surely You're Joking, Mr. Feynman.* New York: Bantam.

———. 1988. *What Do You Care What Other People Think?* New York: Bantam.

Fielding, Linda C., and P. David Pearson. 1994. "Reading Comprehension: What Works." *Educational Leadership* 52 (February): 62–68.

Fletcher, Ralph. 1993. *What a Writer Needs.* Portsmouth, NH: Heinemann.

Fraser, Mary Ann. 1994. *Sanctuary.* New York: Holt.

Freedman, Russell. 1980. *Immigrant Kids.* New York: Scholastic.

Freeman, Evelyn B., and Diane Goetz Person. 1992. *Using Nonfiction Trade Books in the Elementary Classroom: From Ants to Zeppelins.* Urbana, IL: National Council of Teachers of English.

Fritz, Jean. 1977. *Can't You Make Them Behave, King George?* New York: Coward McCann.

Gardner, Howard. 1991. *The Unschooled Mind: How Children Think and How Schools Should Teach.* New York: Basic.

Gerstein, Mordecai. 1987. *The Mountains of Tibet.* New York: Harper Trophy.

Gollenbock, Peter. 1990. *Teammates.* San Diego: Harcourt Brace.

Gore, Rick. 1981. "When the Shuttle Finally Flies." *National Geographic* 15 (March): 317–347.

Grand, Gail. 1995. *Free (and Almost Free) Adventures for Teenagers.* New York: John Wiley.

Graves, Donald. 1989. *Investigate Nonfiction.* Portsmouth, NH: Heinemann.

———. 1994. *A Fresh Look at Writing.* Portsmouth, NH: Heinemann.

Green, Chuck. 1996. "Smoke 'em at 'Creek,' But not at 'Big Mac.'" *Denver Post,* September 13.

Guinness Book of World Records. Stamford, CT: Guinness Media.

Hammond, Margo. 1993. "President's Life Is an Open Book." Rocky Mountain News. January 20.

Hamner, William. 1994. "A Killer Down Under: Australia's Box Jellyfish." *National Geographic* 186 (August): 116–130.

Hansen, Jane. 1987. *When Writers Read.* Portsmouth, NH: Heinemann.

Harvey, Stephanie, et al. 1996. "Teacher Researchers Study the Process of Synthesizing in Six Primary Classrooms." *Language Arts* 73 (December): 564–574.

Harwayne, Shelley. 1992. *Lasting Impressions: Weaving Literature Into the Writing Workshop.* Portsmouth, NH: Heinemann.

Hawking, Stephen. 1988. *A Brief History of Time.* New York: Bantam.

Hindley, Joanne. 1996. *In the Company of Children.* York, ME: Stenhouse.

Hopkinson, Deborah. 1993. *Sweet Clara and the Freedom Quilt.* New York: Knopf.

Hoyt-Goldsmith, Diane. 1994. *Day of the Dead: A Mexican-American Celebration.* New York: Holiday House.

Janeczko, Paul. 1990. *The Place My Words Are Looking For.* New York: Macmillan.

Johnson, Delores. 1993. *Now Let Me Fly.* New York: Macmillan.

Keene, Ellin Oliver, and Susan Zimmermann. 1997. *Mosaic of Thought: Teaching Reading Comprehension in a Reader's Workshop.* Portsmouth, NH: Heinemann.

Kids Discover. 1995. Vol. 5, no.10 (December).

Kilpatrick, James. 1997. "The Writer's Art." *Rocky Mountain News,* June 1.

Kobrin, Beverly. *The Kobrin Letter,* 732 Greer Road, Palo Alto, CA 94303.

Koss, Amy. 1987. *Where Fish Go in Winter and Answers to Other Great Mysteries.* Los Angeles: Price Stern and Sloan.

Kramer, Stephen. 1992. *Avalanche.* Minneapolis: Carolrhoda.

Lamb, Brian. 1997. *Booknotes: America's Finest Authors on Reading, Writing and the Power of Ideas.* New York: Times.

Lasky, Kathryn. 1993. *Monarchs.* Orlando, FL: Harcourt Brace.

Leaf, Munro. 1938. *The Story of Ferdinand.* New York: Viking.

Leedy, Loren. 1990. *The Furry News: How to Make a Newspaper.* New York: Holiday House.

Levine, Michael. 1994. *The Kid's Address Book.* New York: Perigee.

Lopate, Phillip. 1994. *The Art of the Personal Essay.* New York: Anchor.

Lopez, Barry. 1986. *Arctic Dreams.* New York: Scribner.

Lowry, Lois. 1989. *Number the Stars.* Boston: Houghton Mifflin.

McCutcheon, Randall. 1989. *Can You Find It? Library Scavenger Hunts to Sharpen Your Research Skills.* Minneapolis: Free Spirit.

McKenzie, Jamie. 1995. "Before Net and After Net." *Multimedia Schools* 2 (3): 6–8.

———. 1996. "Making Web Meaning." *Educational Leadership* 54 (3): 30–32.

Murray, Donald. 1985. *A Writer Teaches Writing.* 2nd ed. Boston: Houghton Mifflin.

———. 1989. *Expecting the Unexpected.* Portsmouth, NH: Heinemann/Boynton Cook.

———. 1990. *Shoptalk: Learning to Write with Writers.* Portsmouth, NH: Heinemann/Boynton Cook.

———. 1992. "A Writer's Habits." *The Writer* 105 (January): 14–17.

———. 1998. *Write to Learn.* 6th ed. Fort Worth, TX: Harcourt Brace.

Mutel, Cornelia, and Mary M. Rodgers. 1991. *Our Endangered Planet: Tropical Rain Forests.* Minneapolis: Lerner.

Ogle, Donna. 1986. "K-W-L: A Teaching Model That Develops Active Reading of Expository Text." *The Reading Teacher* 39: 564–70.

O'Neill, Kevin, Rory Wagner, and Louis Gomez. 1996. "On-Line Mentors Experimenting in Science Class." *Educational Leadership* 54 (November): 39–43.

Oxford Dictionary of Quotations. 3rd ed. 1979. New York: Oxford University Press.

Pearson, P. David. 1985. "The Changing Face of Reading Comprehension Instruction." *The Reading Teacher* 38 (August): 724–738.

Pearson, P. David, and Margaret C. Gallagher. 1983. "The Instruction of Reading Comprehension." *Contemporary Educational Psychology* 8: 317–344.

Pearson, P. David, L. R. Roehler, J. A. Dole, and G. G. Duffy. 1992. "Developing Expertise in Reading Comprehension." In *What Research Has to Say About Reading Instruction,* edited by J. Samuels and A. Farstrup. Newark, DE: International Reading Association.

Perring, Stefania, and Dominic Perring. 1991. *Then and Now.* New York: Macmillan.

Phinney, Margaret Yatsevitch. 1994. *Land Habitats.* Greenvale, NY: Mondo.

Rand McNally Historical Atlas of the World. New York: Houghton Mifflin.

Ringold, Faith. 1992. *Aunt Harriet's Underground Railroad in the Sky.* New York: Crown.

Rudloe, Jack, and Anne Rudloe. 1994. "Sea Turtles: In a Race for Survival." *National Geographic* 185 (February): 94–121.

Salinger, J. D. 1951. *Catcher in the Rye.* Boston: Little, Brown.

Santa, Carol. 1988. *Content Reading Including Study Systems: Reading, Writing, and Studying Across the Curriculum.* Dubuque, IA: Kendall/Hunt.

Santa, Carol, S. C. Dudley, and M. Nelson. 1985. "Free-Response and Opinion-Proof: a Reading and Writing Strategy for Middle Grade and Secondary Teachers." *Journal of Reading* 28 (4): 346–352.

Schnitzer, Denise. 1996. "Navigating the Net for Grant Money." *Educational Leadership* 54 (3): 44–45.

Schwartz, Robert M., and Taffy E. Raphael. 1985. "Concept of Definition: A Key to Improving Students' Vocabulary." *The Reading Teacher* 39: 190–205.

Seifert, Patti. 1994. *Tree Habitats.* Greenvale, NY: Mondo.

Seuss, Dr. 1950. *If I Ran the Zoo.* New York: Random House.

Stamberg, Susan. 1993. *Talk: NPR's Susan Stamberg Considers All Things.* New York: Random House.

Stanley, Diane. 1990. *Good Queen Bess.* New York: Four Winds.

Strunk, William, Jr., and E. B. White. 1979. *The Elements of Style.* 3rd ed. Needham Heights, MA: Allyn and Bacon.

Swerdlow, Joel. 1995. "Information Revolution." *National Geographic* 188 (October): 5–35.

Tan, Amy. 1989. *The Joy Luck Club.* New York: Ballantine.

Tomorrow's Morning. Los Angeles: Tomorrow's Morning.

Turbak, Gary. 1993. *Survivors in the Shadows.* Flagstaff, AZ: Northland.

Turner, Anne. 1987. *Nettie's Trip South.* New York: Aladdin.

Vonnegut, Kurt. 1988. *How to Write with Style.* International Paper Advertising Campaign.

Waldrop, Victor, Debbie Anker, and Elizabeth Blizard. 1988. *The Unhuggables.* Washington, DC: National Wildlife Federation.

Walker, Barbara. 1992. *Supporting Struggling Readers.* Markham, ON: Pippin.

Weekly Reader. New York: Scholastic.

White, E. B. 1952. *Charlotte's Web.* New York: Scholastic.

Williams, Bard. 1995. *The Internet for Teachers.* Foster City, CA: IDG.

Wollard, Kathy. 1993. *How Come?* New York: Workman.

World Book Encyclopedia. 1996. Vol. 19, s.v. "turtles—see turtles," 522–523.

Wright, Courtri C. 1994. *Journey to Freedom: A Story of the Underground Railroad.* New York: Holiday House.

Wright-Frierson, Virginia. 1996. *A Desert Scrapbook: Dawn to Dusk in the Sonoran Desert.* New York: Simon and Schuster.

Yolen, Jane. 1992. *Encounter.* Orlando, FL: Harcourt Brace.

Zinsser, William. 1988. *Writing to Learn.* New York: Harper and Row.

———. 1990. *On Writing Well.* 4th ed. New York: HarperCollins.

Index